INS

TURN CIRCLE

INSIDE THE TURN CIRCLE

Earning My Wings in the F-16
1979-1988

P.K. White, Col (Ret), USA

Paperback: ISBN 978-0-578-70668-9

Cover Photo: TSgt Marvin Krause
Cover Design: Amy Pattee Colvin
Editor: Amy Pattee Colvin

This book is dedicated to my mother and father, David and Ann White, who have provided role models for me that I have strived to honor; and to my son Walker, for whom I've tried to provide a similar example.

CONTENTS

ACKNOWLEDGMENTS

This book would not have been possible without the help, support, and contributions from the following friends:

Thanks to TSgt Marvin Krause, whose photo *Daddy's Home* graces the cover of this book. The photo was taken at Misawa Air Base in December 1996 and is one of our family's most prized possessions.

Many thanks to Weldon Follis, Rick Gile, and Martin Agüera for providing helpful comments and ideas as I worked through the narrative.

Much appreciation is extended to Dave "Stilly" Stilwell, Paul "Gruve" Gruver, Jim "Rev" Jones, Bruce "Rico" Schwab, Siegfried "Ziggy" Von Schweinitz, and Bryan "Shadow" Turner for their suggestions, reflections, and inputs to the Culture, Customs, and Craziness appendix.

To Rabbi Matt Rosenberg and the entire family at Restoration Messianic Synagogue, thanks for the loving help and friendship you have given Wendy, Walker, and me over the years.

Special thanks to Amy Pattee Colvin, whose creative work on editing, formatting, repairing, fixing, and developing made this book possible.

Finally, I give thanks to my wife, Wendy, who was the catalyst behind this effort. Her love, encouragement, suggestions, and constant support have not only been the keys to my writing this book, but to everything I do. Nothing I do in this life is possible without her, and I thank God for her every day.

INTRODUCTION

There is no such thing as an ex-fighter pilot. Once a young man straps on a jet aircraft and climbs into the heavens to do battle, it sears his psyche forever. At some point, he will hang up his flight suit—eventually, they all do—and in the autumn of his years, his eyes may dim, and he may be stooped with age. But ask him about his life, and his eyes flash, and his back straightens, and his hands demonstrate aerial maneuvers, and every conversation begins with "There I was at..." and he is young again. He remembers the days when he sky-danced through the heavens when he could press a button and summon the lightning and invoke the thunder, the days when he was a prince of the earth and a lord of the heavens. He remembers his glory days, and he is young again.

—Author Unknown, from the eulogy for Col (Ret) John Boyd

In April 1988, our son Walker was born at the small military hospital on Hahn Air Base in Germany. By the time Walker was four years old, he had lived at four different Air Force bases in three different countries. One Sunday, during that fourth assignment, we were standing in line for brunch at the Sembach Air Base Officers Club. A friend of ours standing in line with us looked down at Walker and asked, "So, do you want to be a fighter pilot like your Dad?"

Without a second thought, Walker looked up and replied, "No. I want to be something cool. Like a carpenter."

I'll admit it. The reason I am writing these memoirs is I think that being an F-16 fighter pilot in the U.S. Air Force was pretty cool.

INTRODUCTION

I retired from the Air Force after 30 years of service in June 2009. Having grown up in the Air Force as a dependent from the time I was six years old, it was a pretty big day—it was the first time in 47 years I wasn't in the military in one way, shape, or form. I enjoyed a four-month vacation before taking a job with the Federal Emergency Management Agency (FEMA) in Seattle. I enjoyed working in FEMA well enough, but I missed working in the active-duty military—and I especially missed flying fighters and being around fighter pilots.

My new civilian friends were naturally curious about my former career, but even when I tried to tell a few *"There I was..."* stories, I could tell they really didn't understand what I was talking about. I kept in touch with some of the guys from the old days via the internet, but it wasn't the same.

I took more and more to reading books about flying fighters—in Korea, in Vietnam, and in Iraq. It didn't take much to get my thoughts back in the cockpit; reading some of the stories took me back to similar situations, places, and events. I would constantly have dreams I was flying again—they were usually nightmares when I couldn't seem to find my checklist, my flight boots, my Tab-V, or my jet, and it was past step time. I was starting to become a grouchy old former fighter pilot who just wanted to be left alone—and my wife, Wendy, wasn't having any of that.

So, to get me out of my funk, Wendy suggested I share some of my memoirs. I had written a book previously, entitled *Crises After the Storm: An Appraisal of U.S. Air Operations in Iraq Since The Persian Gulf War*, back in 1999 when I was a National Defense Fellow with The Washington Institute for Near East Policy. Excerpts from that book later became part of the Air War College syllabus, but this was something different. Would anyone really be interested in the early days of my Air Force career? Would I be able to write a biographical-style book that would hold someone's attention?

Well, as the saying goes, no guts, no Air Medal.

This book is my attempt to relate what it was like training and becoming an F-16 fighter pilot in the U.S. Air Force from 1979 to 1988. It includes not only life in the air, but life on the ground as well—the culture of the fighter squadron, the joys

2

and challenges of living overseas, the fun adventures and love shared by families depending on each other, and the stresses and pressures inherent in this often dangerous profession.

The book covers a period beginning with the dark days (for the military) of the Carter Administration, to the build-up of the Reagan Years, up until two years short of Desert Storm, where the strategy, tactics, technology, and training established during the post-Vietnam era proved itself in a big way. It was a time where our brand new fighters—the F-15, A-10, and F-16—provided the United States the best fighter force on the planet by a large margin.

It was also a time before the politically-correct culture imposed on our military leadership began to smother the fighting spirit of our elite warrior force. Before sensitivity training to placate an ever-growing list of self-obsessed grievance mongers became the norm. Before a Secretary of Defense decided he didn't like Air Force flag officers with call signs. Before Hog Logs—Hog Logs? What Hog Logs?—had to be kept locked away in the weapons vault to prevent non-squadron eyes from becoming offended. Before a growing number of officers who weren't pilots or navigators were issued flight suits because, well, they just wanted to feel special.

And, it was a time when the O'Club—remember the O'Club?—was packed to the rafters on Friday nights, where the singing of songs, dollar bill games, sockchecks, and a shout of DEAD BUG were guarantees for light-hearted fun and chaos.

When I was a young boy, my great-grandfather, John Lee, had his own room in the back of their house. The walls were decorated with photos of the Old West when my Daddy John had lived in Indian Territory before Oklahoma became a state— so he was a genuine Sooner. There were pictures of cowboys, lawmen, and Native Americans. There were guns, old tools, maps—an entire collection of Wild West memorabilia. I even gave him one of my toy six-shooters to hang on his wall when I was around three years old, and he displayed it proudly with the rest of his collection.

I loved going in that room—every item had a story, and although I knew all the stories by heart, I demanded my Daddy John repeat them to me over and over again—stories about eating dog soup with Quanah Parker, escorting Geronimo at the Hobart train station, the night the Devil chased him home from the barn dance, and many more. He left us a legacy of stories the family still cherishes to this day.

Just like most retired fighter pilots I know, I also have a Daddy John room in our house full of mementos, plaques, and photos of my days in the Air Force—the "I Love Me" room. In some small way, this memoir is an added attempt to leave a lasting legacy for my grandchildren-to-be. I hope to one day be able to sit with them on my knee and tell them mostly-true stories about flying the world's-greatest-sleek-and-shiny-single-seat-single-engine-Viper-jet.

There may be a day in the not-so-distant future where fighter pilots are largely a thing of the past. Some already say the last fighter pilot has been born; future generations may look on fighter pilots as relics from a distant memory, perhaps thankfully forgotten. Hence, this memoir of my days slipping the surly bonds inside the turn circle.

Check Six.

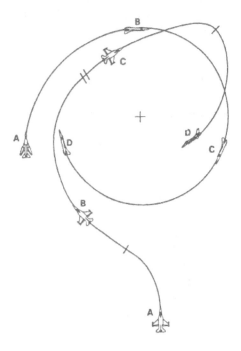

CHAPTER ONE

AIR FORCE BRAT

1956-1979

The military life, whether for sailor, soldier, or airman, is a good life. The human qualities it demands include fortitude, integrity, self-restraint, personal loyalty to other persons, and the surrender of the advantage of the individual to the common good. This is good company. Anyone can spend his life in it with satisfaction.

—Sir John Winthrop Hackett

Everyone knows how these flying memoirs are supposed to start. I was a young lad playing in the back yard of our home in my hometown of Hobart, Oklahoma, a small town of about 5,000 located in the southwest corner of the state about halfway between Altus Air Force Base to the south and Clinton–Sherman Air Force Base to the north.

Aircraft from both bases, with transports at Altus and bombers at Clinton–Sherman, would fly directly over Hobart en route to each other's traffic pattern to practice strange field approaches. I would see and hear them nearly every day, and I was mightily impressed. I wondered what it would be like to fly those big jets; to be able to just takeoff and go wherever I wanted in the sky.

Early on, it was my dream to fly and become an Air Force pilot.

Except that was not the way it happened. Not even close.

I was born in Hobart in 1956. My mother was petite, pretty, and smart, and had a bit of a reputation in town of someone not to be trifled with. Like many girls of her generation, she married her high school sweetheart shortly after graduation. I came along about a year later, and the divorce came not too long after I was born. We lived with my grandparents and mother's younger sister, and my mother worked the night shift at the local telephone office. She met the man who was to become my father working the switchboard late at night—an early example of online dating.

He was an airman working communications at Clinton-Sherman Air Force Base not too far up the road. Dad was a player—voted Most Handsome and Most Popular in his high school yearbook from his hometown in Fayette, Alabama, he was a three-sport athlete, a hit with the ladies, and my mom definitely caught his eye.

Mom loves to tell the story about the first time I met the man who would become my Dad. I was about four years old, and my mother had taken me to see a movie at the local Esquire theater in downtown Hobart. As we were coming out after the movie was over, Dad was coming in with a friend. Mom introduced us—and Dad got down on one knee and said, "How did you like the movie, little boy?" I sighed, rolled my eyes, and looked away. Mom squeezed my hand extra tightly and said, "P.K., Mr. White asked you a question." I looked at him, sighed again, and said, "Well, if I hadn't liked it, don't you think I would have gotten up and left?"

Dad was not intimidated by the tough little Okie girl or her precocious child, but he was in love. Not long after they started dating seriously, Dad was assigned to Wheelus Air Base in Libya. Off he went for a year-and-a-half, and they kept up their relationship via letters and phone calls. When he returned from Libya in early 1963, they were married, and at the age of six, I became an Air Force Brat.

Our first assignment as a family was to Laughlin Air Force Base in Del Rio, Texas. I loved it. I had free reign of the base. I could go to the movies, go to the swimming pool, or go to the mini-mart all by myself. We made frequent trips across the border into Mexico, which was a real adventure. I loved having a father—we would play catch just about every day, he would take me golfing with him, and he even coached our Little

League baseball team. We watched Five Star Shock, the local scary movie television show on Friday nights together, and I remember the three of us watching The Beatles on the Ed Sullivan Show in February 1964.

I was vaguely aware that there were jets constantly flying on base, mostly trainer aircraft, but I assumed that's just what happened on Air Force bases. What I didn't know or could have appreciated at the time was they were secretly flying U-2 spy planes out of Laughlin during the night. They would keep them hangared by day, launch them after nightfall, and land them before sunrise.

One day early on, I got a bit of an education from my new father. Dad was a Staff Sergeant at the time—it was a Saturday morning, and we were driving together to the Base Exchange (BX). I saw a young airman crossing the street, and I noticed he was wearing two stripes. "Ha, ha, look at that guy—he only has two stripes!" I laughed. Dad silently pulled the car over to the side of the road. In quiet but firm tones he explained to me that everyone works hard for their stripes—that it takes time and experience to get promoted—that anyone wearing the uniform in service to their country deserves respect—and that if I ever laughed at anyone again for their (lack of) rank, it was not going to be a good day for me. An early lesson learned which I later passed on to my own son.

In 1965, Dad received orders to Camp New Amsterdam in the Netherlands. We were all excited—especially Mom. Dad wasn't approved for concurrent travel, meaning he had to first deploy by himself and secure a place for us to live before Mom and I were permitted to arrive, so off Dad went to Holland, and Mom and I went back to Hobart, where I started fourth grade.

Around six weeks later, Mom and I arrived in our new house in the Netherlands. Our first house was on a Dutch turkey farm—it was essentially a small summer cottage heated by one kerosene heater in the living room. I can remember it being so cold I was able to see my breath in the morning when I awoke.

Flocks of turkeys followed me to the bus stop to school at the start of every day, and followed me home again when I got off the bus in the evening. A few months later, we moved into a bigger house in a small village. There was a bakery across the street, and I loved running across the street, speaking what little Dutch I knew, and ordering fresh bread and cheese every Saturday for breakfast.

Living in the Netherlands was a wonderful adventure as we adjusted to living on the economy and the European culture and lifestyle. There was no AFN-TV (Armed Forces Network) available in the Netherlands in those days, and Dutch TV didn't start broadcasting until around 4:00 PM. There were some American TV shows—*Bonanza* being the one I remember most—that were shown on Dutch TV with Dutch subtitles. We took to listening to the radio for entertainment, much like in the Forties and Fifties. I remember listening to *Mystery Theater* on AFN radio late at night, in addition to shows like *The Whistler*. It's amazing how terrifying some of those old radio shows were, especially to nine-year-old ears. But mostly, we listened to music. It was the height of the British Invasion in America, with the Beatles, the Rolling Stones, the Kinks, the Animals, the Yardbirds, etc. We had the radio constantly going in the house, and surprisingly, we didn't really miss television all that much.

We made friends with our Dutch neighbors—one family had a son a year older than me. I taught him baseball and football, he taught me soccer, and we spent many days playing outside together with our language differences being no barrier whatsoever.

With about four Dutch guilders to the dollar, our money went a long way. So even on a Tech Sergeant's pay, we were able to make weekend visits to Amsterdam, the miniature city of Madurodam, the tulip gardens of Keukenhof, and the old fishing village of Volendam, where like most American military families, we posed in traditional Dutch costumes for our Christmas cards. Dad and I developed a taste for smoked herring, mostly just to gross Mom out, and I loved Dutch licorice in all its various forms (lekker!).

It was during our year in the Netherlands that Dad brought home a small pamphlet on the Air Force Academy. I remember the pamphlet well—just a tri-fold, but it had pictures of cadets, the campus, and jets. That was the first time I thought about joining the Air Force one day.

After a short but fun year at Camp New Amsterdam, Dad received orders to Lindsay Air Station in Wiesbaden, Germany, in late summer 1966. I was excited—we were going to be able to live in an American military housing area where I would be surrounded by other American kids, and they had AYA (American Youth Association) football there.

We moved into our stairwell apartment on #37 Washington Strasse in the Hainerberg housing area at the start of fifth grade. It was great—surrounded by kids, I could walk to school, the BX, the theater, and I could play organized football and baseball. Living on the economy in Europe is great for adults, but living on base was better for kids, especially at that age.

The start of fifth grade was the first time I really realized I was going to be a small guy, taking after my Mom's side of the family. New guys—especially if they are small—get challenged quite often at that age, and it seemed I got into fights several times a week that first year.

Mom always handled it well. I would come home, nose bleeding, and head straight for the bathroom.

Mom would ask, "What happened?"

"Got into a fight," I would mumble.

"Get any punches in?" she would ask.

"A couple," I would reply, whether I had or not.

"Okay, go get cleaned up," she would mutter, and that would be that.

I learned that all you really had to do was stand up for yourself a few times, and you would be okay.

We later had a series of one-year assignments; I attended 6th, 7th, 8th, 9th, and 10th grades at different schools. As a perennial new kid, I was able to use sports as a great way to get to know other kids in the neighborhood and keep the bullies at bay. On the first day, I would show up to whatever neighborhood game was going on—and be picked last. On the next day, I would usually be picked among the first, and all generally went well from there.

Living in a large American military community like Wiesbaden was quite a bit different than the relatively small base at Camp New Amsterdam. While AFN television didn't come on until the afternoon, it was all American—albeit last

9

year's episodes, or shows that had been canceled. We had spent the previous year in the Netherlands without television for the most part, so the shows were all new to us. *Twelve O'Clock High* and *Combat* were two of my favorites, while my parents enjoyed The *Carol Burnett Show* and *The Smothers Brothers Comedy Hour.*

Football and baseball games were aired on weekends, but they were all replays of the previous week's contests, so we already knew the outcome thanks to the *Stars & Stripes* daily newspaper—for my money, still the best newspaper on the planet. If you wanted live sports, you had to listen to AFN radio. I remember listening to the Green Bay-Dallas Ice Bowl game late at night on New Year's Eve—my Dad was a huge Cowboys fan, and was devastated when Bart Starr stumbled over the goal line to win the game.

We took full advantage of the Armed Forces Recreation Center (AFRC) resorts at Chiemsee, Berchtesgaden, and Garmisch for vacations. We couldn't afford to eat out for every meal, so Mom always hooked Dad and me up with apple butter sandwiches while we were out and about. Every day on every trip, we lived cheap on apple butter sandwiches. I can't stand apple butter to this day.

Another popular pastime was watching the Wiesbaden Flyers play football on the weekends. The Armed Forces in Europe had founded the Continental Sports Conference, with teams representing the bigger U.S. military bases and made up of active-duty soldiers and airmen. We would go to the football stadium at Lindsay Air Station and watch the Flyers battle the Rhein Main Rockets, the Bitburg Barons, the Ramstein Rams, the Sembach Tigers, the Hahn Hawks, or any of the other teams. It was a big deal to go to a game; the bleachers would be packed, and watching the Flyers play was something most everyone looked forward to in the fall.

One of my Dad's friends was rotating back to the States, and gave me his vast collection of *Sports Illustrated* magazines. He had saved three years' worth, and there were over a hundred for me to pour over and digest. I was mostly interested in football and hockey. Still, at age 10, being a military nomad with no real geographic loyalties (except to the University of Oklahoma Sooners), I hadn't yet determined who my favorite teams were. This was 1966-1967—and I kept reading about Dick Butkus, Gale Sayers, Bobby Hull, and Stan Mikita. I was barely aware of where exactly Chicago was, but these guys were cool, and their uniforms were cool. That's what started the passionate fandom I have for the Bears and the Blackhawks, which persists to this day.

During that first assignment at Wiesbaden, I learned another valuable lesson from my father. I was in the sixth grade and had gone to an evening movie with some of my friends. On a dare, I stole some candy from the BX. As I exited triumphantly, a man with a badge walked up and asked me for the receipt for the candy I had just stolen. Busted!

He took me back to the office, took my dependent ID card, and called my Dad. I was terrified that something was going to happen to Dad for what I had just done—maybe lose a stripe! As Dad walked into the office, the official said, "Sergeant White, your son seems to be more worried about you than he is himself."

Dad, in his usual quiet, serious manner, replied, "Well, I think he needs to start worrying about himself."

I was restricted to the house for a while, but the worst thing was I was told I had lost my ID card privileges for 90 days. Without an ID card, I was stranded. No admittance to the Base Theater, or to the BX. No riding the shuttle busses. Torture.

Years later, when I was a squadron commander, I had a situation when one of the dependents of someone assigned to my squadron was caught stealing from the BX. I told the First Sergeant that we would simply have his ID card taken away for 90 days, just like the BX had done to me when I was young.

The First Sergeant said, "Sir, you can't do that. An ID card is a personal, official document—you can't confiscate it."

I told him he was wrong—it had been done to me, and I would prove it. I called Dad up and said, "Dad, remember when I got caught stealing from the BX in 1967, and they confiscated my ID card for three months?"

Dad chuckled and said, "It wasn't the BX that confiscated your card—it was me." Busted again.

After two years in Wiesbaden, Dad received orders to Southeast Asia. Dad had volunteered, so we knew it was coming. Mom and I went back home to Hobart to live with my grandmother for the 7th grade, and Dad flew back with us to get us settled in before he left. On the day of his departure, we all went to my Daddy John's house so Dad could bid them goodbye, then drove back to my grandmother's house to drop me off. Mom stayed in the car—she was driving him to Oklahoma City to put him on the plane—while Dad took me in the house. He went to the kitchen sink, poured himself a glass of water, gulped it down, then wordlessly knelt down and hugged me tightly for a long time before finally walking out the door and not looking back. I tried to be brave, but I couldn't stop the tears for most of that afternoon.

Still, that '68-'69 year back home in Hobart was a good one. Mom immediately got her old job back, working the night shift at the telephone office. Living with my grandmother, I discovered a large collection of my aunt's old 45-rpm records from the late Fifties and early Sixties. I played them on her little portable record player until I had virtually made myself an expert on early American rock'n'roll.

Dad sent me a small Sony portable radio for Christmas—in those days, every G.I. came home from Southeast Asia with a new stereo system, and he had already started buying equipment (Sansui speakers and a TEAC reel-to-reel!). I went to sleep every night listening to radio station KOMA in Oklahoma City—Steppenwolf, The Doors, Jimi Hendrix, Jefferson Airplane, all the awesome bands of the late Sixties.

I played junior high football, basketball, and baseball, and spent precious time with my great-grandparents, grandmother, and other family members and old friends. After three years in Europe, it was fun living in the USA again, with all the luxuries and conveniences we had missed living overseas.

I had always wanted a dog, a dachshund, to be precise, but we never got one because of the demands of keeping a dog with the Air Force nomadic lifestyle, especially living overseas. However, in an effort to provide me a special companion while Dad was gone, Mom brought home a tiny black-and-tan dachshund puppy shortly after Dad's departure. I named her Pandora, because of all the mischief she created around the house. I spent hours and hours with Pandora. Like many young boys with a dog, we were virtually inseparable. Sadly, she came down with a form of canine leukemia, and we had to put her down just a few weeks before Dad's return. We like to think she was put on this earth to keep me company and give me comfort during Dad's absence. She was special.

Dad spent most of his year at Udorn Royal Thai Air Base in Northern Thailand. I missed Dad terribly, but I wasn't particularly worried about him. Dad received the Bronze Star for his actions while conducting special missions during that assignment, and it was only much, much later I learned it was for his activity assembling combat communications equipment and listening devices along the Ho Chi Minh trail, in locations where we technically weren't active during the war in 1968-1969. If I would have understood at the time, I think I would have been a lot more worried.

After Dad's return stateside in the summer of 1969, we were stationed at Kelly Air Force Base in San Antonio, Texas. I spent the 8th grade at Sam Rayburn Junior High, my first real big-city school. We lived in a little apartment complex not far from school, and I made friends with some of the other Air Force kids living there in the same complex. San Antonio had a reputation as The Murder Capital of the USA in those days, and we lived in a pretty rough area. I didn't play any school sports and tended to keep a pretty low profile.

That spring of 1970, my Papa White—my grandfather—unexpectedly passed away. Dad asked for and received a humanitarian assignment to Columbus Air Force Base in Mississippi, so we could be near my grandmother, who still lived just across the state line in Fayette, Alabama.

Moving to Columbus in the summer of 1970, we spent almost every weekend my 9th grade year at the farm in Fayette, and I loved it—running around in the woods, fishing from sunrise to sunset, and working with Dad on the never-ending list of projects he had going there.

School was another matter, however. It was the first year of forced integration in Mississippi, and many of the locals were not too happy about it. The school was divided into three factions—the Air Force kids, the white townies, and for the first time at S.D. Lee High School, the African-American kids.

There were policemen in the hallways, and the tension was ever-present. We Air Force kids had grown up in an integrated environment and had a hard time understanding what the fuss was all about. Neither the white townies nor the African-American locals really trusted us, so we tended to stick together and bond with our own tribe. Although there were no real violent incidents I can remember, it simply was not a good atmosphere.

Towards the end of that year in Columbus, we received great news—we were returning to Lindsay Air Station in Germany. I was delighted—I loved stairwell living in Wiesbaden, all the sports activities, and since it was a four-year assignment, it looked like I would be able to spend the last three years of high school in the same location. We arrived in Wiesbaden in August 1971 and after nearly a month in the Amelia Earhart motel, moved into a stairwell on #2 Arizona Strasse directly across the street from where we had lived in 1966-1968.

Since we had only left Wiesbaden three years previously, it had not changed that much and we settled in quickly. I started playing football again and became seriously interested in music.

My parents had always encouraged me musically—early on, before I could afford them on my own, they bought me the hottest albums on the charts, including the first Beatles and Rolling Stones releases, which I still have. They bought me my first guitar when I was 11. I spent most of my weekly allowance and wages from working at the Mess Hall as a busboy during the summer break on albums—Led Zeppelin, Black Sabbath, Grand Funk, and Alice Cooper were my favorites.

While we could listen to the latest stateside hits on AFN Radio, I preferred the late-night transmissions from The Great 208, Radio Luxembourg, the only independent radio station on the air. Radio Luxembourg was a pirate radio station playing music that the BBC in England tended to neglect, and in the early Seventies U.K., that was T.Rex, Slade, Gary Glitter, David Bowie, Roxy Music, Mott the Hoople, and other bands from the Glam Era in Britain.

I still have a nostalgic and somewhat embarrassed soft spot in my heart for that music. My friends and I spent hours in downtown Wiesbaden at record stores, where one could still listen to an album on headphones before purchasing it, and at the Piano Schulz music store where I gazed longingly at the Les Paul Goldtop guitar displayed in the window.

All of us tended to dress the same way, in the same clothes— the BX was one of the largest in Europe, but the variety was still fairly limited. When the BX received a new shipment of jeans or shoes, word spread quickly, and we all rushed down to buy what was available before they sold out. The next day, we would all show up at school wearing the same thing. Music, football, and girls were my primary focus—in short, I was your typical red-blooded All-American boy.

Now that I was in high school, I figured it was time for me to start thinking seriously about what I wanted to do with my life. Like many young men my age, I wanted to be something cool— like a rock star since I didn't have carpentry skills! In Wiesbaden, I played in a rock-n-soul band named Uhuru, but I knew that making a career in music wasn't a realistic goal for me. I loved playing football, but at 5'8 and 145 pounds, I wasn't nearly good enough to be considered for a college scholarship anywhere. There was no area of study I was particularly interested in outside of music, so essentially I was left with that Air Force Academy pamphlet Dad had brought home years ago.

It seemed to be a reasonable choice. I loved being a military dependent—I enjoyed moving and traveling around the world, I liked the security of living on military installations, I liked attending Department of Defense schools, and I genuinely enjoyed being around military people. I felt at home with the culture and the lifestyle. My Dad was having a phenomenally successful career; he had just pinned on Chief Master Sergeant with less than 16 years of service, and our family lived comfortably. I just didn't really know what I wanted to do in the Air Force.

In those days, the Air Force was much more segregated than it is today, keeping officers and enlisted personnel separate for the most part. Officers had their own housing areas; in Wiesbaden, they lived in Aukumn. The rest of us lived in Hainerberg and Crestview. Officers had their own hotels; in Wiesbaden, they had the Von Steuben. The rest of us had the Amelia Earhart and the American Arms. They had their own clubs—and in the States, officers and their families even had separate swimming pools.

Largely because of the separate housing areas, officers' kids tended to hang with officers' kids, and enlisted kids spent their time with enlisted kids. I didn't really know any officers, I didn't spend time with any officers, and pilots were officers. As a result, although I had spent most of my life growing up on Air Force bases, I didn't have a real connection with pilots or flying. My Dad was in communications, and being a pilot simply wasn't on my radar scope.

At the start of my junior year in the fall of 1972, our high school in Wiesbaden, H.H. Arnold High, introduced Air Force Junior ROTC. I immediately signed up, as did most of my friends. While my parents had saved diligently to have enough money to put me through college, it was understood that I would pursue any scholarships available. While my grades were generally good overall, my math grades were strictly mediocre, and getting an appointment to the Air Force Academy seemed more and more out of the question.

Besides, I had discovered girls in a big, big way, and by that time, I really wasn't interested in attending that School for Boys in the Colorado Rockies. Women weren't permitted at the military academies until 1976. So, I set my sights on an Air Force ROTC scholarship, which provided full tuition, books, and a monthly $100 stipend.

In the Seventies, 4-year AFROTC scholarships were different than they are now. If you accepted a 4-year scholarship in 1974, you were automatically given a pilot slot, meaning that if you continued in the program and met all the requirements, upon commissioning as an officer and graduation from college, you would proceed to pilot training as your first Air Force assignment.

Having been raised on Air Force bases, I knew the difference between an F-4 and a C-141, and had seen the Air Force Aerial Demonstration Team Thunderbirds many times. Still, I had never seriously considered a career as a pilot. Frankly, I didn't think much of it at the time—my goal was the scholarship, not the pilot slot. If I had to agree to be a pilot to get the scholarship, so be it.

Having family connections in Oklahoma, Texas, and Alabama, I applied to all of the colleges in those states that had Air Force ROTC programs. I was accepted by them all except the University of Texas, no doubt due to my low SAT test scores—I killed the ACT test, but didn't do nearly as well on the SAT. However, I did relatively well on the Air Force Officers Qualifying Test (AFOQT), and passed the physical exam, to include the 20/20 uncorrected vision requirement, with flying colors.

I honestly didn't know how well I would compete—my grades were okay, I had leadership positions in Junior ROTC, I had played varsity sports, and I was a military dependent. I was the president of The Revelation Generation, an Up with People-style music group made up of around 60 Catholic and Protestant teens that performed at military chapels around Europe. However, I knew my poor SAT score would not impress the scholarship board, and failing to be accepted to the University of Texas was a significant indicator. I decided that if I received a 4-year AFROTC scholarship, I would attend the University of Oklahoma, and if I didn't, I would attend Troy State University in Alabama.

As a military dependent, one automatically assumes the state residency of their active duty parent, whether they were born or ever lived in that state or not. Therefore, I was technically an Alabama state resident. Of the three Alabama schools that had AFROTC (University of Alabama, Auburn, and Troy State), Troy had the least expensive tuition. In addition, Troy State was well-known in overseas military circles—both the University of Maryland and Troy State had a permanent presence at the Education Offices of every installation in Europe, allowing soldiers and airmen to take night courses in pursuit of their college degrees, as my father had done. Also, one of my close friends had decided on Troy State, so my mind was made up—either OU or TSU.

Finally, sometime in the early spring of my senior year, I received a notice in the mail from AFROTC Headquarters. "Congratulations!" the letter began, "You have been selected as a Primary Alternate for a 4-year AFROTC Scholarship."

My parents and I were disappointed, naturally, but not really surprised. This being 1974, the Air Force was at the start of the post-Vietnam drawdown, and scholarships were at a premium. We assumed that my chances of being picked up as an alternate were slim at best. My game plan was to proceed to Troy State, enroll in the AFROTC program, and hope to compete for a 3-year scholarship while there.

Our high school graduation took place in downtown Wiesbaden at the Kurhaus, the elegant spa resort of the city. It served as Wiesbaden's main convention center, with ballrooms, fountains, and was full of old-world charm. After the ceremony, we were unleashed to attend the numerous graduation parties scheduled throughout the evening in the various housing areas. The first one I attended was held in Aukumn at the home of one of the girls from the Revelation Generation. It was a great party—plenty of food, beverages, music, and it was packed. I was sitting in the den with a few friends, and people started slowly heading to the backyard to attack the grilled delicacies. Suddenly, I found myself alone in the den with Wendy Shelton.

Wendy Shelton was one of the most popular girls in school. She was beautiful, smart, and funny. She had been a cheerleader in our junior year, the first time I really noticed her. Wendy had lived in Wiesbaden since starting her freshman year in 1970; she was a San Antonio girl, and her mother had remarried an Air Force Ears-Nose-and-Throat (ENT) surgeon, Dr. Felix Portelli. Wiesbaden was Wendy's first experience as an Air Force Brat. During one of her first days in school, someone had said, "My Dad is TDY" (Temporary Duty travel), meaning he was away on business.

Wendy replied, "My Dad is ENT!!" She had much to learn about military acronyms.

Wendy was a colonel's daughter and lived in Aukumn. We had taken a Humanities course together in school that senior year. At one point, I played Paris, and she played Helen of Troy in a brief reading of *The Iliad* in class. I sat in the back—she sat in the front by the teacher's desk. We ran in different circles and were barely acquaintances. But I knew her—oh, yes. She was one of the prettiest and sweetest girls in the school, and way out of my league.

Now was my chance...

Being the polished, debonair guy I was, I noticed a guitar sitting by the piano. I picked it up, looked Wendy in the eye, and sang "Ain't No Sunshine When She's Gone."

She smiled—didn't say a word—and after I had finished, people started drifting back in again, and we were no longer alone. That was the last time I saw Wendy—my future wife—until eight years later.

I spent the rest of that summer in Wiesbaden playing gigs with Uhuru, chasing girls, and having fun with my closest friends. All of us went to college—all of us went into AFROTC or the Naval Academy—and all of us went on to successful military careers. One became a 2-Star Rear Admiral, one a Navy Captain, one an Air Force Colonel, and three retired as Air Force Lieutenant Colonels. All of us were enlisted kids. I am still in close touch with each of them today.

I was excited to begin college and return to the States, but I knew I would really miss Wiesbaden.

Although I will always consider myself an Okie and Wendy will always be a Texan, we cherish Wiesbaden as a home of sorts. I had attended nine different schools in twelve years, and until my retirement from the Air Force, Wiesbaden was the place where I had lived the longest since my father had two assignments there. I have fond memories of travel throughout Europe, riding the shuttle buses through the different housing areas and U.S. installations, listening to Radio Luxembourg late at night, strolling downtown in the resort city of Wiesbaden, traveling by train to attend rock concerts in Frankfurt, performing shows with The Revelation Generation and Uhuru, playing football, street hockey, and generally living the carefree life of a high school kid in Germany. It was an exceptional experience and one that Wendy and I are blessed to share.

In recent years, there have been books, movies, and commentaries that overwhelmingly highlight the negative aspects of being raised in a military environment. Several stereotypes exist—the alcoholic, abusive, career-obsessed absentee father; the parent with post-traumatic stress who can't relate to their family; the fanatically-strict father who treats his family like basic trainees at boot camp; the shy, lonely child who is traumatized for life from having to move, attend a different school, and make new friends every year. There is no doubt that these tragic situations truly do exist, and I know that many military brats had—and currently have—significant difficulties growing up. Particularly in more recent years, the challenges military families face have increased dramatically with our never-ending pace of combat deployments. My heart goes out to them, and we need to keep families in mind every time we thank a serviceman for his or her service.

But for me, my wife, my son, and most of my friends, growing up as a military child was an overwhelmingly positive experience. As we attend reunions with our high school classmates and stay in touch via the internet, what remains is a clear sense that we had a very special childhood that most of us appreciate for its adventure, uniqueness, and the friends we made. I wouldn't have traded it for the world.

A few weeks before my 18th birthday, my parents put me on a plane at Rhein-Main Air Base in Frankfurt and sent me back to the States for the first time in three years. I first flew to Hobart to spend some time with family there.

Being in America again took some getting used to, but I still had some old friends who remembered me, and they helped me adjust. After a few weeks, my parents joined me in Oklahoma, and we drove to Alabama to spend some time with family in Fayette before heading to Troy State.

At that point, amazingly enough, I didn't even really know what I wanted to study. I looked over the course guide and finally decided to major in Business Administration, with an emphasis in Economics. I had taken an Economics course as an elective in high school and enjoyed it, so I figured it would be a safe bet.

We made the drive from Fayette to Troy, and it was an eye-opener for me to see where I would be living for the next four years. I had never really lived in Alabama and had never visited Troy. There was no internet in those days, so I didn't really know what to expect. Troy appeared to be just another mid-sized southern town, and the campus seemed to be small, tidy, and cozy. We drove straight to the Alumni Hall dormitory where I would be staying, and while I was unpacking, Dad disappeared.

He reappeared about twenty minutes later. "I just popped into the AFROTC office to check in and say hi," he said. "You got it!"

I didn't quite know what he meant. "Got what?" I asked.

"You got the 4-year scholarship!" Dad said with a huge grin on his face.

I was absolutely stunned—but he was ecstatic, and so was I. Uncle Sam was going to pay for my education, I had a job waiting for me after I graduated, I was going to be an Air Force officer, and I had a pilot slot!

We ran downstairs to tell Mom—she couldn't come into Alumni Hall since it was a male-only dorm. She was beside herself with joy as well, but there were mixed feelings; in a few minutes, I had to say goodbye to my parents, as they departed to make their way back to Wiesbaden. I would rejoin them in Germany for the Christmas holidays.

That first quarter at Troy State was an enjoyable adjustment to a new life. I roomed with a good friend of mine, a fellow Air Force Brat I had known in Wiesbaden. We didn't know anyone else, and neither one of us could drive, since the driving age in Germany was eighteen.

Some guys living next door in the dorm took us under their wing—they were from Mobile, were intrigued with our military background, and amused that we were both in AFROTC. They helped introduce us to life in America, took us to their homes on weekends, and generally took care of us—true Southern hospitality.

The change from living in a military environment overseas to a civilian environment stateside wasn't as difficult as I thought it would be. We were all living in the same dorm with the same academic challenges, so it was fairly easy to settle in with the help of these new friends.

I took quickly to college life; the burden of a scholarship made me get serious about my grades, and I aced all of my courses, including College Algebra—surprise! I played intramural football, became active in AFROTC extra-curricular activities, and enjoyed living with a fair amount of independence.

The AFROTC detachment there at Troy State was outstanding. Even though this was the end of the Vietnam War and the beginning of the drawdown in overall military strength, the detachment had about 140 cadets enrolled in AFROTC. Since Troy State was well known in military circles through its presence in Education Offices at bases all over the world, we had a large prior-enlisted population, which gave our cadet corps an added maturity and experience. Plus, this was the Deep South—the military was still highly respected. There were no anti-war protests at Troy State during the Sixties or early Seventies, and certainly no attempts to burn down the ROTC building, as was fairly common at other colleges and universities throughout the nation during that period. I continued to excel during that first year, and life was good.

In the summer of 1975, after completing my freshman year, I rejoined my parents, who had since been reassigned to Tinker Air Force Base in Oklahoma City. The big activity during that summer was getting my driver's license and buying my first car—a school-bus-yellow 1972 Ford Maverick. Two more good friends from Wiesbaden decided to attend Troy State after I conducted an aggressive drafting campaign to have them join me, and my sophomore year was a repeat of the fun and success of the first.

Now that I had a car, I was able to drive up to the farm in Fayette for weekend visits with my grandmother on a fairly regular basis, and I enjoyed occasionally getting away from campus and being spoiled by my Mama White. My Brat friends and I did all the things guys did in college during those years—study, drink beer when we could afford it (Coors was highly valued and hard to come by east of the Mississippi River), watch TV (*Happy Days*, *Three's Company*, and my favorite, *Monty Python's Flying Circus* on PBS), and spend time with our girlfriends. We went to rock concerts in Montgomery and Dothan, where we saw Kiss, Blue Oyster Cult, Aerosmith, and a host of other hard rock bands we all liked. We would occasionally drive down to the beaches at Pensacola or Gulf

Shores on weekends, and since all of us were in ROTC, we stayed busy with the myriad of events that were part of the program.

At the conclusion of my sophomore year, I was scheduled to attend AFROTC Field Training at McConnell Air Force Base in Wichita, Kansas, over that summer of 1976, and it was there that I flew an airplane for the first time.

Part of the Field Training program was to give us future Air Force officers an orientation flight in the Cessna T-37. The T-37 Tweet is a small, twin-engine trainer used during that time as the primary jet trainer at Air Force Undergraduate Pilot Training (UPT), with the instructor and student seated side-by-side. The cockpit was unpressurized, so it had a service ceiling of 25,000 feet. It was fully acrobatic, could endure up to 6.7 Gs, and had a maximum speed of about 350 mph. It was notorious for the loud, high-pitched screech of its engines—many called it The 6,000 Pound Dog Whistle.

The Air Force flew our group of Field Training cadets from McConnell AFB to Vance AFB in Enid, Oklahoma in a C-130 for our orientation rides. We were all ushered into the Base Theater, where we were given a welcome and basic briefing as to what to expect. Much attention was paid to the location and use of airsickness bags. As I learned later, T-37 pilots hated these 20-minute ROTC orientation rides, as they tended to be puke-o-ramas.

When my turn came, I was ushered into the light rain and out to my Tweet, with its left engine still running. I jumped into the right seat and shook hands with the pilot whose face I couldn't see because of his mask, helmet, and dark visor. The crew chief strapped me in, the pilot restarted the right engine, closed the canopy, and off we went.

This is the part of the typical flying biography where I am supposed to say that I fell in love with flying with that first flight. Yet again, this was not the case with me.

We were in and out of the clouds for most of the flight, and I remember just concentrating on the pilot's running narrative, his stick and rudder movements, and being fascinated with all the cockpit instruments. He did a few aileron rolls, but since we were mostly in the clouds, it wasn't that impressive. Although we were briefed that we wouldn't get a chance to fly, I did get a little stick time, but nothing more than keeping the jet straight-and-level and on speed, with a few easy turns to a set heading. The ride was over before I knew it. I had enjoyed the flight okay and didn't get sick, but I can't say it was the thrill that I secretly hoped it would be.

Nevertheless, it was during my junior year that I first started to seriously consider becoming a pilot. I had entered my AFROTC freshman class of about 50 at Troy State as one of three 4-year scholarship winners. By the start of my junior year in 1976, one of those guys had dropped out, and the other had failed a physical, so I was the only pilot candidate in my class. As I continued through the AFROTC program, I began to appreciate more and more what a gift I had been given to have the opportunity to fly. After quite a bit of study and contemplation, I decided that I wanted to fly the A-10 Thunderbolt II, better known as the Warthog, after I got my wings.

The mission of the A-10 was a concept that appealed to me. Through my AFROTC studies, I started to become keenly interested in military history. When I wasn't preparing for my college classes, I studied military history, biographies, and especially enjoyed reading about strategy and tactics — Clausewitz, Jomini, B.H. Liddell-Hart.

I wasn't reading much about air power outside my AFROTC studies, but I was fascinated with armies, troop movements, and warfare. While I understood that the F-15 was the jet all the die-hard fighter-pilot-wannabees wanted to fly, I liked the idea of an A-10 flying low, dropping bombs, strafing with that huge 30mm gun, and providing Close Air Support (CAS) to troops on the ground.

The F-16 was still in development, and seemed to be a magic jet; I preferred something with a bit more traditional stick-and-rudder application, flying a mission I appreciated and could understand. Plus, the A-10 just looked cool to me — a brutal, flying beast made for maximum violence.

For that reason, I requested and received an assignment to Myrtle Beach AFB, South Carolina, for the Third Lieutenant program in the summer of 1977, between my junior and senior year. The Third Lieutenant program allowed future Air Force officers an opportunity to spend some time with an active unit, and gain some hands-on experience.

Myrtle Beach had an operational A-10 wing, and I wanted a chance to get up close and personal with the Warthog. While I was actually assigned to a UH-1 Helicopter Rescue Unit for the program, I was able to fly the A-10 simulator a few times, and while I wasn't ready to solo by any means, I could manage to takeoff, fly, and land the A-10 simulator without crashing most of the time.

I also gained a whole new appreciation for the guys flying helicopters; it's a vital, gutsy mission, but I decided it was a miracle of the Lord every time a helicopter got airborne, and probably not for me.

At the start of Spring Quarter in my senior year, I began the AFROTC Flight Screening program. This was a program set up to give AFROTC pilot candidates a chance to take basic flying lessons at a local civilian airport and solo out in a Cessna 150, a light-weight, single-engine, propeller-driven airplane commonly used for basic flight training. The real goal of the course was to weed out anyone who had a fear of flying, or who simply didn't have an aptitude for it.

My lessons were conducted at the Ozark, Alabama airfield, about 45 minutes south of Troy. Ozark was the home of Fort Rucker, where both the Army and Air Force conducted their basic helicopter training. I took to flying the little C-150 quickly, but for me, it was a task to be mastered more than taking delight in flying an airplane. We practiced stalls, spins, engine-out procedures, traffic patterns, and touch-and-go landings. I soloed out after 10 hours, passed my check ride after 20 hours, and finished with 22 hours in the C-150.

As we neared graduation and commissioning in June 1978, we all looked forward to our first Air Force assignments. My number one choice for pilot training was Williams AFB near Phoenix, Arizona. It had great weather, was located near a metropolitan area, and had a reputation as the premier UPT base. I was delighted when I was notified about my assignment to Williams in early Spring. Another bonus—at least I considered it a bonus—was that due to the post-Vietnam drawdown and reduction-in-force for pilots, there was a backlog at Air Force UPT bases. I wouldn't have to report to Williams until almost a year after commissioning. This provided an opportunity for me to complete my master's degree before entering active duty.

In anticipation of this delay, I had begun taking electives in Political Science, with the hopes that I could earn a Master of Political Science after earning my bachelor's degree in Business Administration. The one drawback was that you were not paid during this interim period, and there was no scholarship money available. As a result, I applied for admission to the University of Oklahoma's master's degree in Political Science program and planned on living at home with my parents in Oklahoma City during my studies.

The day of commissioning and graduation arrived. My parents and aunt attended the ceremony. My father was still active duty, wore his uniform, and rendered my first salute as an Air Force Second Lieutenant. As I handed him the traditional silver dollar for that first salute from my Chief Master Sergeant father, I got a little choked up. Dad had foreseen this day ever since bringing home that Air Force Academy pamphlet when I was nine, and that day had arrived. It was a big day for our family.

Knowing that I couldn't rely on scholarship money to pay for my master's degree, I knew I would have to work part-time. So, on the same day I became a commissioned Air Force Second Lieutenant, I reported to McDonald's that evening to begin my summer job cooking hamburgers during the night shift.

While waiting for confirmation that I had been accepted into the University of Oklahoma for the fall semester, I took two masters-level Political Science courses at Troy State over the summer. Within a few weeks, I received notification that I had been accepted to OU. I finished summer school and moved back to Oklahoma with my parents to continue work on my master's degree.

Although I took a heavy class load to ensure I could complete my degree before entering active duty, I thoroughly enjoyed my classes at OU. I worked on my master's thesis, *Reactions of the American Military Community to the Baader-Meinhof Terrorist*

Bombings, using texts and articles from German magazines and newspapers, and sent surveys to friends who had lived in Wiesbaden during that period.

Many of my classes were attended by Iranian students, who were extremely vocal about their support for the Islamic Revolution, the evils of the Shah and the American CIA, our support for Israel, and the great changes the new Ayatollah Khomeini was creating. It was quite an eye-opener, and I think many of us could see future storm clouds rising. Still, it was a different area of study for me, and I immersed myself in it.

There were a few active duty Air Force officers who were also getting their master's degrees in Political Science at Oklahoma. Two of them were enrolled in the Air Force Institute of Technology (AFIT) program; they were both Intelligence officers. Another officer flew the E-3 AWACS out of nearby Tinker AFB and was taking night classes. They took me under their wing, and I hung out with them during the day between classes.

It was through them that I first learned of the German Air Force pilot training program at Sheppard AFB in Wichita Falls, Texas. The program was strictly for German and Dutch student pilots, and the instructors were a mix of German, Dutch, and U.S. flyers. The flying syllabus was quite a bit different and more aggressive than the USAF syllabus; all of the graduates would go on to fly fighters in their own country, so the basic syllabus reflected the need for more advanced training, including more low-level visual navigation and formation flying. I filed that tidbit of little-known information away for future use.

My report date to Williams was set for May 12th, 1979. I finished work on my master's degree on May 9th—the plan had worked perfectly. I packed up my car, said goodbye to my parents, and headed down I-40 to life in the active-duty Air Force. I had been on a pilot roster for five years, and it was time to finally get started.

CHAPTER TWO

EARNING MY WINGS

Williams Air Force Base, AZ

1979-1980

How much more there is now to living!... There's a reason to life! We can lift ourselves out of ignorance, we can find ourselves as creatures of excellence and intelligence and skill. We can be free! We can fly!

—Richard Bach, *Jonathan Livingston Seagull*

Anyone who has ever made the trip west on I-40 knows what a lonesome stretch of interstate it is. Between Oklahoma City and Flagstaff, Arizona, where you turn south and take I-17 on into Phoenix, there is Amarillo, Albuquerque, and Gallup—and that's about it. Nearly 870 miles of straight-ahead highway with mostly flat, brown desert terrain to keep you entertained. It gave me plenty of time to think about what I was about to do. I hadn't thought about flying much since commissioning; I was too busy trying to finish my master's degree. I wasn't sure what lay ahead, but I thought I was ready. I had done well during flight screening, and I tended to hold my own academically and in sports, so how hard could it be?

Williams Air Force Base, or Willie as it was generally called, was located in Chandler, Arizona, about 30 miles southeast of Phoenix. It opened as a training facility during WWII and was considered the Air Force's primary pilot training base. The base had three long runways and was led by the 82nd Training Wing commander. Besides T-37 and T-38 training, it also ran an F-5 conversion training program for various allied air forces. Coming through the main gate, I drove around the base for a while, trying to get the lay of the land. It was a nice base— mostly modern buildings with only a few WWII-era relics, and spotless, as most Air Force installations tend to be. I checked in to the Orderly Room, filled out a stack of documents, and was given the key to my room in the Bachelor Officers Quarters (BOQ)—hopefully, my home for the next ten months as I sought my wings.

My BOQ room was fairly standard for the times. It was a one-room efficiency-style apartment, with a private bathroom and a shared kitchen with the room next door. It was furnished with the same bulky furniture you found in every Air Force quarters throughout the world with a single bed, a desk, a small couch, a coffee table, and a chest-of-drawers. Washers and dryers were located in a separate room on each floor of the two-story building. It was more than enough room for me and my belongings, and I felt right at home.

I met my kitchen mate, a Virginia Tech grad, who was also in my class. He was a nice guy; he had worked selling cars while waiting to enter active duty, and seemed to be as nervous and excited as I was. It was a Saturday, so we had all day Sunday to unpack, explore the base and downtown Chandler, and worry about what Monday had in store for us.

Early Monday morning, we departed together for our in-processing appointment at the Base Administration office. We were ushered into a large auditorium-like room, and it was full of restless, talkative guys in mostly ill-fitting short-sleeve blue uniforms like the one I was wearing. The first thing I noticed was many of the guys had 3 x 5 cards they were studying intently. "Whatcha got there?" I asked one of them.

"Boldface," he replied without looking up.

"What's boldface?" I asked.

He looked at me like I had three heads. "Boldface are emergency procedures you have to have memorized—it's pass-fail, and we'll probably be tested on them later this week."

Uh-oh. Someone forgot to give me the memo.

I quickly learned that I was already way behind the power curve. My class was designated Class 80-05, meaning we would be the fifth class scheduled to graduate in fiscal year 1980, estimated to be sometime in late April. There were 60 of us— the largest class in several years, and the beginning of a pilot build-up after the Air Force realized, not for the first time, and not for the last, that it cut too many pilots during the post-Vietnam Reduction-In-Force (RIF).

Of those 60, eleven had been navigators or non-flying officers who had received pilot slots, six were Air National Guard products, and the rest of us were brand new lieutenants who had received their commissions through AFROTC at universities throughout the U.S. There were no Air Force Academy graduates; since it was May, the latest Academy class had not yet graduated, and Academy grads didn't have the nearly year-long wait most of us had prior to entering active duty. I could tell by eavesdropping in on other conversations that everyone else appeared much more prepared than I seemed to be. I tried not to panic.

After filling out paperwork all morning, we received some much-appreciated advance pay and our new active duty military identification cards. I surrendered the dependent ID card I had since I was ten. Getting an active duty ID was pretty neat, I thought, as it was another symbol of my transition into adulthood.

We then proceeded to the academic building to be issued around 30 pounds of books: the T-37 Dash One, Air Force Regulation 60-16, Air Force Manual 51-37, and many more regs and manuals we would all strive to memorize.

We were then directed to report to the supply hangar, where we were issued our flight gear. Now, this was more like it! We were fitted and issued our flight helmets, oxygen mask, helmet bag, flight boots, flight gloves, two flight suits each, a light-weight flight jacket, a pressure-resistant wristwatch, and a pair of Joe Cool Air Force-issue aviator shades. We were finally done for the day, and I'm sure every one of us rushed back to their rooms and did exactly as I did—put on all the new flight gear and stare in the mirror with self-admiration at the Air Force's newest student pilot.

The rest of the week was devoted to more admin, in-processing, and academics. We were separated into two training flights; half of us would be in Jack Black flight, and half of us would be in No Loss. I was assigned to No Loss, as was my kitchen mate. We wouldn't even see an airplane or get to the flight line for several weeks, after we had many hours of academics, completed Life Support training, and numerous sorties in the T-37 simulator.

We were also given physicals once again, mostly to ensure we were all healthy and still had 20/20 uncorrected vision. One of the things they did during that physical was take our footprints. Odd, I thought—I understood fingerprints, but footprints? I asked the physician's assistant why.

"If you crash and burn, usually the only thing remaining is your feet—the thick leather flight boots tend to protect them from disintegration. Your footprint may be the only way we can identify the body." Nice to know.

Another shock was to learn that a score of 85% on all tests was the minimum passing grade—84% was considered a failure. This was a whole new standard, and I spent every evening that first week studying like a madman, trying to memorize the T-37 boldface procedures, catch up with the rest of the class, and prepare for that first test on Friday.

The first test was a separate boldface test; we learned we would be tested weekly on the boldface, and if we even missed one comma, jot, or tittle, we would be grounded. The other test was our first academic test, dealing primarily with T-37 cockpit instruments and switches—functions and characteristics of the attitude indicator, altitude indicator, speedometer, gear and flaps switches, etc. I was relieved to pass the boldface test, but almost fell out of my chair when I got my first academic test score—an 86%.

I had almost flunked my first test. I took furtive glances at some of the other guy's test results and saw mostly high-90s and 100% scores. How hard can it be? Pretty hard, at least for me, I guess.

That evening brought a newly-learned tradition—heading to the Officer's Club and bar every Friday after the last jet had landed. After surviving the first week, the entire class was ready for our first experience rubbing shoulders with the instructors and students who were in classes ahead of us.

A couple of guys from my flight and I entered the bar through a side entrance where a captain stood at the door. "Come on in, gents!" he smiled as he opened the door for us.

My kitchen mate stepped in first, and with his first step, someone loudly rang a bell over the bar, and the entire room erupted in applause and hoots of laughter. He had been slow to take off his hat—and a time-honored Air Force tradition, we learned, was that you never wear your hat in the bar, out of respect for those who have gone before. The penalty was buying a round for the entire bar, signified by the ringing of the bell, and there was absolutely no getting out of it.

The whole base knew there was a new class in town, and they were eagerly welcoming us novices to Willie by cordially opening the door for us and greeting us with the bell. That captain stayed by the door most of the night—the bell must have gone off a dozen times.

I had never been much of a drinker; having been raised in Germany, there was no real mystique about alcohol for me, and I didn't drink much in college, mostly because I couldn't afford it. Well, I could afford it that night, since it was free beer all night long with the continuous clanging of the bell—and another new experience was the massive hangover I had the next morning.

The next few weeks were more of the same—T-37 academics, Life Support training, and simulators. We were tested often, and I finally settled down and started to pass the tests comfortably. I especially liked Life Support training—we learned and practiced Parachute Landing Falls (PLFs) from different heights, and each of us took a ride on the Led Sled—an ejection seat simulator where you enjoyed the instantaneous 14-g shock of an ejection. We were put in the altitude chamber, where we were able to experience different pressure altitudes and taught to recognize our individual hypoxia symptoms, should our oxygen system fail.

Finally, we went parasailing so we could experience what it was like to drift down under a parachute canopy and perform a real PLF. To do this, they took us out to an old abandoned runway in the middle of the desert, attached us to a parachute harness, held the parachute in back of us, tied us to a truck, and told us to start running as soon as the truck started rolling. We would be airborne, they assured us, very quickly. "Whatever you do, don't stop running after you get airborne—you might float back down still attached to the truck and be dragged along the ground at 40 mph."

After we got airborne under the inflated chute at the height of about 200 feet, they would cut us loose from the truck, and we would (hopefully) safely float down and be graded on our PLF. I volunteered to go first—as a lightweight I was airborne in seconds, it went just as advertised, and was a lot of fun.

The simulator missions began to get more challenging as we got closer to our first flight in the Tweet. The emphasis shifted from ground operations, start, taxi, takeoff, and landing, to emergency procedures. First, we were given simple emergencies, such as electrical failure, then progressed to boldface emergencies such as engine failure, then on to multiple simultaneous emergencies. On our first day of academics, our instructor had said, "The Air Force can teach a monkey to fly—so we should do okay with you guys."

One of my classmates later muttered, "They may be able to teach a monkey to fly, but I'll be darned if they can teach a monkey to fly that dang simulator!"

The big day finally came, and we were sent down to the flightline and introduced to our flying instructors in No Loss Flight. Each instructor had his own table in a large open room and had three to four students assigned to him. I hit the jackpot—my instructor pilot (IP) was a former RF-4 pilot with combat time in Vietnam. There were only two instructors in our flight who had fighter experience. The rest of the IPs were bomber-tanker-transport pilots or were First Assignment Instructor Pilots (FAIPs)—pilots who became instructors right out of pilot training. Most of us wanted an IP with fighter time, and I had gotten one of them.

My IP was your typical Vietnam-era fighter pilot. He was cocky, brash, bald-headed, big mustached, and every other word was a curse word. His favorite expression was "F%#k me dead!" as he would roll his eyes with any question we failed to answer to his satisfaction. He never smiled and looked thoroughly unimpressed as the four of us who were assigned to him introduced ourselves.

His introduction went something like this, "I ain't your buddy. I ain't your friend. I could care less if you get your wings or not—that's up to you, not me. It's gonna be tough, and it's gonna be tough every day. You better come here every day ready to fly. You better be prepared, and you better bring me your best. If I sense you are slacking off or being lazy, you are done. You better not embarrass me by screwing up, on the ground or in the air. I will have your butt, and I will personally kick you off this base. Questions?" I immediately idolized him.

One of the first things our new IP emphasized was the need to have Chapter 8 of our Aircrew Operational Procedures T-37 manual completely memorized. Chapter 8 dealt with Local Area Procedures and provided specific guidance on everything we needed to know about flying out of Williams AFB. It included ground operations, getting to and from the airspace reserved for flying training, traffic pattern procedures, and, most importantly, to our IP, standard radio calls. "I don't want you toads humiliating me on the radios—you better not mess up your comms." He spoke much about the need for chair flying.

"Get in your rooms, shut all the curtains, turn off the TV and stereo, and fly the mission—the entire mission—in your heads. Make all the radio calls, and say them out loud as you visualize start, taxi, takeoff, working in the areas, recovery, and landing. Strap your checklist to your leg, and refer to it just as you would in flight. What airspeed do I need to have at this point? What altitude restrictions do I need to meet? Fly the entire mission sitting in your chair in your BOQ—don't just study Chapter 8, fly it! Do it over and over again until it's flawless—then do it some more. Think about what you're going to say on the radios before you hit the mic button—rehearse your radio calls just like you'll do them in the cockpit. Don't stop until it becomes second nature. You may not be very proficient yet, but at least you'll sound like you know what you're doing."

It was wise advice, and I spent many hours chair flying in my room. Sometimes, I'd even put on my helmet, mask, and gloves just to try and make it as realistic as possible. It was a useful lesson I carried with me my entire career.

Finally, nearly a month after our arrival, I was scheduled for my dollar ride. New pilots were expected to give a dollar bill, which was signed and dated, to your IP after that initial sortie, and most IPs kept their collection of bills under the plexiglass at their tables. There was a palpable excitement in the flight, as guys would return from their first flights and relate their experiences. I was nervous, obviously, but mostly because I was afraid I would let my IP down.

I also worried about the spin recovery in the T-37—it was a complex, boldface maneuver that couldn't adequately be practiced in the simulator. I still remember the T-37 spin boldface to this day:

1. Throttles - Idle
2. Rudder and Ailerons - Neutral
3. Stick - Abruptly Full Aft and Hold
4. Rudder - Abruptly Apply Full Rudder Opposite Spin Direction (Opposite Turn Needle) and Hold
5. Stick - Abruptly Full Forward One Turn After Applying Rudder
6. Controls - Neutral After Spinning Stops and Recover From Dive

It sounded like a pretty violent maneuver on paper, and more than one of the students in my flight had confessed to getting sick during their dollar rides. I imagined the outrage my IP would have if I were such a "weak d#%k," as he put it, to vomit in his cockpit. Still, I felt ready and wanted to get it started.

We briefed the mission. My IP gave me an outline of how the mission would go overall and what he expected. Essentially, he was along for the ride.

He would expect me to start, taxi, and takeoff on my own and make all the radio calls. He would point out area references, and then once we got to the area, he would demo each maneuver first, then expect me to do it.

I briefed him how I was going to actually perform the maneuvers—an aileron roll, a loop, and a spin would be all we would do on this first sortie. I would then fly back to the traffic pattern, again making all the radio calls, until we got to the pattern.

He would demo a straight-in touch-and-go landing, then we would go back out, and I would do it. Then he would take the jet for the overhead pattern for a demo, again pointing out visual references for inside and outside downwind, then I would perform overhead touch-and-gos until we landed full-stop.

We processed through Life Support—I grabbed my helmet, mask, and gloves, stored away a few airsickness bags in my helmet bag just in case, and donned my parachute. We caught the crew trolley outside Life Support, gave them our tail number, and were driven out to the jet.

It was the middle of June in Arizona; the temperature was 100+ degrees, so we both had water bottles stashed away in our flight suits. We had our ear protectors on—the high-pitched wail of multiple T-37s with engines running sounded like a gaggle of angry banshees, and you were guaranteed hearing loss without the noise protection. A running joke was the Tweet converted jet fuel into noise, and it was easy to see (hear) why.

I looked at the 781 forms to review the status of the jet— what repairs had been performed, how many hours it had flown, when it was next due any specific maintenance actions, etc. My IP asked me a few questions to ensure I knew what I was looking for, then followed me around as I performed the exterior inspection, again, asking a few questions to ensure I knew what I was doing and following the checklist. We then jumped in the jet—me in the left seat, he in the right. We strapped in, put on our helmets, and he looked at me and said, "ready when you are."

I did okay on the ground ops; later, I would complete them much faster, but I didn't make any mistakes. My IP had his helmet and visor on, but his mask was hanging loosely and on cold mike, meaning his mike wasn't automatically trans-mitting. He appeared to be bored and didn't say a word. We kept the canopy open due to the heat. I called for taxi as I had practiced in my room about a bazillion times, and off we went.

My IP remained silent, mask hanging loosely, still on cold mike. I got us to the end of the runway, got clearance for takeoff, called, "canopy clear!" and lowered the canopy.

My IP finally put on his mask and went back to hot mike; I could hear him breathing, but he still remained silent. I got us into position, recited my final pre-takeoff checks—"line on line, point on point, four green, no red, no amber"—slowly pushed the throttles forward to military, or full power, and we started rolling forward.

The two little J-69 engines only provided about 1,000 pounds of thrust each, so we accelerated slowly—slower than I anticipated. We finally started picking up speed; I rotated and raised the nose about ten degrees at 75 knots, and the aircraft slowly became airborne at 90 knots. After we were safely airborne, I raised the gear and flaps, made a left turn out of traffic as required, and flew the departure course to the training area. As I made that left turn, I noticed my IP again dropping his mask and going cold mike. Still, he said not a word.

As we gained more altitude, he put his mask back on and started pointing out visual references. As we entered the working area, I made a radio call in the blind that we were entering the area at our altitude to ensure no one had overstayed their allotted time and to verify that the area was free for us to work.

My IP then took the jet, did some clearing turns, pointed out a few more area references, then performed an aileron roll. He talked his way through it, and I listened intently and watched his stick and rudder movements. He then gave it to me to try. An aileron roll is a simple maneuver, but mine was sloppy; I hadn't gotten a feel for coordinating rudder inputs very well yet, so my nose wandered more than it should have. I tried a few more, with some improvement.

He next took the jet for a loop, pushing the throttle forward and heading down about 45 degrees nose low to pick up speed. He then initiated a 4-G pull to the vertical, continuing to talk as if we were taking a Sunday stroll while I performed my L-1 straining anti-G maneuver. I did get a little greying visual sensation—it was the first time I had pulled that many Gs, and it was kind of exciting. He continued over the top, talking all the way, completed a perfect loop, then handed me the jet. I was slow to blend into the 4-G pull, and pulled too much coming over the top rather than releasing back pressure as I had been instructed, so we were slow on speed. Still, I completed the loop, and after a few more tries, was performing them fairly decently. My IP then took the jet to demonstrate a spin entry and recovery.

I had performed spins in the Cessna 150 during flight screening at Troy State, but I suspected this would be a different kettle of fish. It was. After performing a few more clearing turns, the IP pulled the throttle to idle, and began slowly but steadily pulling back on the stick to almost pure vertical. We quickly started to get stall indications—the IP described it as, "First you feel cats dancing on the wings, then dogs, then pigs, then elephants. You're about to stall when you feel the elephants." The stall warning horn went off, the IP applied full left rudder, and we snapped—and I mean snapped—into a left spin.

The T-37 entered a spin much quicker and more aggressively than I remembered the Cessna 150. The IP continued to talk, drawling out the spin recovery boldface, while I watched the world rotate below and tried not to hyperventilate. I noticed that Step 5—Stick - Abruptly Full Forward was very abrupt, almost a pop of the stick from full aft to full forward. However, that action broke the stall, and the jet easily recovered from the dive.

He then gave me the jet for my first attempt. My IP continued to talk me through the entry, and as we entered the spin, I began to recite the spin boldface—slower than my IP, so the spin really started to wrap up tightly. When I shoved the stick forward to break the stall, I held it forward too long, and the nose almost tucked under with negative Gs—not very comfortable at all. My IP cursed under his breath, but I recovered the jet successfully. He sternly let me know what I had done wrong, and we set up for another one. This time my stick technique was better, and then it was time for us to head back to the traffic pattern for my first landings.

On the way back to Willie, my IP continued to point out area references, including a swimming pool on long final, "where a babe likes to sunbathe in a yellow bikini." She wasn't out that day, or any other day, for that matter.

We completed the Before Landing checks, and my IP took the jet to demo a straight-in landing. It seemed easy enough, not much different than the Cessna. He gave me the jet as we turned downwind, and continued to point out area references. I executed the Chapter 8 straight-in procedures, and my first landing was okay; I held the jet off a little higher than optimum, and while a little long, the landing wasn't too firm. My IP explained that I wanted to be just a few inches above the runway, feel the cats dancing on the wings, and land on speed within the first 500 feet.

He then took the jet and turned crosswind for the outside downwind pattern, continuing to point out visual references all the way. As we came up initial, he emphasized clearing the pattern and making sure there were no traffic conflicts; with training going on from sunrise to sunset, the traffic pattern was usually very busy with students like me practicing their patterns and landings.

We went into the break about half-way down the runway—a pull of about 3-Gs, which surprised me, and entered inside downwind much closer to the runway than I anticipated. "I don't want to ever see you fly a wide bomber pattern—you fly with me, you fly like a fighter pilot," he said with an I'm not messin' around emphasis.

The final turn was also more aggressive than I was used to, and a bit intimidating. He executed a perfect touch-and-go landing, then requested a closed pattern to inside downwind. I heard the controller say, "Closed approved," and the IP snatched the jet into a tight, 3-G pull up to closed downwind.

I was caught by surprise again by the aggressive pull to closed, and was feeling a bit disoriented as he said, "Your jet!"

I put the gear down about half-way downwind, followed by the flaps—dropped the speed brake, ensured the landing light was still on and departed the perch. "Gear down, three green, flaps, landing light, speed brake," I whispered to myself as a final pre-landing check—something I did as a ritual my entire career. My final turn was not aggressive enough, and I overshot the runway.

"Go around," my IP muttered. I executed a go around, requested a closed, and tried to fly as aggressive a closed pattern as my IP had done. I overshot downwind altitude by about 200 feet, earning more muttered scorn from my IP, but got the jet settled down, flew the pattern, and this time made the runway with another fairly long but decent landing. We continued to fly a few more patterns, each getting better, until we were low on gas, and it was time to call it a day. On landing roll, I performed my post-flight checks and felt a huge feeling of relief. I had survived my dollar ride without getting sick or getting us killed.

As we turned off the runway, my IP said "canopy clear," opened the canopy, dropped his mask, and returned to cold mike. It was amazing to me how good that cool 100+ degree outside temperature felt. The T-37 had a horrible cockpit cooling system. We had been warned that cockpit temperatures often reached 130 degrees in the summer, contributing greatly to the number of airsickness and manifestation of apprehension episodes that often led to new pilots being eliminated from the program.

For the first time, I realized I was absolutely drenched in sweat, and my mask felt wet and slimy on my face. I figured out that was why my IP kept his mask off as much as possible, to keep his mask dry, and to direct what little cooling air there was onto his face. My mask was full of sweat, and a nice little pool of liquid sludge had pooled around the microphone attached inside. After an hour-and-fifteen minute flight, I was exhausted.

We taxied in, shut down, and walked back to Life Support. My IP didn't say a word. We processed back through Life Support, paying extra attention to swabbing out our masks. "I'll meet you in debrief in 15 minutes," he said.

As I walked back into the flight room, the dollar ride post-flight ritual continued, with my classmates all coming up and asking, "How was it? How did you do? Did you get sick?"

I told everyone it was awesome, I loved it, and I didn't get sick. However, to be honest, I was working too hard to really enjoy flying a jet for the first time. As had been the case for me before, at this stage, flying was a task to be mastered more than enjoyed. The enjoyment would come after I got good at it.

I sat down with my IP, took out a dollar bill, signed and dated it, and gave it to him. He slipped it without ceremony under the plexiglass to join his large collection, then began the debrief. We talked about what I had done wrong, what I had done well, and what to expect for the next sortie. The entire debrief only lasted about 20 minutes; my IP had to get ready for the next sortie and another dollar ride with one on my table mates.

Our gradesheets were marked *Unsatisfactory, Fair, Good*, and *Excellent*. An *Unsat* obviously meant you had failed the ride and would have to repeat it. A second *Unsat* meant you would get some practice rides, then proceed to an Initial Progress Check (IPC) to see if you were still doing well enough to stay in the program. If you failed your IPC, you were given a few more practice rides before proceeding to your Final Progress Check (FPC). If you failed your FPC, you were out of the program, would be re-classified as non-rated, and given a new non-flying assignment. Most of us were getting *Fair* or *Good* overall grades—an *Excellent* was almost unheard of at that stage. I got a *Good* grade on my first sortie. Success!

The next several weeks were filled with more of the same—academics in the morning or afternoon, depending on if you were on an early week or late week schedule for flying, followed by either flying, or a hop in the simulator where we mostly rehearsed emergency procedures.

We continued working on aileron rolls, loops, and spins, as well as traffic pattern stalls, power-on stalls, slow flight, Lazy 8s, Cuban 8s, Split S maneuvers, Chandelles, Immelmans, Barrel Rolls, Cloverleafs, steep turns, and other area maneuvers. We practiced patterns and landings both at Willie and at the auxiliary field, nicknamed Headpin. I occasionally flew with some of the other No Loss instructors but was scheduled primarily with my regular IP. I continued getting *Good* overall grades, generally didn't make my IP very angry, and things were progressing nicely.

After my 8th training sortie, following the debrief, my IP asked me to step outside with him. We found a bench in the shade, sat down, and staring off into the distance, in his usual no-nonsense tone of voice, my IP said, "We just got a new instructor in the flight. He was a B-52 pilot and is fresh out of Pilot Instructor Training (PIT) at Randolph. He's going to be your new IP starting tomorrow."

My mind raced—What? Just a few rides before solo, and you're changing IPs on me? Why? What did I do wrong? I didn't say anything, but my IP could tell I was devastated.

"Look," he said, as his voice got softer—a tone I had never heard before. "You are doing great in the program, and you're gonna keep doing great. I've got four studs, and as you know, most IPs have three. I need to give one of you guys up to the new guy. I know you can handle the change to a new IP, so you're the one."

Still—I was crushed. I was losing my experienced fighter pilot IP to an inexperienced bomber IP who had never even taught UPT students before.

I loved my old instructor. Naturally, we students talked a lot about our IPs. Some guys had screamers, who would yell, harass, and pound the cockpit dashboard throughout the flight. Some guys had Chatty Cathys, who wouldn't shut up for the entire flight—constantly in instructor mode. Some IPs were a little skittish—one hand always hovering over the stick, always fidgeting and flinching. My IP was a hard guy, but he was an excellent instructor, confident, knew his business, and I was thriving under his tutelage. I was afraid it was all going to change.

I met my new IP the next day. He was originally from Guatemala and had a slight accent. He had an easy-going personality and was quick to laugh. He wasn't intimidating at all, nor did he try to be. He called me Lieutenant rather than P.K., and I was going to be his only student until I soloed, and I would have his undivided attention.

Being newly arrived from PIT at Randolph AFB in San Antonio, he was still in learning mode himself. On our first flight together, he stayed hot mike the entire flight. However, he said very little, and hardly ever took the jet to demo a maneuver, even on a first attempt; he was content to have me give it a go, then would verbally critique my performance and have me do it again as required. His grades were consistent with what I had been getting from other IPs, and I found myself looking forward to our flights and simulator missions together. This was going to work out fine.

I continued to progress to the day of my solo flight. Some of my classmates had already flown their solo rides, the earliest being the guys who had hundreds of hours of private flying time before joining the Air Force. After 17.4 hours in the Tweet and having been at Willie for nearly two months, my day arrived. My new IP and I took off on a pattern only ride, since the initial solo was to be flown only in the local traffic pattern. This gave the IP one last chance to ensure the student was familiar with all the necessary radio calls, visual references, Chapter 8 procedures, and flying skills to successfully takeoff and land the jet with confidence.

After a few rotations around the pattern and a few touch-and-goes, we taxied back to parking. I shut down the right engine, my IP unstrapped, reached out his hand, and said, "Good luck, Lieutenant!" In his hand was a pair of wings. "Those are mine. Bring them back to me in one piece!" He laughed, patted me on the helmet, and I was on my own.

I don't remember much about my initial solo in the Tweet. I had chair-flown my missions as instructed, and my only fear was being thrown a curveball. What if the pattern was really congested—could I keep track of all the jets flying around? What if I had to break out of the pattern and re-enter somewhere on outside downwind or initial? I had done these things once or twice but wasn't totally confident in my ability to maintain situation awareness in a busy pattern. My landings would be graded by the controller in the Runway Supervisory Unit (RSU). Due to the high volume of traffic pattern activity at training bases, the RSU controller actually controlled traffic for the T-37s on the inside T-37 runway, leaving the center runway and big picture control to the controllers in the Tower. The T-38s followed the same protocol on the outside T-38 runway. As it turns out, the pattern was not too busy, my solo flight was uneventful, and I taxied back and shutdown after my full stop landing with relief.

Our T-37 squadron had a dunk tank outside the building. It was used for special occasions—an instructor's last flight before re-assignment, or, more commonly, to celebrate a student pilot's initial solo. Another tradition was to throw in a new IP the first time he soloed out a student. My IP was waiting for me in Life Support with congratulations as I walked back in. I gave him back his wings with thanks and a chuckle, and as we walked back into the No Loss flight room, both of us were swarmed by IPs and my fellow classmates. They hoisted both of us up, carried us outside, and threw both of us into the dunk tank together. The water felt good in the hot Arizona summer sun, but what felt better was that I had soloed and was doing relatively well in the program.

The next milestone was our first check ride—the Mid-Phase Check. This sortie occurred after around 25 hours in the jet and was intended to serve as the first big opportunity to wash a guy out of the program. The ride was conducted by specially-designated Check Section instructors—the Darth Vaders of UPT.

The mission began with a ground eval, where the Check Section IP would grill you for about 30-45 minutes on your knowledge of everything you had been taught so far—T-37 Dash One Operating Manual numbers and restrictions, local Chapter 8 requirements, Air Force Regulation 60-16 rules, etc. You would then fly the ride. In addition to spins and stalls, the IP would direct you to fly two or three acrobatic maneuvers, and then you would fly back and execute patterns and landings from the straight-in and overhead.

Nothing much different than what we had been doing up to this point, but the pressure was on. A few of my classmates, mostly the guys sailing through the program with lots of private flying hours, had already taken their Mid-Phase Checks. I had flown well up to this point—all *Good* grades—and my new IP sent me to my check ride with confidence.

The ride went great. I did well on the ground eval, and the flight went just the way I had trained and practiced. The only glitch was I was assigned an operating area I had never been to before. However, I had studied the map and ground references, drafted a few radial/DME cuts so I could help maintain myself in the area using cockpit instruments, and therefore wasn't too concerned. My area work was solid, my patterns and landings good, my radio comms within the standard, and after the flight was over, I sat down with my Check Section IP with confidence. He let me know how well the ground eval and flight went overall—and was sorry he had to bust me. I had failed the Mid-Phase Check.

I was stunned. What? Where? Why? It was a great ride—you said so yourself! I hadn't said anything, but I'm sure the look of shock on my face was evident.

"What were the altitude restrictions in the area we were assigned?" he asked.

I told him that the area was capped at 22,000 feet, unlike the other areas that were capped at the T-37 service ceiling of 25,000 feet.

"How high did you climb when you were setting up for your spin entry?" he asked.

I didn't really know—I began the pull to vertical at the same altitude I always did, and, uh-oh.

"Yeah, that's right. We didn't roll into the spin until 23,000 feet, so you busted out of the area by 1,000 feet."

Well, that was that. I went back and reported to my new IP. He was as shocked and embarrassed as I was, and while I wasn't the first in my class to fail the Mid-Phase Check, it was still a mighty blow to my pride for my classmates to learn I hadn't measured up in this first big flying test.

My IP went down to Check Section to speak with my check ride IP and inform the No Loss Flight Commander, came back not too long afterward, and let me know that I would get two practice rides before proceeding to my Initial Progress Check. Also—I would be flying the practice rides with my old IP. Yikes.

For the most part, my practice rides were uneventful. I was initially somewhat nervous to be flying with my original IP again; I was prepared for sarcasm and comments on what a "weak d#%k" I was for having busted my Mid-Phase, but there was none of that. If anything, he was looser and even joked around a bit, although he still flew most of the ride in cold mike. I went on to my IPC as scheduled, passed without incident, and went back to flying with my new IP.

UPT is an extremely competitive culture. While you grow close to your classmates, you are constantly aware that you are in competition with them, and virtually everything you do is graded. At the end of training, you would be given your choice of assignment based on your ranking in the class.

As graduation neared, the Air Force would send a list of available cockpits for your particular class assignments. The #1 guy would probably get his first choice, as indicated on his Form 90 Dream Sheet, where you indicated your Top 3 choices. The further down the class you were ranked, the less chance you had of getting one of your top three.

We were still months away from having to fill out our Dream Sheets, but most of us knew who wanted to fly what. Surprisingly, many of the eleven previously non-flying captains who had been given UPT slots wanted to fly transports, which was fine with the rest of us lieutenants who wanted to fly fighters. Everyone knew of my desire to fly the A-10, but I would have to finish pretty high in the class to get one. I was sure my stock had fallen considerably with my failed Mid-Phase Check.

Following the Mid-Phase, we were now required to perform duties in the RSU as spotters and recorders occasionally. The RSUs were manned by four individuals—a controller, an observer, a spotter, and a recorder.

The controller was an experienced instructor who would operate the radios and issue directions to jets in the traffic pattern—closed approved, cleared to land, and other guidance as required to keep the pattern running safely and smoothly. The controller faced the approach end of the runway; the observer, usually a newer instructor pilot, faced the departure end and kept the controller informed of traffic and the position of various jets in the pattern to help the controller keep track of each jet's position.

The spotter was a student pilot, facing the approach end with a pair of binoculars—he would confirm gear down for the controller prior to the controller giving a clearance to land. There were flare guns mounted in the RSU that a controller and observer could activate as a last-ditch warning if someone showed up on short final without their landing gear down.

46

Finally, the recorder wrote down land times for each jet and would write comments issued by the controller for each, such as landings long and hot, patterns too wide/long final, or radios below standard. Performing observer and recorder duties gave us an opportunity for the first time outside academics to observe our classmates in action; we soon were able to judge who was strong, who was weak, and who was merely talking a big game.

As we grew more comfortable in the program, we began to spend more time in leisurely pursuits. Friday nights at the Officer's Club was a must, of course, and it was always packed. Most of us were single, so we tended to venture downtown to Tempe and the bars and clubs near Arizona State University on Saturday nights. Most of the ASU coeds weren't nearly as impressed with our being Air Force jet pilots as we were with ourselves—but then again, the movie *Top Gun* hadn't come out yet. Go figure.

The next phase involved missions leading up to our Final Contact Check. We would continue to refine the maneuvers we had already practiced but would fly more single-engine landings, no-flap landings, and add more solos, night flights, and visual navigation to our profiles. I had flown three rides following my IPC, when suddenly I had trouble clearing my ears. It seemed crazy to be getting a cold in early August in the Arizona desert, but I dutifully reported to the Flight Surgeon, and he put me on DNIF status—Duty Not Including Flying—and gave me a week's worth of medication.

I couldn't fly, but I could still perform RSU duties, attend classes, and complete simulator missions. No one wants to be DNIF; pilots tend to avoid Flight Surgeons like COVID-19, since they have the power to ground you. You especially didn't want to go DNIF for too long at UPT, for fear of not keeping up and being washed back a class. This didn't seem too serious, however, and since I was still a little ahead of the rest of the class despite the added missions with my IPC, I wasn't worried.

On the second day being DNIF, I tried to clear my ears, and blood spurted out my nose. Not good. That night, after I had been in bed for a few hours, I woke up with a sharp, stabbing pain in my chest every time I took a breath. The deeper breath I took, the worse the pain was, and it was not going away—it was getting worse.

I staggered out of bed, taking short, rapid breaths to limit the pain—I didn't know what was going on. I threw on a robe, stumbled to my car, and drove myself to the emergency room at the Base Hospital, which was only about five minutes away. I walked up to the desk, and the nurse on duty took one look at me and started yelling for help. "Not good," I thought.

They grabbed me, threw me on a gurney, wheeled me into one of the side rooms, put a mask on me, and started feeding me 100% oxygen.

"You've got severe cyanosis," the nurse said loudly. "Your lips are dark blue—what's going on?"

I gave her the details, and the flight surgeon on duty showed up with my medical records. I was able to breathe a bit more normally by then, so they ordered some x-rays. The flight surgeon reappeared soon after that, and gave me the diagnosis; I had bronchial pneumonia and would be admitted to the hospital for an undetermined time. Again, not good.

I ended up being grounded for 18 days. I spent six days in the hospital, where I received excellent care. I had a private room, and my classmates brought me all of my books for study and kept me up to speed on my academic assignments. I had a steady stream of visitors, including my IP, who much to my relief informed me that while I would have a lot of catching up to do, I probably wouldn't have to be washed back a class. After I was discharged from the hospital, I sandbagged a few simulator sorties to get back in flying mode and was able to complete four graded simulator sorties before coming off DNIF status and returning to flight. When I was able to get back in the air, finally, my IP was pleased to report that I hadn't really regressed that much and that I should be able to seamlessly flow right back in with the rest of the class.

We continued our normal routine of academics, flying, and simulators leading up to the Final Contact phase. During that time, Williams AFB was given an annual readiness inspection by the Inspector General's office of Headquarters Air Training Command (ATC), based at Randolph Air Force Base in San Antonio, Texas. Inspectors reviewed paperwork, practices, operations, and daily conduct of every unit on base, including our T-37 training squadron and the instructor pilots of No Loss Flight. The inspection included written tests for both instructors and students, as well as flight evaluations. I was selected as one of the students to fly with an ATC Evaluator. Whether by random or by selective choice, I didn't know. While it would be just another graded syllabus ride for me, my performance would reflect on No Loss and the rest of the squadron, so I wanted to do well. We flew a standard contact profile—the HQ ATC IP was pleasant and talkative, and after we returned to the traffic pattern, he ended up flying the rest of the ride himself. I got my standard *Good* grade and was glad when the day was over. The squadron ended up passing the inspection without too much trouble.

My Final Contact Check was scheduled for a Friday. I felt pretty confident, but I had felt that way during my Mid-Phase Check as well, so I walked down the hall to Check Section for my mission brief and ground eval with some trepidation. It would be a standard profile, with some acrobatics, the stall series, a spin, drop into the auxiliary field for some overhead patterns, recovery to Willie for a no-flap straight-in, single-engine overhead, then an overhead full stop. As I walked back to the No Loss flight room to retrieve my checklist, I noticed the flight was in the middle of conducting the weekly BoneHead Award.

Every Friday, at the conclusion of the initial mass briefing, the floor would be open for BoneHead nominations. This gave the IPs an opportunity to point out which student had done the stupidest thing for the week—an incorrect radio call, taxiing the wrong way, giving the wrong answer during an oral quiz, or something similar where the student had embarrassed himself or done something funny.

The nominations, all in good fun, were generally offered with humor and were mostly true. After the nominations, a winner was declared, and that student received The BoneHead—a life-size stone skull with a leather flying cap. The Bonehead of the Week had to keep the skull on his table in No Loss until hopefully relinquishing it the following week. I thought, "Well, I've got a pretty funny story..."

I raised my hand as I retrieved my checklist and was heading out the door, and was recognized. "All of you know my IP—the Ricky Ricardo of No Loss," I began with great fanfare, to muffled chuckles. "Earlier this week, we were flying an instrument sim. I was climbing to altitude and overshot slightly. I bunted over fairly aggressively with a fair amount of negative-G to get back to altitude. As I executed the bunt, I heard this 'Ungh! Ungh!' sound coming from the right seat. I looked over, and there was my IP, both arms raised over his head and frantically waving his hands, and he cried, 'Help, Lieutenant, help! There's too many neggies—I can't get my hands on the stick!!!'"

His observation that I was producing negative-G on the jet trying to maintain altitude was spot on, and hilariously enacted.

The entire room exploded with laughter, but I had to leave for my check ride. I met my Check Section IP in Life Support, and off we went. Everything went fine until we were descending out of the area into the auxiliary field. I heard several simultaneous radio calls from jets trying to proceed to the aux field entry point at the same time as me—it was going to be a busy pattern. I didn't have a visual on the two jets, and they sounded like they were going to create a conflict with each other, so I stopped my descent, circled at altitude, and waited until I had sight of both of them before I continued on to the entry point myself. It was a fairly non-standard maneuver, but I thought it was the safest thing to do at the time.

The rest of the mission was going well until I was on inside downwind back at Willie. If there was a jet on a straight-in inside two miles, you were not supposed to roll off the perch into your overhead-final-turn-to-landing unless you had the straight-in aircraft in sight. I was approaching the perch when I heard an aircraft declare, "two miles, gear down, full stop."

I acquired the straight-in visually and informed my IP, so I was technically cleared to begin the turn. However, something didn't feel right to me—even though I had sight of the straight-in, it looked to me there would be a conflict between us. So I called, "Gambler breaking out," raised the gear, flaps, and speed brake, and executed the Chapter 8 breakout procedures for a re-entry into outside downwind—something I had only done a few times before.

Again—a fairly non-standard maneuver, but I had made the call. The rest of the mission went fine, but after landing, as I was walking down the hall for the debrief, I wasn't sure how the IP would grade me, or even if I had done the right thing. My mind kept going back to my Mid-Phase Check when I was so caught by surprise with a bust.

The Check Section IP reviewed the flight in the standard manner, what we had done, and how I had performed well overall, but then he paused, "That circling maneuver you did at the aux field—was outstanding. You displayed excellent situation awareness, just like you did at the perch back here when you executed the breakout. That was the right call—we definitely would have been a conflict. Great job!"

He shook my hand and gave me my gradesheet. I couldn't believe it—my first *Excellent*. To say I was happy would be an understatement. Coming off the results of my busted Mid-Phase Check and being DNIF for almost three weeks, I couldn't have asked for a better result. As I hustled back to No Loss to inform my IP of the good news, I noticed The BoneHead on his table. I had also successfully boned my IP. It was a good day—and one that would have repercussions.

Following our Final Contact Check rides, there was only about a month left in T-37s. The remaining rides were mostly navigation and instrument missions, with some cross-country out-and-backs and strange field instrument approaches. Our final check ride would be an Instrument Check to a strange field—most probably Luke AFB to the northwest in Glendale, or Davis-Monthan AFB to the south in Tucson. Finally, we would be given eight basic formation rides, for which we would be graded, but for which there would be no check ride. We could all see the light at the end of the Tweet Tunnel, and we were excited for the chance to fly formation.

Something magic happened in those final weeks in the T-37. All of a sudden, I started to get *Excellent* grades on most of my rides. I didn't think I was necessarily flying any better than I always had, but I had a hunch. With the results of my Final Contact Check, I now had a reputation for excellence. I also sensed I was now a bit more likeable with the other IPs since I had the hutzpah to Bone my IP. In addition, we were nearing the end of our T-37 training, so I suspect the IPs were in a better mood as well. At any rate, I breezed through the instrument and navigation phase, flew my Instrument Check ride to Luke AFB and got a *Good* grade, and started the formation phase with eagerness and excitement.

Formation flying was the most fun I had ever had in the air. We practiced fingertip formation, formation takeoffs and landings, crossunders, echelon turns, pitchouts and rejoins, close trail, and extended trail. Throughout T-37 training, I had continued to approach flying as a skill to be mastered; I enjoyed it well enough, but I can't say I was having a lot of fun. Well, flying formation was pure joy. I loved it, and I couldn't wait for the next mission.

On about my fifth formation ride, I was flying with my regular IP, as always. Our wingman was another student whose IP was the only other fighter pilot in No Loss besides my original IP. He was an F-4 pilot, and fairly young; this was his second flying assignment, and he didn't have Vietnam experience, but he had that fighter pilot swagger, gave us all a good-natured hard time, and was fun to be around.

We were flying off their wing, and they gave us the call to go extended trail. Extended trail was the closest thing we had to being in a dogfight, except there was no fight. The lead jet would fly a series of predictable acrobatic maneuvers, and the job, as trail, was to maintain about 1500 feet back in a 30-45 degree cone—an area that came close to simulating the vulnerable zone for a close-in heat-seeking missile, or a long-range gunshot.

Maybe because it was a Friday, maybe because the T-37 program was almost over, maybe because I enjoyed flying formation rides so much, or maybe because I was just feeling a bit extra cocky that day, but when we were established in extended trail position, I barked out, "guns, guns, guns!!!!" over the radio.

There was a slight hesitation, then the lead aircraft exploded in the vertical and started to try and loop us. Immediately my IP and I knew what was going on—the F-4 pilot was about to

52

teach the too-cocky student a lesson. Both my IP and I were howling with laughter as I tried to stay in position—to no avail. Within a few loops and turns, he was in back of me, and we heard, "guns...guns...guns" slowly and sarcastically over the radio.

After landing, we all had a good laugh during the debrief, but the F-4 IP let me know with a smile that I was out-of-line, and probably shouldn't do that again.

That night, at the Officer's Club, I was sitting at a table with a few of my classmates when the F-4 IP walked up. He had two whiskeys in his hand, and he handed me one. "Fun times out there today," he said and clicked my glass. I wasn't a whiskey drinker, but I managed to down it, as he did his. He then sat down with us and told us stories of flying the F-4. We were mesmerized—and I felt honored to have hoisted a drink with him.

A few days prior to our last T-37 flights, I was called into the No Loss Flight Commander's office by the Assistant Flight Commander. He told me to take a seat. We made some small talk about moving on to T-38s, when he said, "How did you like flying the Tweet?"

"It was fine," I replied, and I told him how much I had enjoyed the formation phase.

"Ever think you might want to come back as a Tweet IP?" he smiled, looking me straight in the eye. Wow. I had not been expecting this.

I stuttered and stammered a little about how I liked flying the T-37, but I really had my sights set on the A-10.

He said, "Okay. Just something to think about." With that, I was dismissed.

I didn't know what to think. By this time in training, the class had pretty much figured out who was at the top, and who was at the bottom. The guys who had arrived with hundreds of hours of private flying time had excelled initially, but our learning curve was much steeper than theirs, and any advantage they may have had early on had pretty much evaporated.

A couple of the prior non-rated/navigator captains were clearly at the top, as were a few of the lieutenants who had started strong and were finishing strong. I had busted my Mid-Phase, and was average in academics at best. I still tended to score in the mid-low 90s on most of my exams, where some guys had not even missed a single question. However, I had finished strong, and I knew I had a pretty good reputation with my classmates and with the No Loss IPs. I figured I was probably in the Top 30%—probably not good enough for an A-10 at this stage, but I had high hopes.

As we transitioned to T-38s, we were moved to the T-38 squadron with an entirely new set of instructors. Our flight was Boomer flight, and my assigned IP was a former FB-111 pilot—not a real fighter necessarily, but at least the FB-111 had a pointy nose. He was a Citadel graduate, and was the Class Commander of 80-05, meaning he was the officer primarily responsible for our overall training and graduation in the T-38 phase. For that reason, he was not a dedicated flight line IP, and just like in T-37s, I would be his only student until my solo.

He was pleasant and easy to talk to but tended to be all business. One of the first things he said to me was, "You know, the rumor is you're going back to Tweets when you get your wings."

I repeated my desire to fly the A-10, and that being a Tweet FAIP would not be on my Dream Sheet.

He said, "Don't worry about it. Most of your assignment will hinge on how well you do in the Talon."

The T-38 Talon is a two-seat, twin-engine, supersonic jet trainer still flown by the Air Force as of this writing. Unlike the T-37, with side-by-side cockpit seating, the T-38 cockpits are in tandem with the student in the front and the IP in the rear. It had a max speed of 1.3 Mach, a max G of 7.33, and a max service ceiling of 50,000 feet. It was called the toy fighter in some circles, and the true fighter version of the T-38 was the F-5 Tiger II, a lethal, lightweight fighter in its own right. It was sleek and sexy looking.

In addition, unlike the T-37, we had to wear G-suits in the T-38. Most of us couldn't wait to get out on the flight line wearing our G-suits—go fast pants, or speed jeans—and get our pictures taken in front of the T-38 for our Christmas cards.

Flying the T-38 was an entirely different challenge than flying the T-37. You could really ham-fist the Tweet; it was sturdy, reliable, slow to stall, and slow enough that you rarely got behind the jet. Not the T-38; you had to have some finesse to really fly it well, and your instrument cross-check had to be faster to keep from getting behind the power curve. Approaching the stall, it went from cats to elephants much quicker due to its stubby wings, so you had to be a bit more cautious about horsing it around in the traffic pattern.

Just walking out to the jet for the pre-flight felt different; this was a real fighter-like jet, that demanded respect. I always felt like a rookie in the T-37, but flying the T-38 made me feel special. The Tweet was a training platform; the T-38 was cool.

Our initial sorties were very similar to the T-37, minus the spin training. We flew aerobatics, stalls, slow flight, steep turns, unusual attitudes and recoveries, constant rate climbs and descents, and traffic pattern work. Our simulator sorties concentrated on emergency procedures and instruments—again, very similar to the Tweet contact phase. My grades were also similar to my T-37 grades—a few *Fairs*, a few *Excellents*, but predominantly *Goods*.

On my fourth ride, my IP experienced a severe sinus blockage, so I had my first emergency declaration. We had been doing area work between 20,000 and 30,000 feet, and during the descent for the return to Willie, he was unable to clear his ears. The T-38 has a pressurized cockpit with steady pressurization beginning as you climbed past 8,000 feet, but the high altitude we were working in still led to a build-up of pressure in his sinuses. He was pretty much incapacited being in so much pain.

"My cranium feels like it's gonna explode," he moaned.

He talked me through declaring the emergency, informing the RSU controller that we had a physiological incident, and that we needed a flight surgeon to meet us after landing. I landed uneventfully from a straight-in, and the fire trucks and ambulance met us after shutdown. It was kind of exciting—my IP was grounded for a few weeks while he recovered, but he was okay. I ended up soloing just before Thanksgiving and successfully completed my Contact Check with a *Good* around two weeks later.

One of my best friends ended up washing out of the program during the T-38 Contact Phase. He was one of the Air National Guard guys and had an O-2 Duck assignment waiting for him in Southern California after graduation. His parents had a house on Lake Havasu, and a few of us spent several weekends enjoying the water there. It was hard to say goodbye to him— we had all gone through a lot together. Because he was in the Guard, he was allowed to proceed to Navigator training, where he became an F-4 Weapons System Operator. A few years later, he and his front seat pilot were killed after failing to pull out from a pop-up attack on a controlled range.

We started formation rides immediately after our Contact Checks, and just like before, I absolutely loved formation flying. I was able to complete four formation rides before the Christmas break.

My Dad had since retired from the Air Force, and they had moved to a lake north of Montgomery, Alabama. He now worked as an Emergency Planner with the State of Alabama, and my parents were enjoying this second career. I went home full of myself; I was doing well in the program and was confident I would be getting my wings within less than four months. I still wanted that A-10, but I could see that the guys who were strong in the T-37 were also strong in the T-38. There had not been much change in the pecking order.

I still considered myself to be in the Top 30%—prime FAIP territory, for First Assignment Instructor Pilots. While none of us really knew how the assignment system worked, it was generally understood that the top 20% had a good chance of getting one of their top choices, while those in the 20-30% range were often retained as FAIPs in the T-37 or T-38, regardless of whether one wanted the assignment or not. I remained a little nervous about the prospect of staying at Willie as a non-vol Tweet FAIP but tried to stay positive.

Returning after the Christmas break, we continued the formation phase, which progressed from 2-ship to 4-ship formation rides. We performed wing takeoffs and landings as well as the standard area work with fingertip flying, crossunders, pitch-outs-and-rejoins, echelon turns, close trail, and extended trail. In the T-38, flying extended trail seemed much more like you were actually in a dogfight than in the T-37, but I did not make the same mistake of transmitting a guns call.

The 4-ship work was initially challenging, but still a load of fun. During the latter part of the formation phase, we flew night rides, including a night solo, and flew some team rides, where we were able to fly in the same jet with one of our student pilot classmates.

We also flew our boom rides, where we broke the sound barrier for the first time. These sorties had to be flown above 30,000 feet to prevent any impact of the sonic boom on the civilian population below. While the transition through Mach airspeed wasn't that dramatic, it still felt pretty exciting to know you had flown faster than the speed of sound.

We all started to feel pretty confident in ourselves. Besides my friend who had washed out, we had only lost three other guys, so our class as a whole was doing quite well. I successfully completed my Formation Check Ride with another *Good*, and moved on to the final Navigation phase.

I enjoyed flying low-level navigation sorties even more than my formation rides. We weren't allowed to fly any lower than 500 feet, but it was absolutely exhilarating. We flew out-and-back missions all over the southwest—Kirtland AFB, Norton AFB, March AFB, Yuma MCAS. I flew my solo out-and-back to Nellis AFB, and it felt cool to land at the Home of USAF Fighter Aviation.

I flew a weekend cross-country mission to Mather AFB near Sacramento with my IP, where primary navigation training for the Air Force was conducted. The Mather O'Club seemed much larger than the club at Willie, and there were scores of apparently unattached single women there. My IP—a fun, semi-crazy Australian exchange pilot, explained that they bussed in girls from off base to the Mather Club every Friday night. Good times indeed.

The final check ride in pilot training was a navigation check. A Check Section IP informed you a few days in advance where you would be going; it would be an out-and-back mission, where you flew the majority of the ride under the bag. On these missions, there was a cloth shield you could attach to the inside of the front seat canopy, and during certain phases of the flight, the IP would direct you to pull the bag forward, thereby almost totally restricting your visibility outside the cockpit and simulating as if you were totally in the soup and in poor weather conditions.

We flew my navigation check on 7 April to Vandenberg AFB. On the return leg to Willie, while under the bag, my IP also conducted the ground eval. I was relieved after landing and debrief to have earned a *Good* on my final check ride in UPT. My performance during the T-38 phase had been solid—while I didn't have some of the highs I had experienced in the latter part of the T-37 phase, I hadn't busted any rides. With Assignment Night approaching, we were all happy to have finished the program and looked forward to learning what our futures would be.

A few weeks earlier, we had completed our assignment Dream Sheets, an opportunity to indicate your top three preferences for the aircraft you wanted to fly, and to highlight any special reasons you might have to warrant your selection.

I knew that my chances of getting an A-10 assignment were slim, but I still put it down as my first choice. For my second choice, I put an OV-10; the OV-10 was used primarily in the Forward Air Control (FAC) mission, and I figured it was a close cousin to the A-10, and I would have a better chance of getting an A-10 later. For my third choice, I put an RF-4; besides it being a nod to my favorite IP, I assumed that since it was such a limited mission that it might also give me a chance to transition to another jet like the A-10 a little further down the line. I also hoped that by selecting two aircraft not normally on anyone's Top 3 like the OV-10 and the RF-4 that I might avoid getting FAIP'd. None of us knew what jets might be available to our class, and none of us knew exactly where we were ranked. Again—I hoped for the best.

Our graduation was scheduled for 25 April, and Assignment Night was scheduled on a Friday night a couple of weeks before graduation. After completing our navigation checks, we had a few more contact and formation rides, but they were mostly relaxed and fun missions, with the IPs taking a lot of the stick time.

Two days before Assignment Night, my IP/Class Commander pulled me aside in the parking lot outside the squadron. "PK," he said with a serious look on his face. "If you were going to get a Tweet assignment—and I'm not saying that you are!—where would you want to go?"

Well, that's all she wrote, I thought. I had anticipated the possibility of getting a T-37 FAIP assignment, but I had not considered I would actually get a choice of location. My mind quickly thought back to that tidbit of information revealed to me while I was getting my master's degree in Oklahoma. "Well, if I've got to fly Tweets, I'd like to go to the German Air Force program at Sheppard."

My IP smiled, and said "Okay!" and that was it. I didn't tell anyone about the conversation, but for the next 48 hours, I was on pins and needles.

Assignment Night was held at the Officer's Club. The entire room was packed; in addition to our class, most of the other classes at Willie were there as well just to see what kind of assignments were coming in. There were chairs lined up for all 54 of us, and up front next to the Master of Ceremonies podium was a table full of 54 glasses of whiskey. We were told that our names would be drawn out of a hat, and when called, we were to come forward, down the glass of whiskey handed to us, and announce our assignments to the crowd. Our new assignments were taped to the bottom of the glass, and as you drank your whiskey, you would see your assignment. Bottoms up.

Most of us knew what everyone's top choices were. As our names were called, loud cheers came for those who got their first choice, and muffled polite applause for those who didn't. Some didn't make it all the way through their whiskey, either choking or spitting it out as they realized what jet they were getting. Finally, my name was called. I sprinted up to the table, grabbed my glass, downed it in one swallow, and my assignment was revealed. "Tweet to Sheppard," I announced and walked back to my seat. The room was almost silent, with a few half-hearted hand claps.

"Boy, he got screwed," I heard someone whisper as I took my seat.

They were wrong. I got the assignment I deserved, as did nearly all of us. For the 54 members of my class, there was one F-16, two F-15s, three A-10s, four T-38s, and four T-37s. There were two F-4s, two OV-10s, and one T-33, but the rest were all heavies—bombers, tankers, and transports. Of the guys who received fighter assignments, I knew I had not performed better than any of them. Of the FAIP assignments, I was the only non-volunteer, but based on my self-estimated ranking in the class, it was probably as good as I could have hoped for.

One of the guys in the other flight in our class got a T-38 to Sheppard; he had no clue that Sheppard even had a training program, and didn't know where Wichita Falls was. When I told him about the advanced German Air Force syllabus, he was pretty enthused. Hardly anyone knew about the program at Sheppard, so I spent the remainder of the evening at the bar with the rest of the class bragging about the fighter-oriented syllabus, and how awesome it was for me to be going there, especially since it was less than two hours from my hometown in Hobart, Oklahoma.

Having lived in both Germany and the Netherlands, I felt uniquely qualified for the assignment. I didn't get the A-10 I had dreamed of—I had fallen short of my goal, but I went to bed that night satisfied that the Air Force had done right by me. Furthermore, the A-10 was still in reach; FAIP assignments generally lasted only three years, and you were then given another opportunity to compete for an operational aircraft after successfully competing your FAIP tour.

My parents flew out to Willie for graduation, and it was a grand affair. Since my Dad had gotten my first salute as a new second lieutenant, I let my Mom pin on my wings. I later gave those first gold bars and that pair of wings to my parents, who still have them framed and displayed along with that first silver dollar I gave my Dad for getting that first salute.

While my Mom was pinning on my new silver wings, the general officer who had been the speaker at our graduation walked up and congratulated me on my assignment. "There are some great and unique things being planned for Sheppard," he said with a wink. "You are going to love it!"

I was not a Distinguished Graduate—my mediocre academic scores had taken care of that. The only comment on my UPT Training Report was, "Lt White's military bearing, dress, and personal appearance are excellent."

You're darn right—my Dad was a Chief Master Sergeant.

The night before graduation, the news on television was singularly-focused on our failed rescue mission attempt in Iran. President Carter had ordered Operation Eagle Claw in an effort to rescue 52 American hostages held at the U.S. Embassy in Tehran. The team attempted to link up during a dust storm at a staging area in a remote location in the middle of the Iranian desert prior to proceeding to the target area. The storm led to the decision to abort the mission. During departure, in significantly reduced visibility, a helicopter collided with one of the transport aircraft, killing eight servicemen. As we pinned on our wings, it was a sobering reminder that we were in a vital and potentially dangerous business.

My report date to Sheppard was not until early June, so I had some free time available. I took ten days of leave to spend some more time with my parents, then returned to Willie on casual status while awaiting my training date at Sheppard.

Most FAIPs got their instructor training and certification via the Pilot Instructor Training (PIT) program at Randolph AFB in San Antonio, Texas. However, since the German Air Force program had a slightly different syllabus than our American one, my PIT training would be conducted at Sheppard as well.

During my time on casual status back at Willie, I completed a few special projects for my class commander, sandbagged a few T-37 simulator rides just to get myself familiarized again with the Tweet, and mostly spent a relaxing few weeks studying the T-37 Dash One again. At the end of May, I started back up I-17 north to make the long drive back across the desert plains on I-40, where I had first traveled almost a year before. I would spend a few days with family in Hobart before heading on into Wichita Falls and my new assignment as a T-37 Instructor with the German Air Force Flying Training Program at Sheppard AFB.

CHAPTER THREE

TWEET FAIP

Sheppard AFB, TX

1980–1983

But of course! Not only the washed-out, grounded, and dead pilots had been left behind—but also all of those millions of sleepwalking souls who never even attempted the great gamble. The entire world below...left behind! Only at this point can one begin to understand just how big, how titanic, the ego of the military pilot could be. The world was used to enormous egos in artists, actors, entertainers of all sorts, in politicians, sports figures, and even journalists because they had such familiar and convenient ways to show them off. But that slim young man over there in uniform, with the enormous watch on his wrist and the withdrawn look on his face, that young officer who is so shy that he can't even open his mouth unless the subject is flying—that young pilot—well, my friends, his ego is even bigger! So big, it's breathtaking!

—Tom Wolfe, *The Right Stuff*

My report date for my new assignment at Sheppard was scheduled for Monday, June 2nd, so I planned my arrival for the previous Friday to allow myself the weekend to get acquainted with the area. I thoroughly enjoyed the two-hour drive from Hobart to Wichita Falls. It felt like home, driving through the rolling hills of southwest Oklahoma into the flat plains of north Texas.

On the way, I stopped at Frederick, Oklahoma—not only were the Frederick Bombers one of the chief rivals of the Hobart Bearcats, Frederick was also home to Sheppard's T-37 auxiliary field, where I would spend many hours flying patterns and landings with my students, in addition to numerous tours sitting in the RSU. I stopped and watched the Tweets shooting touch-and-goes for a while, and began to get even more pumped up about what the future held.

Sheppard was one of the USAF's Technical Training Centers, and one of the largest training bases in the Air Force. It housed a large regional hospital and shared one of its three runways with Wichita Falls Municipal Airport. It was a large base, well kept, had a large commissary and BX, and plenty of housing.

It was led by the 82nd Training Wing Commander, who was responsible for schools of instruction for aircraft and avionics maintenance, civil engineering, munitions, several medical fields, and other career tracks. The German program fell under the 80th Flying Training Wing, which was a tenant unit to the 82nd.

Wichita Falls was a typical mid-to-large sized Texas town. It had a population of approximately 100,000 and was located a few miles south of Sheppard. In the Fifties and Sixties, Wichita Falls had been home to several large oil companies that had since failed or moved on with the drop in the Texas oil business. There was one shopping mall, a small university, and a downtown area that had seen better days as small retail stores steadily lost business to the big superstores in the suburbs.

A devastating tornado had struck Wichita Falls on April 10th, 1979, when I was still at the University of Oklahoma. The impact of the storm was felt all the way to Oklahoma City. It was a monster tornado, and 42 people were killed. The city was still recovering from its effects more than a year later. However, in typical Texas fashion, the people were upbeat, friendly, and generally welcoming of the military presence in their city, which provided more local jobs than any other entity.

I checked into base billeting that Friday afternoon, expecting to be assigned Bachelor Officer's Quarters somewhere on base.

Silly me. Unless you were in one of the training programs, bachelors were expected to find their own quarters off base. However, they did permit me to check in to Visiting Officer's Quarters for a period not to exceed 30 days until I could find off-base quarters of my own.

With some time still left in the day and with absolutely no forethought, I drove outside the main gate. After passing the standard collection of bars, tattoo parlors, and pawn shops typically located near military bases, I pulled into the first apartment complex I saw, only about a mile from the gate. I strolled into the office and asked if there were any one-bedroom furnished apartments available. I was in luck—there would be one available in about a week. The office manager showed me a typical one-bedroom apartment, and it was fine, if a little run-down, furnished with olive green carpet, olive green refrigerator and stove, olive green fake leather couch, and a white plastic dining room set that looked like it had once belonged to The Jetsons. Perfect.

The price was right, and the location was as close as I could get to the base, so I made the deposit and started making plans for moving in. I later learned that I was one of the few officers living in the complex; most of the rest of the bachelor officers lived in the much-nicer and more expensive apartment complexes near Midwestern State University about 20 minutes from the gate. If I had done some homework and taken some more time, that is probably where I would have ended up as well, but I was happy enough with my simple-if-somewhat-shabby abode and being a mere 10 minutes door-to-door from the squadron.

The next day, I was driving in downtown Wichita Falls, exploring my new city. While stopped at a red light, a snazzy-looking convertible pulled up next to me. I looked over, admired the car, and looked at the driver. I couldn't believe it. I rolled down the window. "Jake?" I yelled.

"P.K.?" he answered back.

It was Jake Dixon, one of my friends from high school in Wiesbaden. Jake had received the 4-year AFROTC scholarship from high school, for which I was an alternate. He had attended Duke University, and we actually bumped into each other when we attended ROTC Field Training together in Wichita, Kansas, in the summer of 1976.

We pulled over and quickly got reacquainted. Jake had gotten married, earned his wings at Columbus AFB in Mississippi, and had been a T-38 FAIP at Sheppard for a few months. I had known Jake well in high school, although we didn't hang out much. He was popular, friendly, and had been our class president every year.

He invited me to their house for dinner on Sunday evening. I met his lovely and charming wife, Janice, and we spent most of the night telling old Wiesbaden stories and catching up on mutual friends. He told me he had remained in constant contact with Wendy Shelton, who was now living in San Antonio. Jake hinted that we would all have to get together someday, emphasizing that Wendy was still single. I told him the "Ain't No Sunshine story," and we had a laugh. Being in a new town and at a new location, it was nice to have a familiar face at my new base.

Bright and early Monday morning, I drove out to the 88th Flying Training Squadron to which I was assigned for the Pilot Instructor Training program for in-processing. The 80th Flying Training Wing and its squadrons were located about a mile north of the rest of the base proper. All the operations—T-37, T-38, and academics—were housed in the same building, in addition to a small cafeteria.

I reported in to the orderly room and was directed by the secretary to take a seat. A few minutes later, I heard a loud boom as the door to the Senior Enlisted Advisor's office flew open. There before me stood the meanest looking Senior Master Sergeant I had ever seen. He was huge—took up most of the door space—and he stood there with a scowl on his face. He was Native American and looked like Geronimo must have looked like on a bad day at Fort Sill. I nearly shat myself.

"Lieutenant White!" he barked at me. "Would you step into my office—NOW."

"Oh, Lord," I thought to myself. What had I done? I'd been in the office for less than five minutes, and it looked like I was already in trouble—what a great way to begin my new career. I gulped, stood up, and timidly walked into his office.

He held the door open for me and slammed it closed as I walked in. He strode back to his desk, sat down, and the scowl never left his face. He leaned back, put his arms behind his head, and it looked like he had two footballs stuffed in his biceps. He stared hard at me and standing at semi-attention, I prepared for the worst. He then leaned forward, grinned, and said, "Your Dad said to say 'Hi.'"

I almost collapsed with relief as he nearly laughed himself to tears. "You son-of-a-gun," I nervously chuckled, not entirely sure if it was really a joke or not.

Still laughing, he explained that it had been a plot launched between my Dad and a close friend of ours who had also recently retired. The friend knew this Senior Enlisted Advisor well and knew I would take the joke as it was intended—as a humorous welcome-to-the-family gesture. I spent most of the morning in his office, filling out in-processing paperwork while he patiently answered all of my new guy questions.

The 80th Wing was a fairly small operation as Flying Training Wings go. There were three squadrons—the 88th for academics and ground training, the 89th for T-37s, and the 90th for T-38s. In the 89th and 90th, there were only two flights for each squadron, with about a dozen students in each flight, meaning there were less than 25 students per class. With only two classes going through training at a time, Sheppard's training load was quite a bit smaller than the other UPT bases.

Accordingly, the instructor pilot cadre was also small; I was the first T-37 FAIP to be assigned in nearly a year. The instructor pilot cadre was made up of a mix of about 30% German and Dutch fighter pilots; the remaining 70% were American pilots with a representative cross-section of various weapons systems—fighters, tankers, bombers, and transports.

The student pilots were all German and Dutch; around 80% German, 20% Dutch, but all instruction was conducted in English. The student pilots also tended to be younger than their American counterparts, especially the Dutch students. It wasn't unusual for a Dutch student to enter the program barely out of his teens.

In addition to the German Flying Training Program, the 80th also conducted training for helicopter pilots transitioning to fixed-wing aircraft assignments. And, unlike standard practice at Willie, the aircraft and flightline maintenance for the German Air Force (GAF) program was conducted by civilian contractors instead of the active-duty enlisted force. All in all, it was a small, compact cadre with a unique mission. It all seemed very exotic and thrilling to me.

I dropped by the PIT flight I would be assigned to for T-37 Instructor Training. It was a small room with only a few tables, and three or four IPs were just hanging out. I introduced myself, and they all seemed happy to see me. The PIT flight also did the T-37 transition training for the former rotary-wing pilots, of which there were only a couple going through training at the time.

My arrival was similar to the Maytag Repairman finally getting a customer; I was the first guy going through instructor training in a few months, and they were looking forward to some new blood. The vibe was informal and laid back, and I knew I was going to enjoy the course.

I spent most of that first week with more in-processing appointments, moving into my off-base apartment, and T-37 academics, which was taught one-on-one to me by one of the T-37 PIT instructors. I was also introduced to the GAF-contracted simulators, which were Sixties-era Link trainers, with no visual screen or computer-aided presentation or avionics. The GAF believed that it was worth the extra expense to fly as many missions as possible, rather than trying to maximize the amount of simulator sorties in an effort to save money, as the USAF was doing. As a result, most simulator missions at Sheppard were very basic and devoted to switchology, emergency procedures, and instrument procedures. Most instrument training missions would actually be flown in the aircraft—another bonus with this syllabus. I liked the new assignment more and more.

My first flight in the Tweet was on Monday of the next week. It was my first flight in a T-37 in eight months, but everything came back quickly. My instructor was also a FAIP, the only one in the PIT flight. It was a partly cloudy day, with thick, towering white puffs of clouds in the area. After some area orientation, acrobatics, stalls, and spins, my IP took the jet and said, "Let's have some fun!"

At full throttle, we raced along the edge of the cotton-candy canyons. We zoomed past the tumbling mirth of sun-split clouds. We looped and rolled through the foot-less halls of air, climbing and diving in the delirious, burning blue, laughing, yelling, and whooping with the profound joy of flying. It was my first real experience in flying for the sheer fun of it. Even in my area solos in the T-37 and T-38 at UPT, it was all business and executing the task at hand. This was something different— it was absolutely exhilarating, and almost a life-changing event for me. I think I really fell in love with flying on Monday, June 9th, 1980.

After the flight, I couldn't wipe the smile off my face. And, during the debrief, the day topped off with an *Excellent* grade on my first ride back in the Tweet. The rest of the summer was much of the same; relaxing and enjoyable flying at a leisurely pace with laid-back instructors who liked to have a bit of fun.

The PIT syllabus was broken into two phases. The first phase was the proficiency phase, where you flew sorties and were given check rides in contact, formation, instrument, and navigation. This phase was flown from the left seat, just as if you were a student at UPT. The second phase was the instructor phase, where you transitioned to the right seat, and flew sorties with the IPs simulating being student pilots, and making typical student errors for you to observe, correct, evaluate, and grade.

The IPs had a lot of fun in this phase, making typical student errors, sometimes speaking in German accents in simulation of our GAF students, and exercising their best Oscar-winning acting skills. The instructor phase mirrored the proficiency phase with check rides in contact, formation, navigation, and instruments. During the instructor phase, the IPs continually told stories regarding episodes that demonstrated the joys— and hazards—of flying with students.

The following two stories are my favorites—the 10% Rule applies.

The first story involves an IP flying with a German student on his first T-37 sortie. Just as in every orientation mission, the

IP was pointing out landmarks to help the student find his way around the traffic pattern. "There is the fork in the river for the initial entry point. There are the cattle pens for turning outside downwind. There is the cotton gin for turning towards final."

As they continued around the pattern, the IP would repeat the area references as they passed them, "River fork. Cattle pens. Cotton gin." Suddenly, as the IP said, "Cotton gin," the student shut down the right engine. Holy Smokes! Not a good thing to do in a Tweet, especially low level in the traffic pattern on a hot day.

The IP screamed, "What are you doing??!!!"

The student stammered, "But sir, you said to cut engine!!"

The second story involves another IP flying with a student in the initial stage of training. The IP noticed that during the first two sorties, when they would approach the VFR entry point for the traffic pattern, the student would say "Sir, could you take the jet for a moment—I'm feeling a little sick."

The IP would take the jet, the student would take off his mask for a few moments, and after the IP passed the VFR entry point, the student would make a miraculous recovery, put his mask back up, and continue the flight.

The IP began to suspect that the student really didn't know how to find the VFR entry point. Sure enough, on the third flight, as they neared the VFR entry point, the student repeated his mantra, "can you take the jet, I'm feeling sick."

The IP said, "Nope. You fly this jet, and you take us to the VFR entry point."

The student, with a bit more urgency in his voice, said, "But sir, I'm really feeling kind of sick."

The IP sternly replied, "Nope. Fly the dang jet!"

Just about then, the student's hand flew up to his mouth, and the fruit salad lunch he had eaten started spewing between his fingers onto the cockpit instruments.

The IP said, "I've got the jet," took the controls, and started clearing extensively to the right side of the cockpit so he wouldn't have to look at the mess blasted on the left. The IP requested a straight-in full stop, put down the gear and flaps at the appropriate time in preparation for landing, and asked the student to put down the landing light, which was located on the left side of the cockpit and where only the student could reach.

The student, still feeling miserable and a bit disoriented, said, "Sir, I can't find it."

The IP, still not wanting to look to the left at the smelly carnage, replied, "It's up there on the left console, right above your left knee."

"Sir, I'm sorry. I don't see it," moaned the student.

The IP took a quick glance at the left side of the cockpit. "It's underneath the strawberry."

There I was... stories like this, whether entirely true or not, were educational as well as being humorous. Flying Tweets may not have been all that glamorous, but it certainly presented distinct challenges.

The time passed quickly, and I successfully completed PIT by the end of August. However, before moving down to the T-37 squadron as an instructor, you were taken on your Spin Ride. Each T-37 squadron had a couple of Spin Pilots who had gone through special training to enter, recognize, and recover from spins you were never supposed to get yourself into—inverted spins, landing configured spins, accelerated spins, and those unusual situations where you might find yourself if you let your student go just a little too far.

Naturally, this ride was infamous for making even the most seasoned pilot airsick, so I looked forward to my ride with apprehension. The sortie took another see-one, do-one approach, and it wasn't too bad. The T-37 is tough and reliable, and as we put it through its paces, it quickly recovered every time, just as advertised. The ride went a long way towards giving you confidence that you could recover the jet in just about any situation.

I was doing fine until we descended out of the area; it was a typical blazing hot summer day in Texas, and the lower we got, the hotter the cockpit got. For the first time in my short flying career, I started to feel a little queasy. My IP chuckled at this announcement, said it was not unusual, and we landed from an overhead full stop. While I enjoyed the ride, I was glad when it was over, and happy that I hadn't needed to use the airsickness bag.

During that summer, an announcement was made revealing the changes hinted at by the general officer who spoke at my UPT graduation. In the fall of 1981, the 80th Flying Training Wing would transition from the German Air Force program to the Euro-NATO Joint Jet Flying Training program (ENJJPT). ENJJPT would expand its operations beyond the Germans and Dutch to involve participation by most of our NATO allies. It would be the world's only multi-nationally manned and managed flying training program, chartered to produce combat pilots for NATO.

The flying and training activities at Sheppard were expected to expand significantly, and a cadre of U.S. student pilots would participate along with those from the NATO-member nations. We all felt fortunate and were invigorated by realizing we would be on the ground floor of such a unique and ambitious program. It was something to look forward to, but it was still over a year away. For now, my focus was on being the best Tweet instructor pilot I could be.

As a brand new flightline IP, I was assigned to B Flight in the 89th Flying Training Squadron. The flight was commanded by a former OV-10 pilot who had been promoted to major three years below-the-zone. There were about six other IPs in the flight—two were German fighter pilots, but the rest were American IPs who had all been heavy drivers in their previous lives. They were open, friendly, and welcoming—I noted immediately that the general atmosphere was much less tense than it seemed in my T-37 and T-38 flights at Willie.

All of the students in the flight were German, and they were nearing completion of the Final Contact phase. They were respectful, if a little wary—I was the only FAIP in the flight, and one of only a few in the entire squadron. I learned that the GAF had requested a minimum number of FAIPs in the program; they desired a more experienced instructor cadre. With about 150 hours in the Tweet by that point, I was more experienced than the students, but not by much.

During my introduction, the flight commander remarked that I had lived in Germany and graduated from high school there. The students quickly tested my German language skills, although they all spoke excellent English. While it quickly became apparent to them that my German was strictly elementary at best, they now knew they probably couldn't get away with muttering something inappropriate in German without my understanding. I was assigned a couple of students, and after reviewing their grade books, it was clear I was given two of the stronger performers in the class.

I wanted to model myself after my favorite IP—the first one I had at Willie, who had flown RF-4s in Vietnam. I wanted to appear cool, calm, collected, and confident. Not talking too much—not hovering over the stick—but always striving for perfection. I knew I wouldn't be able to pull off being a hardass; as a FAIP, that would have been laughable, and besides, it wasn't my style. I had also learned from and appreciated the things I had experienced from the IPs in PIT; flying was fun, but it wouldn't be fun if your IP was a screaming, nitpicking terror.

Most of the IPs in B flight had similar approaches—in fact, the toughest IPs were probably the German fighter pilots. All of these German students would be graduating to fighters back in Germany, so obviously, there was a common bond between them, and perhaps a little more at stake. As I prepared for my first real instructor sortie, I knew the importance of making a good impression.

The briefing and ground operations went smoothly. As predicted, my first student was proficient and confident in his abilities. We flew to the working area and started the planned profile. After each maneuver, I pointed out what he did well and what he could do to improve his performance. After four or five comments from me, he finally said, "OK, I got it. Let's get on with the program."

He was tired of my yacking away at things he probably already knew. In PIT, we were expected to critique and correct each maneuver in order to display our instructor observations. I had begun my IP career doing exactly what I was taught, but I could see that wasn't always going to work. I could have taken the jet and taught the young man a lesson, or put him in a brace to show who was boss, but I didn't; he was right to feel a little frustrated with this rookie IP. It was an early lesson for me and did much to refine my instructor style.

I eventually became one of the more popular IPs with the students. I was closer to their age, I could speak a little German, and I tended to be relaxed and liked to have a little fun. I didn't critique each maneuver; if it was performed within standards, I was good with that and would provide techniques for improvement if required during the debrief. However, when a maneuver was performed poorly, I calmly provided on-the-spot instruction, and if necessary, would demonstrate the proper technique. I could also fly the Tweet fairly well, so I had some credibility as a solid stick-and-rudder guy.

That November, I was sent to the Air Force Survival Schools, required training for all USAF pilots. The Survival, Evasion, Resistance, and Escape (SERE) training course was conducted at Fairchild AFB in Washington state, and the Water Survival course took place at Homestead AFB in Florida.

The SERE course was about a week long. It involved classroom instruction and some demonstration of simple survival skills on the base before turning us loose in the forests of Eastern Washington. Groups of eight of us were assigned an enlisted SERE instructor who marched us through the woods and taught us more complex survival skills—land navigation, radio operation, building a fire in the rain, how to catch game, how to eat strange and horrid tasting plants and critters, building a campsite with gear from your survival kit and parachute, and various evasion techniques.

We were then separated into pairs and given assignments to try and successfully make it from Point A to Point B without being caught by instructors simulating the bad guys. In addition to these adversarial trackers, helicopters were searching overhead for us as well. My partner and I successfully completed our trek. Once, we were in visual contact with one of the instructors tracking us. We hid and remained silent; he eventually moved on to other prey, but I'm pretty sure he knew exactly where we were the entire time.

After this escape and evasion piece, we were all placed in a simulated POW camp for a couple of days. We all had to agree not to reveal what went on during this resistance phase; all I can say is that it was much tougher than I expected and very revealing. I was surprised by how we new pilots—that the Air

Force had just spent millions of dollars in training for us to get our wings—could be treated so harshly. I was shocked, I tell you, shocked! However, these were lessons we would never forget, and for some of us, they would come in useful a little later down the road.

Transitioning from the cold, wet forests of Eastern Washington to the warm, sunny coast of Southern Florida for water survival was absolute bliss. After that week of living off the land and limited rations at SERE training, several of us spent that first night in Florida at a steak house gorging ourselves.

The course only took a few days, and culminated in parasailing off the platform of a ship and landing in the water with everything you would have if you ejected into the Atlantic Ocean just off the coast. You were expected to successfully get in your life raft, employ your radio, and vector in a rescue helicopter that would hoist you up.

We were not allowed to wear our flight boots, for fear of damaging the life rafts, so we had to wear tennis shoes. We were instructed to place black socks over our shoes, for if the barracudas see white shoes, they may think they are fish and take a bite. Wonderful.

I had never been a strong swimmer, and never really felt comfortable in the water. Before the final exercise, the instructors stated that if anyone couldn't swim well and wanted special attention, to request a red helmet (versus the standard white they used for training) for easy identification. Everyone was probably too embarrassed to ask for a red helmet—but not me. I wanted all eyes on me.

With much trepidation, I successfully parasailed into the water, got in my raft, made my radio calls, and while waiting to be picked up, took off my helmet and started bailing water out of my raft. Looking down, I saw something large and black swim underneath me. Forget this—I put my helmet back on and just stared quietly at my feet until I was picked up.

That graduation night at Homestead, we learned that Ronald Reagan had beaten Jimmy Carter in a landslide—Reagan would be the next President of the United States. Everyone I talked with was happy with that result. The military had suffered under Carter's leadership in many areas, and Reagan had promised a return to a stronger Army, Air Force, Navy, and Marines as we continued to confront the Evil Empire of the Soviet Union. I returned to Sheppard full of optimism—for the United States, for the Air Force, and for my future as a pilot.

Although I was still a new guy, I quickly became immersed in the culture of flying and working with German and Dutch pilots. For the NATO instructors, an assignment at Sheppard was a real plum. They had a unique opportunity to live in the United States for three years, and their instructor duties were not very demanding.

All of us U.S. instructors were given the lion's share of additional duties—scheduler, grade book monitor, safety officer, standardization-evaluation monitor, etc. The unionized German instructors took their flying duties very seriously, but it was rare for one of them to put in more than an 8-hour day.

One of the favorite activities was darts; it seemed that every IP, including the Americans, had their own personal set of darts, and during breaks in flying, you would find most of the IPs gathered around several dartboards we had established in one of the break rooms. Another aspect of the culture was the hearty consumption of alcohol. The Germans and Dutch hated what the Americans called beer in those days. Who could blame them? So they had monthly shipments of their favorite beer and spirits flown in on a German C-160. The German IPs would always ask us deprived Yanks what we wanted—I developed a taste for Pilsner-Urquell, a Czech beer better known as PQ to the Germans. Through my European friends, I also had my first taste of apfelkorn—yum!—and aquavit—yikes!

The O'Club had two bars—one larger, formal bar generally inhabited by Sheppard's non-flying cadre, and Duffy's, a smaller, informal bar mostly populated by the instructor and student pilots. Friday nights were a madhouse at Duffy's. The place was always packed wall-to-wall.

One of the special missions that Sheppard AFB was responsible for was the MIMSO program—Military Indoctrination for Medical Service Officers. It was a two-week course whereby civilian doctors and nurses without an academy or ROTC education could enter active duty after completing this training; the military is always short on doctors and nurses. The classes were made up mostly of nurses, and there was a new class once a month. These new nurses were generally unfamiliar with all things Air Force and were probably more impressed with flight suits than they should have been. Fighter pilots from all over the U.S. would fly into Sheppard on MIMSO Fridays, and Duffy's would be rocking. As a young bachelor blonde-haired-square-jawed lieutenant pilot, I fell in love with a new nurse every month.

I developed a routine that generally characterized my time at Sheppard. I worked hard at both my flying and non-flying duties during the week, alternating between early and late weeks. I played on the squadron intramural football and softball teams, so there were practices and games on many evenings. I would go to Duffy's on Friday nights and the occasional weekend party, usually at one of the German or Dutch pilot's homes.

On Saturday mornings, I would go to the commissary for groceries. My shopping list consisted mostly of coffee, Dr. Pepper, and snacks as I usually ate lunch at the flightline cafeteria, and stopped at Del Taco on the way home at the end of the day. Most Saturday afternoons, I'd often visit the record store in the mall on a quest to add to my growing music collection. Sundays would be laundry and house cleaning days. Once every couple of months, I would travel to Hobart on weekends to visit my grandmother and great-grandmother, but my routine fundamentally remained the same.

My first student class in B Flight soon moved on to T-38s, and now I'd experience taking a new T-37 class from start to finish. I was assigned two students, both of average capability. I followed the same tradition from Willy when I soloed out a student for the first time—I handed him my wings and told him to bring them back in one piece.

The Germans had a different tradition for solo celebrations; instead of being thrown in a dunk tank, they essentially turned you into a cake. After he landed successfully, my new solo student and I were dragged outside Life Support and sprayed down with a hose. One of the German IPs then came up and poured sacks of flour over our heads, followed by the second

German IP who cracked about a dozen eggs on our heads and faces.

I had always been allergic to eggs—egg whites, to be specific, so I simply avoided eating anything with eggs in it. However, I hadn't counted on the effects of egg slime dribbling into my eyes; my eyes, nose, and head started to swell up like a balloon, and I had some difficulty breathing. They rushed me to the shower room, hosed me down, again, and took me to the hospital. A nice dose of Benadryl put me to rights, but it was an unusual way to celebrate my first solo student.

One of the students in this class had some real difficulties right from the start, and there were some concerns he would end up being washed out. He was huge—about 6 feet 4 inches of solid muscle, blonde, blue-eyed, crew cut—a perfect German poster boy. Although he wasn't my student, I flew with him once. He was extremely nervous and unsure of himself and tended to be very tentative in his actions.

One day, the flight commander called me into his office. The German IPs were there as well. He told me that this student was in real danger of not completing the program and that the young man had requested that Lieutenant White be his IP. Would I agree? I agreed, of course. We made quite the pair; walking out to the flightline together, we looked like Baby Huey strolling next to Tweety Bird. We got him back on track, and he remained my student for the duration of the program and ended up being one of my all-time favorites. Some years later, I learned that he returned to Sheppard with his family as a T-37 instructor in his own rite. We still remain in touch.

Occasionally, I would invite some of my students over to the house for beer and pizza. Once, I put on a documentary of William Shirer's *Rise and Fall of the Third Reich*, narrated by Richard Basehart, on my new cutting-edge video cassette recorder. They were absolutely fascinated; it was film footage most of them had never seen before, with much of the history of the Nazi Party and fascism in Germany not thoroughly discussed in German schools at the time.

Since they were all going to be fighter pilots, I would play the song "ME-262" by Blue Oyster Cult for them as well.

"It is quite heroic, is it not?" marveled one of the students. I think they were so used to Germans in WWII being portrayed as villains that they were surprised by the song's narrative.

Later, one of the students built a beautiful model of the ME-262 for me that I kept until a steady stream of Air Force moves damaged it beyond repair, and another student did a large charcoal drawing of the ME-262 in flight, which I had framed.

Flying with students was fun and challenging. It wasn't long before I could generally predict what a student was going to do before he did it. I was ready with instruction and rarely caught by surprise, although, on occasion, surprises surfaced.

Over the next few months, I found myself in a landing-configured spin with a student hamfisting a nose-low traffic pattern stall; an over-G when I was demonstrating runaway trim to a student who simply let go of the stick; and an unusual attitude recovery with a student who became disoriented pulling a closed in the traffic pattern—"Recover, now, please." These were all good lessons in not becoming too complacent, which could be easy to do if you weren't careful.

One of the VR routes for flying our low level training missions passed almost directly over Hobart. Whenever I was scheduled to fly that route, I always called my grandmother and told her what time I would be passing by so she could come outside and perhaps see me flying overhead with my student. I would then call her that evening, "Did you see me?"

"Yes!" she would always exclaim, but she continued to tell her friends that her grandson flew the big ones, so I don't think she ever really understood that I flew Tweets. I'm pretty sure she never really saw or heard me doing a fly-by.

There was a program created between Air Training Command (ATC) and Tactical Air Command (TAC) whereby around once a year, TAC would fly a fighter into an ATC base and give orientation rides to four deserving FAIPs interested in flying fighters. I was one of the lucky selectees and was given a backseat ride in an F-4 based out of Seymour-Johnson AFB in South Carolina. What a monster! You could feel the Phantom absolutely powering its way through the sky with its big twin J79 engines. While it didn't seem as agile as the T-38, there was no denying its capability.

We flew formation with another F-4 with a fellow orientation pilot. I was impressed with the responsiveness of the throttles, and how sensitive my front-seater was to a potential over-G from the ham-fist flying in the back. Other than a few warnings to ease off the stick, I flew it well enough. Nevertheless, it felt like I was trying to harness a big overpowered tank rather than the swift and stealthy fighter I had imagined. During the debrief, I got my first real taste of anti-FAIP bias. The F-4 pilot told me how surprised he was that I could fly as well as I could, being a Tweet FAIP and all.

In July 1981, after eleven months as a flightline IP, I was moved to Check Section as a check ride evaluator, playing the Darth Vader role mentioned earlier. Although viewed as a promotion, being in check section wasn't as much fun as being a flightline IP. You couldn't develop relationships with your students; you didn't do any real instruction, and you had to put up with irate IPs who were disappointed with some of the grades I gave to students for sub-par performance.

I still occasionally flew with B Flight as a guest IP but felt pretty isolated with my fellow black-hatted evaluators back in the Check Section office.

However, there was a growing sense of anticipation at Sheppard. The ENJJPT program was fast approaching, with opening ceremonies scheduled for late October. We would be creating new flights and welcoming new instructors from Canada, the United Kingdom, Norway, Denmark, Belgium, Greece, and Turkey to accompany our German and Dutch cadre. We would also begin teaching U.S. student pilots for the first time, and we were all curious about how the new blend was going to work.

In early October, an announcement was made regarding the new ENJJPT PIT flight, the instructor course for the soon-to-be-arriving IPs from our NATO allies. I was surprised to find my name listed as a PIT instructor in the new flight. Seven of us were selected, two of us FAIPs, and the rest highly-experienced instructors.

This was going to be a big challenge for me. I barely had 14 months' experience as a T-37 IP, and this first PIT class would be comprised of not only fighter pilots, these pilots were also their particular nation's senior representatives for ENJJPT. They would all be lieutenant colonels or their equivalent. I was honored to be chosen, but it was going to be quite a change for me in how I flew and taught others to fly the Tweet. I would be teaching other older and far more experienced pilots how to teach.

The ENJJPT PIT course was unchanged from the GAF PIT course I had completed earlier. The first half of the course would entail teaching pilots to fly the T-37 in contact, instruments, navigation, and formation. The second half was devoted to teaching student pilots, simulated by us PIT instructors, those same maneuvers.

Not surprisingly, this initial cadre was mature and generally easy to work with. However, their English skills were often not as strong as those of the younger student pilots, and I was surprised that not all of them seemed to be good sticks. I learned that just because you were a fighter pilot doesn't mean you were going to be God's Gift to Aviation in the simple little Tweet.

In addition, many of this senior cadre had recently come from staff jobs, so some of their flying skills were a little rusty. Still, all of them tended to perform well enough, except for one crusty old lieutenant colonel.

He was overweight, in his 50s, his English skills were poor, and the ENJJPT assignment was probably his last tour—a gift allowing him to spend his last three years on duty flying in the U.S. He had probably been a solid pilot in his younger days, but his biggest problem was that he just didn't seem that interested in the program. Maybe he thought that as the senior representative to his country, he would be able to waltz through with little effort. Unfortunately, it showed in his flying and academic performance. He just didn't seem to care. Because of the sensitivity of possibly having to wash out a senior officer from the first-ever ENJJPT class, he only flew with our most experienced PIT IPs.

One day, we were flying a formation proficiency ride. The lieutenant colonel was in a jet with our flight commander, and I was flying with another PIT student who was doing well in the program. We were doing pitch-out-and-rejoins—they were in the lead, and we were flying fingertip on the right wing. Since it was a proficiency sortie, the flight commander and I were in the right seats, students in the left. They gave us the pitch-out-and-rejoin signal, and my student acknowledged with a head nod. Then the lead jet, flown by the lieutenant colonel student, hesitated.

Do you believe in guardian angels? I do. At that moment, it came to me as clear as day. Unbelievably, they were going to pitch into us, not away from us! My student was looking to his left, waiting for the lead to pitch away from us so we could complete the rejoin, thus he did not see my hand coming forward to grab the stick. Sure enough, the lead pitched up hard into us, and I jammed forward on the stick as forcefully as I could.

We were flying the standard three-feet-wingtip separation, so I don't know how close we came to being hit as they passed over the top of us. I had always thought in that situation, I would do a loaded roll around any jet breaking into me, but for whatever reason, my instinct told me to duck under.

"Knock it off!!" calls filled the radios as we gathered our wits and emptied our underwear. The ride was terminated. We flew back to the base, and the lieutenant colonel eventually ended up eliminating himself from the program and going back home to Europe.

To this day, I don't know exactly why I knew—yet I knew, without a shadow of a doubt—that he was going to break into us. However, I do believe in guardian angels, and mine saved four lives that day.

After graduating our first class of senior officers, subsequent classes consisted primarily of majors and captains. We also started to see more U.S. instructors entering PIT, to include newly-assigned FAIPs from other UPT bases.

Not everyone made it through the program. Once, I was flying with a B-52 pilot who was having all kinds of problems with the T-37 transition. We were doing a touch-and-go following an instrument approach into Lawton-Fort Sill Regional Airport. After the wheels touched down, we continued down the runway. "There's something wrong with the engines! We're not accelerating!" he sputtered.

"You forgot to put the throttles back up to mil," I replied, both horrified and amused.

I guess he routinely thought a co-pilot would work the throttles for him—I don't know. Anyway, he slammed the throttles up to mil, and I slammed them right back to idle—there wasn't enough runway remaining to continue the takeoff at that point, so we did a low-speed abort. Much to our embarrassment, we had to taxi back around, contact tower, and request another clearance for takeoff. He was later eliminated from the program and given a non-flying assignment.

A few of the new NATO instructor candidates were eliminated as well, primarily due to challenges with English proficiency. Their flying skills were fine, but several of them had trouble understanding the air traffic controllers, much less trying to instruct a student who already only understood English as a second, third, or fourth language.

I was most impressed with the new instructor candidates from Denmark and Norway. They were competent, relaxed, confident in their flying skills, and their English was better than mine.

Being in ENJJPT PIT, I worked daily almost exclusively with NATO fighter pilots. I enjoyed flying with them and listening to their stories. We flew T-3 sorties once or twice a week, whereby you would fly with one of your fellow instructors just to get some stick time and not let your own flying skills erode while in constant instructor mode.

I especially enjoyed flying formation with the guys and started to get a better understanding of what extended trail and gun/missile envelopes actually represented. I seldom got spit out when flying in extended trail anymore, and on more than one occasion was cocky enough to transmit the guns call.

I became known for my hair-raising rejoins, which, looking back on it, was a stupid way to prove my manhood among the fighter jocks. Knowing that it would take Tweet engines a long time to spool back if reduced to idle, I would come screaming in with supercharged overtake speed, but rather than reduce the throttle past the thrust attenuators, I fanned the speed breaks in and out instead. This technique usually resulted in a perfect, albeit very aggressive, rejoin. It left little room for error, but in my immaturity, I confess I enjoyed occasionally scaring my more experienced students and fellow IPs with the technique. One of the advantages of being a PIT instructor was that you got plenty of stick time since half the syllabus involved your simulating a student pilot for your PIT student instructors to evaluate.

My desire to fly the A-10 had not waned, but the fighter pilot cadre around me thought I was daft. Why would anyone want to fly a slow and ugly ground-pounding machine like the Warthog—a jet with a titanium cockpit designed to take hits?

Almost all of my friends and fellow IPs adored the F-15. It had the more glamorous air-to-air mission, and we had several former F-15 pilots in our instructor cadre who passionately preached its advantages to me. There were no F-16 pilots in the cadre—the jet was still too new, and only one IP in Sheppard's history had ever received an F-16 assignment, and that guy later went on to be a 4-Star general.

I started to come around to my companions' way of thinking, but I still wasn't that interested in the F-15. I wanted to drop bombs, fly fast and low, and take it to the bad guys in a meaningful way. As someone once said, you win a war by killing in the thousands, not one at a time at 20,000 feet. I still favored the A-10, but the F-16? Maybe—but for now, I was excelling as a Tweet IP, and loving life.

One Friday evening in July 1982, I was at Duffy's as usual. My friend from high school, Jake, was there with a friend from out of town. We spent some time chatting about the possibilities for our future assignments. Jake desperately wanted to fly an F-15, and I told him about my conflicting desires.

He and his friend were going flying the next day; Jake often flew privately out of the local airport. I had to get up early the following day to drive to Hobart to spend the weekend with my grandmother, so I called it an early night. When I returned to my apartment on Sunday afternoon, I picked up the Sunday paper off my doorstep and carelessly threw it on the couch as I walked in the door. The phone rang before I had taken a few steps.

"Lieutenant White," I answered, as I always did.

"Hello...is this P.K. White?" a female voice asked.

"Yeah," I replied pleasantly. Hmmm. I wondered if this was a nurse acquaintance from one of the MIMSO classes?

"P.K., this is Wendy Shelton from Wiesbaden."

Wow!! I was delighted! I had often thought of Wendy over the years since that high school graduation night in 1974. I recalled that Jake mentioned that Wendy was living in San Antonio. I hoped she was in town.

"Hi, Wendy!" I laughed. "How are you doing? It sure has been a long time!"

There was a slight hesitation on the other end. "Yes," she stammered, "it has been a long time. I was just calling about Jacob Dixon."

"Ha!" I laughed again. "I just saw Jacob on Friday night. We've been talking about all of us getting together one of these days. Are you at Jake's right now?"

Another pause. "P.K.," she said. "Jacob is dead."

"Jake Dixon??!!" I blurted. I felt like I had been hit by lightning. I don't exactly recall what we said next; she mentioned something about Jake and a friend dying in a plane crash Saturday morning. She had been notified by Jake's wife, who was out of town visiting her mother. I started sobbing and really couldn't talk, so I took her number and told her I would call her later. Almost immediately, as I hung up, the phone rang again.

"Lieutenant White," I choked.

"P.K., it's Zeke." Zeke was my best friend at Sheppard and a fellow T-37 FAIP.

"What happened?" I asked.

"Don't look at the paper," he said before going on to explain what he knew. As far as he understood, Jake and his friend had crashed in a Cessna 150 almost immediately after takeoff, and an FAA safety board had been convened to investigate the cause.

I hung up the phone, and of course, opened the Sunday paper. There on the front page was a photo of Jake's body, tangled up in the twisted metal of the Cessna. It was shocking and horrific. I couldn't believe they had printed something that grisly—that insensitive—on the front page of the newspaper.

I was really shaken up. This was not the first time I had lost a friend in an aircraft accident. It was an occupational hazard, something you came to expect and accept. But this, for some reason, was different. Maybe it was because I had known Jake since I was 15 years old. Maybe it was because he was the only local tie I had to a former life before the Air Force.

After a mostly sleepless night, the first thing I did the next day was report to the Wing Commander's office and volunteer to escort Jake's body back home for burial. I had met Jake's parents in Germany on several occasions and thought they might appreciate a familiar face being there for them.

However, I was informed by the Wing Executive Officer that Jake's wife had already requested one of Jake's best friends from the T-38 cadre perform the escort duties, which of course, made total sense. The Exec told me how livid the entire wing was over the front-page photo, and how the Wing Commander had written a formal letter of outrage to the newspaper. Everyone, especially those who knew Jake in the 90th FTS, was in mourning.

That evening, I called Wendy. We talked for quite a while. Wendy had been much closer to Jake than I was in high school, and had remained close with him and his wife over the years. We shared a few stories and grieved together. Wendy asked if it was okay if she drove up from San Antonio the next weekend, just to be with someone who had also known and appreciated Jake. I naturally agreed; I thought it might help us both heal from the shock of losing a friend, and I would enjoy getting to know another fellow Wiesbaden Air Force Brat.

The next Saturday, I woke, showered, straightened up and cleaned my apartment, and put on what I thought was a flattering t-shirt and trousers. I expected Wendy around noon, and as the hour approached, I nervously paced back and forth between my window to look out on the parking lot, and to make sure the apartment was ready for a female visitor.

I was looking out the window when I saw a vision of absolute loveliness come strolling up the sidewalk. She had short dark hair, wore a purple summer top and blue jeans, and I could see the flash of her blue eyes from my second-story window. I was thunderstruck—I was gobsmacked—and I said a quick prayer that it was Wendy. It was.

I met her at the top of the stairs. "Wendy?" I asked.

"P.K.?" she smiled.

We shared a friendly hug and entered my apartment. We spent most of that afternoon looking at old yearbooks and photos, talking about Jake, telling stories from our high school days, and generally catching up. There were some tears, but mostly laughter.

Just as I remembered her in high school, she was stunningly beautiful, smart, funny, and delightful company. When I reminded her of the "Ain't No Sunshine" incident on our high school graduation night, she laughed, "No way!! That was you?"

That evening, we went to a Chinese restaurant, and I told her my plans for my Air Force career, emphasizing my desire to return to Europe and fly fighters. That night, I gave her my bedroom while I slept on the couch, but I had difficulty falling asleep knowing Wendy was in the next room.

Sunday morning, we went to breakfast at Denny's, and as she was getting in her car to return to San Antonio, I worked up enough courage to try and kiss her. She was prepared and returned my kiss in kind. As she drove away, I waved goodbye with the certainty that there was no doubt about it—I was in love with Wendy Shelton.

I called her that night just to ensure she had made the five-hour drive back to San Antonio safely. We discussed trying to get together again as soon as possible, and I made plans for taking a cross-country to Kelly AFB, located in San Antonio, the very next weekend.

I flew in with a buddy that Friday afternoon, and Wendy met us at Base Operations. "Are you a model?" my friend stammered; he was mightily impressed.

Wendy wasn't a model, but her mother was. Dolores left Kansas City as a young woman and moved to New York, where she did vaudeville and modeled for top fashion designers. She met and married Boyce Shelton—a Texan who had flown 37 B-17 missions during WWII as a top-turret gunner and then studied art at the Acadamie in Paris.

Back in Wendy's tiny efficiency apartment, Wendy was in the kitchen, and I was watching television. "That's Mom!" Wendy called from the kitchen.

"Huh?" I wondered aloud—where?

"That's Mom on the television!" Sure enough, Dolores was there in a GM Truck commercial, and Wendy heard her voice.

Wendy had inherited her good looks from her mother, and her artistic talents from her father. She showed me around San Antonio, took me to meet her parents, Felix and Dolores Portelli, and before I left, we expressed our love for one another. It was turning into a whirlwind romance, and we continued to make plans to see each other as much as possible.

A year remained in my Sheppard assignment, so I spent the next months in my normal flying routine, altered by my visits to San Antonio and Wendy's visits to Wichita Falls. Shortly after Christmas, Wendy moved to Dallas, where she lived with her father, Boyce, and was only a short two-hour drive away.

We spent nearly every weekend together and grew to hate Sunday afternoons when we would have to say goodbye. By February, I worked up enough courage to propose, and she said yes. We drove to Alabama to introduce her to my parents in March, and they fell as much in love with her as I. We made plans to be married in late May, and I was happier than I had ever been in my life.

By that March, I had finally made up my mind that I wanted to fly the F-16. It was the newest, hottest fighter in the Air Force inventory, and it had a multi-role mission.

The F-15 was strictly air-to-air—F-15Es hadn't been fully developed yet. The A-10, which I still greatly admired, was strictly air-to-ground. The F-16 was designed to do it all. After much deliberation and discussion with my fellow IPs, I put F-16, A-10, and F-15 in order on my assignment Dream Sheet. I felt I would compete fairly well. I had continued to progress and perform strongly as a Tweet IP in PIT, and coming from the new fighter-based program at ENJJPT, I hoped to have some advantage over the other FAIPS throughout Air Training Command in my same rotation cycle at assignment time.

In late March, my flight commander notified me that my assignment had come in. I was scheduled to meet with the

Wing Director of Operations—a German colonel—that afternoon. I had flown with him several times when he was going through PIT, and we knew each other well. I tentatively walked into his office and reported in. "Well, P.K., I have your assignment—are you ready?" he asked with a big smile on his face.

"Yes, sir!" I replied—this had to be good news.

"How would you like to fly the A-10?" he asked.

"I would love it!" I exclaimed. "Thank you, sir!" It wasn't the F-16 I hoped for, but I had wanted to fly the A-10 for so long that I thought it must have been fate. I was genuinely happy with the news.

He viewed me with a puzzled look on his face, wrote something on a piece of paper, and handed it to me. "Here is the number for fighter assignments at Randolph. Give them a call." I took a look at the paper.

On it was a phone number, and underneath it was written, "It's really F-16."

I let out a war-whoop as he collapsed in laughter. He came around the desk, shook my hand, and congratulated me on my good fortune.

I flew up the stairs back to my flight, where everyone anxiously awaited my news. There were more whoops, more back slaps, and words of congratulations. I felt like a million dollars.

I called Wendy immediately; I heard her softly crying on the phone, but they were tears of joy and pride. That night, I bought the bar at Duffy's with a couple of other FAIPs who had gotten their assignments. One had received his first choice of an F-15, and another had gotten an A-10. A fighter sweep for Sheppard FAIPs; it was a good day.

I called fighter assignments at Randolph, and they informed me that I could expect to attend Lead-In Fighter Training (LIFT) at Holloman AFB in New Mexico sometime in early summer, followed by F-16 training at MacDill AFB in Florida immediately after that. I wouldn't receive my official F-16 assignment until after I neared completion of the F-16 Replacement Training Unit (RTU).

It was an exhilarating time. I spent the next several weeks reading everything I could about the F-16, and planning for the wedding, which was booked for the end of May at the main chapel at Randolph AFB in San Antonio. Wendy and I then planned to spend our honeymoon on Padre Island in the Gulf of Mexico.

Shortly after receiving the F-16 assignment, I received more news. I had been selected to attend Squadron Officer School (SOS) at Maxwell AFB in Montgomery, Alabama, starting in the middle of May. The course lasted until the middle of June. It was a good career opportunity; all junior officers were expected to complete SOS by correspondence or in-residence, and I had not yet finished it by correspondence.

However, it would interfere with our wedding, and possibly my slot at LIFT and F-16 RTU. I called Wendy and told her the news. We agreed that we didn't want to delay the wedding; besides, the chapel at Randolph had to be booked well in advance, and Wendy's mother had already made arrangements for the special day.

I called the SOS folks at Maxwell, and they told me I could expect to be allowed to take two-to-three days of leave to get married without interfering with the class schedule. Wendy and I decided that the honeymoon could wait, and we would proceed with the wedding as planned.

With some nervousness, I then called the F-16 assignment guys and informed them of my dilemma. Would I lose my F-16 slot, since my projected report date to RTU at MacDill interfered with SOS? No worries—they desired incoming F-16 pilots to have SOS completed, and they would merely shift my class dates. However, due to previously scheduled classes, I would not be able to start LIFT until October. I could expect to be assigned to the second-ever F-16 class at Luke AFB in Arizona instead of MacDill.

It meant a few extra months at Sheppard, but I thought that would be okay for us newlyweds as we made the big lifestyle adjustment. But what a way to start a marriage! I would fly into San Antonio from SOS on Friday night, get married on Sunday, and kiss Wendy goodbye to return to SOS at the crack of dawn on Monday. A great introduction to married life in the Air Force for my new bride.

I reported to SOS as scheduled, and had about ten days there before the wedding. My parents still lived just north of Montgomery, so I spent some quality time with them in addition to my participation in SOS. With their help, I found an apartment in Montgomery that accepted month-long leases, so Wendy and I would have a place to stay off base after we were married. I confess that my mind wasn't totally on the SOS course work; much of it seemed barely a step above many of the things we had already been taught in AFROTC. I had other concerns.

When the wedding weekend came, I arrived in San Antonio to be met at the airport by Wendy. She drove me to the Ramada Inn her mother had booked for the rehearsal dinner, and where all of us out-of-town guests would be staying. Besides my parents, grandmothers, aunts, and uncles, several of my high school buddies were there, as well as some of my pilot comrades from Sheppard and my UPT class at Willie. All of Wendy's out-of-town family and guests were staying there as well. We owned that Ramada.

The rehearsal dinner was a riot of stories and toasts, as rehearsal dinners tend to be. My Uncle Lloyd and Wendy's father Boyce spent most of the evening arguing over the greatest WWII bomber; the B-17, which Boyce flew, or the B-24, which my Uncle Lloyd flew. It turned out to be a tie.

After a boys-night-on-the-town, we retired back to the hotel, where my fellow aviators and friends had set up more libations in one of the rooms. I was relaxing on the bed as we were telling old war stories when one of the guys yelled "Now!!!" and they all jumped on top of me, turned me on my stomach, held my arms and legs down, and started taking down my pants—which was a little alarming.

One of the guys then produced a collection of colored magic markers, and they all took turns autographing my bare butt. When they were finished, they released me so I could admire their artwork. Some of my old girlfriends names were inscribed, as well as a few "Hi, Wendy!" messages and directional guides to other parts of my body. As hard as I scrubbed later in the shower, I could not make the messages to my sweet wife disappear. She would get quite the surprise on our wedding night.

Our wedding was held at the old Spanish Chapel on Randolph AFB, a real gem. The chaplain was an old friend of Wendy's family, and the ceremony was perfect. My father was my best man, and Wendy was escorted down the aisle by both her father and step-father. When the "Wedding March" began on the big church organ, and the back doors opened, I lost my breath. Wendy was a gorgeous, radiant vision of grace and beauty.

After the photos were complete, we gathered at the reception held at the Randolph Officers Club. Wendy's mother had planned everything with precision, and everyone had a fantastic time. We then bid the crowd good-bye and spent our wedding night at La Mansion Del Rio on The River Walk in downtown San Antonio. Its elegant Spanish ambiance was beautiful, and it was very hard to wake up in the dark the next morning, say goodbye to Wendy, and return to Maxwell.

Wendy was scheduled to leave San Antonio on Wednesday and make the drive to Montgomery to join me sometime Thursday evening. However, I was in bed late Wednesday night when I heard a knock at the door. It was Wendy; she had driven all the way from San Antonio to Montgomery non-stop. Ah, newlyweds.

While still immersed in the SOS curriculum, we needed to get Wendy officially entered as an Air Force Dependent. We spent a fair amount of time at the Maxwell Personnel Office, and it was a real thrill for Wendy to be re-issued an ID card and go shopping at the BX and base commissary, something she hadn't been able to do since she left Wiesbaden.

Wendy helped me with some of my SOS assignments, but the course began to be more of a distraction as Wendy and I concentrated on building our new life together. I ended up completing SOS in a purely mediocre fashion.

One afternoon just before graduation from SOS, Wendy got a hint of what life with the White family might be like. We had just finished an SOS soccer game, where we were clobbered. I stalked off the field, angry at my teammates, and frustrated with myself for our poor performance. Wendy was in the bleachers, and seeing the look on my face, stood up and shouted, "Don't be so mad, honey! It's only a game!"

I shot her back a look she probably hadn't seen before, so she said, "Gee—stop pouting!"

"You've gotta learn," I growled.

"You're the one who has to grow up and learn!" she retorted.

We drove in relative silence to my parent's home for dinner. As soon as we walked in, Wendy said, "Can you believe your son? He's all upset just because they lost a stupid soccer game."

My mother raised her eyebrows and quietly replied, "They lost?"

To which my Dad immediately said, "Wow. What was the score?"

We've always been a competitive bunch. Welcome to the family.

Upon completion of SOS, we returned to Sheppard for the remaining three months of my assignment there. I continued my duties in PIT, and Wendy began adjusting to life as an Air Force pilot's wife. We discussed career possibilities in detail and agreed that it would be a dream for us to be assigned to fly F-16s at Hahn Air Base in Germany, which was the only F-16 base in Germany at the time.

In preparation for the AT-38s I would fly at LIFT, I was given three front-seat rides in the T-38. With much relief, I found the transition back to flying the T-38 wasn't nearly as difficult as I thought it would be. In late October, I had my finis flight in the T-37; we packed up and started down the road to Holloman AFB in Alamogordo, New Mexico.

More than three years earlier, I had been disappointed with my T-37 assignment. I was now heading to fighters and the hottest jet in the Air Force inventory, and I was a much better pilot with the more than 1,000 hours I had spent flying and instructing in the Tweet.

More importantly, I had found and married the love of my life. How many times, I wondered, had I passed Wendy in the hallways of H.H. Arnold High School in Wiesbaden, never guessing that my lifelong companion was right there in front of me? Life was sweet, and we headed west with joy, looking forward to our new life together.

CHAPTER FOUR

VIPER SCHOOL

Luke Air Force Base, AZ

1984

You love a lot of things if you live around them. But there isn't any woman, and there isn't any horse, not any before nor any after, that is as lovely as a great airplane. And men who love them are faithful to them even though they leave them for others. Man has one virginity to lose in fighters, and if it is a lovely airplane he loses it to, there is where his heart will forever be.

—Ernest Hemingway

Wendy and I made the trip from Sheppard to Holloman in close trail, me in my black Celica Supra GT, and she in her silver Buick Le Sabre. The few household goods reserved for shipment would be stored until our arrival at Luke, so we would essentially be living out of a suitcase for the two months at Holloman and LIFT. We checked into billeting and were issued a small efficiency apartment in the Transient Living Quarters (TLQ) on base. It would suit us well, knowing we would spend our first Thanksgiving and Christmas together there.

Holloman AFB was located a few miles west of Alamogordo, New Mexico, about halfway between El Paso and Albuquerque. Alamogordo was a smallish town of about 30,000 and had a nice, friendly feel to it. Like more than a few towns in the U.S., its economy depended largely on the local military presence.

The base hosted a number of missions, to include an F-15 Tactical Fighter Wing and the White Sands Missile Test Range. The 479th Tactical Training Wing conducted the LIFT mission, and I would be assigned to the 435th Tactical Fighter Training Squadron Black Eagles.

On the first day of in-processing, we received our patches and a blue squadron scarf. I was officially a part of Tactical Air Command (TAC) and I carried myself a few inches taller wearing a TAC patch instead of the ATC patch I wore for four years.

My LIFT class was small, with only about a dozen students. Two other officers were going to F-16s besides me; one a fellow captain making the transition from O-2s to F-16s, and one a lieutenant I'd known as a student pilot at Sheppard. The three of us were assigned to the same F-16 class at Luke, scheduled to begin in early February. The remaining students in our class were all butter-bar lieutenants, newly graduated from pilot training, and they were all going to A-10s. I was the senior ranking officer in the class and was, therefore, named the class commander. While some of the guys were married, they all left their wives behind. Wendy would be the solo accompanied spouse.

We would fly the AT-38B, the fighter-modified version of the T-38. AT-38Bs could carry gun pods, rockets, or practice bombs, and the syllabus consisted of flying basic combat maneuvers and air-to-ground weapons delivery on a controlled range. The AT-38 was much cheaper to fly than our operational fighters, and LIFT provided TAC the opportunity to wash out anyone who clearly was not meant to fly in the tactical fighter role. We spent the first few days in the classroom, discussing the course, getting to know the AT-38, and being indoctrinated into the world of fighter jets and the fighter pilot culture. It was awesome.

Our first few rides involved getting to know the handling characteristics of the AT-38 and tactical formation flying in both two and four-ships. Most of the LIFT instructors were good guys. The training atmosphere was generally relaxed, and the pace not too demanding. Wendy was amused to see me chair flying all the radio calls and local flying procedures from our little TLQ room, but as usual, it paid big dividends in the air.

The Basic Fighter Maneuvers (BFM) portion of the syllabus was fairly canned, as we rehearsed entry into the turn circle from above, below, or level with an adversary. On offense, we worked on getting ourselves into valid missile parameters and flying our way into a guns tracking solution, the success of which we were able to view on film during the debrief. On defense, we strived to maintain sight of our opponent in a high-G environment and defeating those missile and gun attempts. One of the biggest challenges was making radio calls that made sense while flying the jet in this alien regime. I would walk around our little apartment muttering radio calls and trying to make it second nature. I earned *Excellent* grades and was having a ball.

My class commander duties were minimal, so Wendy and I had plenty of time for relaxation and exploration outside of my chair flying and academics studies. We spent Thanksgiving at The Inn of the Mountain Gods at nearby Ruidoso, and Wendy went snow skiing several times on the slopes at Cloudcroft. In December, she got a part-time Christmas-help job at Hastings Book & Record store in Alamogordo. Her primary responsibility was decorating the store for the holidays. We spent Friday evenings at the Officer's Club on base, where Wendy felt obliged to dance with just about everyone in our class. She loved being back in the Air Force and was enjoying herself as much as I.

Making the transition from air-to-air to air-to-ground was a new challenge. The concept of flying BFM felt somewhat related to the acrobatic and extended trail maneuvers I flew in the T-37 for the past three-plus years, but now we had to BFM a target on the ground. I chair-flew myself silly trying to make myself comfortable with the radio calls and hurling myself at a target on the ground at a much faster speed than I was accustomed to. The AT-38 had a gunsight, and our bomb and rocket attacks were all manually employed, unlike the computerized solutions I would later experience flying the F-16. However, the hard work paid off, and most of my scores were counters.

We received a few days off for Christmas, so Wendy and I spent the time exploring the countryside and the Sacramento Mountains. On Christmas morning, I was soundly sleeping when I heard, "Thump! Thump! Thump!" as if someone was doing jumping jacks in our little kitchenette.

I opened my eyes, and there was Wendy. She was inside a full body-sized Christmas stocking, wearing nothing but her birthday suit, and hopping her way to the foot of the bed. "Merry Christmas, baby!" she giggled. Ah, newlyweds.

Our orders to LIFT had specified that we were to bring our black winter Mess Dress uniforms so we could all attend the base New Year's Eve party. It was only a few days before our graduation date and was a fitting way for us to end our LIFT experience as we welcomed 1984. All of our class made it through without any significant difficulty.

Since the F-16 course wasn't formally scheduled to begin until early February, we knew we would have a couple of weeks on casual status. I'd have time to get to know Luke, reacquaint myself with the Phoenix area from my UPT days at Willie, find an apartment, and prepare for the challenges of mastering The Mighty Viper.

We out-processed from Holloman early on a Friday morning and faced an 8-hour drive to Luke. Our desire was to make it to the Luke AFB Housing Referral Office before closing, get registered, and spend the weekend looking for an apartment near the base.

In 1984, the speed limit was still 55 mph, so it would be virtually impossible unless we pushed it up a little. We took off in tandem, again me in my Celica and Wendy in her Le Sabre, screaming across the desert plains on I-10W, trying to keep a close lookout for the Highway Patrol.

We did great until we got to the hills and small canyons just outside Tucson, where we were both pulled over doing 75 mph. The officer was very genial and sympathetic with our plight and appreciated the fact he was talking to a future Air Force fighter pilot, but not forgiving enough to let us off with only a warning. So, on Monday morning, my initial introduction to my new squadron commander would include two pretty impressive traffic tickets. How am I doing so far, boss?

Luke AFB, located about 15 miles west of Phoenix, was home to initial conversion training for both the F-15 and, just recently, the F-16. Most primary F-16 training was still conducted at MacDill AFB in Florida, but plans were already in place for Luke to assume the bulk of F-16 conversion training requirements for the USAF. The 58th Tactical Training Wing was responsible for F-16 training, and the 405th Tactical Training Wing oversaw the F-15 program.

It was a perfect location for fighter training, with excellent year-round weather and plenty of training airspace, including the Barry Goldwater Tactical Range consisting of nearly two million acres of mostly desolate Sonoran Desert. I would be assigned to the 311th Tactical Fighter Training Squadron Sidewinders, and we would be their second-ever F-16 RTU class.

Early Saturday morning, we toured the base to get ourselves oriented, and we drove past the flightline. Flying had not yet started for the day, so the air was still and quiet. My heart leaped in my throat when I saw row upon row of F-16s lined up on the ramp. I had seen a real F-16 only a few times up to this point, usually as a static display at one of the annual Open House/Airshows at Sheppard, so this was quite a thrill to see so many of them. I was in love.

The General Dynamics F-16 Fighting Falcon is better known in the fighter world as The Viper after the starfighters in the *Battlestar Galactica* television series. A single-seat, single-engine jet fighter aircraft originally designed as a lightweight day air superiority fighter, it had quickly evolved into an all-weather multirole aircraft.

The F-16 had a frameless bubble canopy for increased visibility, a unique side-mounted control stick to ease control while maneuvering, a seat reclined 30 degrees to reduce the effect of G-forces up to 9 Gs on the pilot, and the first use of a fly-by-wire flight control system to make it the most maneuverable jet fighter aircraft in the world at that time. It had an internal 20mm Gatling gun and eleven locations for mounting bombs, missiles, pods, and other mission equipment. It was capable of speeds up to Mach 2 and had a service ceiling of 50,000 feet. It had a thrust-to-weight ratio greater than one, which provided enough power to accelerate in a vertical climb. As a Tweet FAIP, it would be like transitioning from a Ford Pinto to a Ferrari.

I reported in to the 311th squadron commander first thing Monday morning. Looking at the plaques and memorabilia in his office, I immediately saw that he had been a Misty FAC in Vietnam. Those guys had balls the size of water towers, and I was very impressed. He had a max-relax demeanor and seemed to have a permanent Mona Lisa-type smile on his face.

He welcomed me to the squadron, laughed off the speeding tickets, and told me I would be assigned to the Assistant Operations Officer for the next two weeks on casual status until the course formally began.

I found the Assistant Ops Officer in his office down the hall and reported in. A gruff, all-business kind of guy, he told me I would be helping him revise and update the briefing room maps and diagrams while on casual status. He then took a glance at my training report from LIFT. "Should be a contender for Top Gun at RTU and progress well ahead of contemporaries, eh? Well. We'll see."

I spent the next couple of weeks working in and around the squadron. I came and went as I pleased, as long as I got the work in the briefing rooms done. Wendy and I found an apartment in Glendale about 20 minutes from the base and started settling in.

More and more guys who would be in the course starting drifting in. There were 14 of us—three FAIPs (I was the only Tweet FAIP), two former O-2 pilots, and nine first-assignment lieutenants. They were all good guys, easy to get to know, and as excited as I was to start the course. One of the T-38 FAIPs outranked me, so I would not be the Class Commander this time. I was relieved as it would allow me to concentrate more fully on the training.

I observed the general working climate of the squadron and the personalities of the instructor pilots with interest. The squadron commander continued his easy-going ways with that ever-present, semi-amused grin on his face. A couple of older, chain-smoking majors laughed and joked around with us, but most of the captains came off as pretty hardcore.

Few of the IPs had ever flown the F-16 in an operational unit. Most of them had transitioned from the F-4 and were assigned directly to F-16 RTU. I assumed the tough, no-nonsense atmosphere was just the way of TAC and fighter jocks. It brought me back to a conversation I had at the O'Club with another Lieutenant Colonel Assistant Operations Officer back at Sheppard, on the night I received my F-16 assignment. He said, "You know, TAC...is different. The fighter pilot community is different. Don't be surprised if you find yourself wanting to come back to ATC one day."

I thought that was a heck of a thing to say to me on that day of all days, but I wasn't going to let it damper my enthusiasm then, or my determination to succeed in TAC now. Still, I could tell things were, indeed, going to be different.

The course began similarly to the UPT schedule—front-loaded with academics and simulators for several weeks before our first flights. The instructors in the academics squadron were great, and I continued with my typical middle-of-the-road test scores in the mid-low 90s.

At home, Wendy was extremely patient with me as I spent most evenings pouring over the F-16 Dash One, memorizing the boldface called Critical Action Procedures (CAPs), and studying operational procedures and limitations. I built a large stack of 3 x 5 cards, where I would write a subject like Airspeed Limitations on the front, and the answers on the back. I quizzed myself constantly with those cards. With my self-imposed all-work-and-no-play schedule, Wendy started taking classes at Glendale Community College in a quest to finish her bachelor's degree.

Sometime during the second week of the course, I was introduced to "Hooter," the IP who would take me to my F-16 Instrument/Qualification check ride. His first words to me were, "I don't think Tweet FAIPs should be allowed in the program."

Wow. I laughed and asked, "Why do you think that?"

He replied, "Because if you were good enough to fly fighters, you would have gotten one out of UPT."

I said, "Fair enough. But don't you think it's possible to have improved one's flying skills after flying three years in ATC?"

"Nope!" he snorted.

This was going to be a challenge. I couldn't tell if he was just a jerk, or if the entire TAC-RTU instructor cadre was like this. Nevertheless, I was the student, and I had to adjust if I was going to succeed.

The F-16 RTU course was broken into three phases; Conversion, Air-to-Air, and Air-to-Surface. A numerical course grading criteria in TAC was used instead of the Excellent-Good-Fair-Poor criteria in ATC. A 4 grade reflected an unusually high degree of ability; a 3 meant your performance was correct, efficient, skillful, and without hesitation; a 2 indicated your performance was essentially correct, recognizes and corrects errors; a 1 showed your performance to be safe, but indicates limited proficiency and makes errors of omission or commission; and a 0 said your performance indicates a lack of ability or knowledge.

If a 0 grade was due to an element marked Dangerous, the gradesheet was marked with a red border. You would receive a NE/SNP, meaning Non-Effective for Student Non-Progress on any 0 graded mission; an IP could also give a NE/SNP on an overall 1 grade depending on the severity of the error or lack of progress.

Our initial simulator sorties were devoted to switchology and learning how to safely and efficiently start, taxi, and takeoff our F-16A Block 5 jets. Programming the INS (Inertial Navigation System) and FCNP (Fire Control Navigation Panel), turning on the HUD (Heads Up Display), SMS (Stores Management System), RWR (Radar Warning Receiver), and REO (Radar/Electro-Optical display) were all new actions for us. Doing the BUC (Backup Control) check took some finesse with the sensitive Pratt & Whitney engine.

The F-16 side-stick and 30-degree reclined ejection seat felt amazingly natural; you wondered why all airplanes weren't built like the F-16. The cockpit fit like a glove; there wasn't much room for extraneous stuff, so cockpit management of checklists, maps, charts, and aids was another skill required.

With so many new and cool things to look at, my instrument crosscheck was much busier than required in the T-37 or T-38. I hardly looked at the information provided by the HUD. I found the FPM (Flight Path Marker) useful, especially for fix-to-fix navigation and as a landing point-of-reference. Other than that, I stuck to flying off the round dials for navigation, airspeed, and altitude control, just as I had always done. I generally emerged from the simulator dripping in sweat, as if I had actually been flying the jet.

While I felt reasonably confident in my academics classes, I worked hard to keep up in the cockpit. I plodded through those initial simulator sorties, with Hooter and I developing an uneasy and uncomfortable relationship. I didn't like him much, and I knew he didn't like me. I had to admit I was pretty stressed, and I wasn't enjoying myself the way I thought I should. Nevertheless, I felt if I just kept at it, kept pounding away, and kept a positive attitude, things would eventually improve.

The day for my first flight in the F-16 arrived on March 2nd, 1984. Our first four sorties took place in the D-model, the two-seater version with the student in the front, and the IP in the back. We were to fly out to the operating area, perform some handling characteristics maneuvers, which included an introduction to the sensation of a 9-G break turn, a few acrobatic maneuvers, then a return to the base for traffic patterns and landings, to include the SFO (Simulated FlameOut) pattern.

Frankly, I was more nervous than excited to finally fly the world's newest and most awesome fighter jet aircraft. Obviously, Hooter expected me to stumble through the sortie, and I was determined to prove him wrong.

Ground ops were fine, much slower than they would be later, with me carefully programming the FCNP and performing the BUC check. I was impressed with how the jet seemed to want to leap away from the earth during the BUC check and was slightly taken aback by all the banging and movement of the jet during the FLCS BIT (Flight Control Systems, Built-In Test) check, hoping it wouldn't interrupt my INS alignment.

We were expected to be able to taxi ten minutes after engine start, but we were given a pass on these initial orientation missions. All of us had been warned continuously about throttle movements during ground ops. Too much thrust and you could blow over fire bottles, crew chiefs, and crew shacks, so I was a bit tentative in running the engine up for the BUC and EPU (Emergency Power Unit) checks. However, I made it to the runway well enough, and after final checks by the arming ground crew, I was cleared for takeoff.

Taking the center of the runway, I pressed down on the brakes and ran the engine up to 80% for a final systems check—all good. I released the brakes, and steadily pushed the throttle forward first to MIL (Military, or 100%) power, then to AB (AfterBurner). The jet quickly accelerated; I needed to lean forward to keep my head from tilting back. I could feel the jolt of acceleration with each stage of the AB as it lit off. Before I had time to note abort or refusal speed, I was rotating the nose and airborne, rapidly approaching the 300-knot maximum landing gear speed. I lifted the gear handle, made my initial radio calls, and tried to settle down to the business of flying The Viper.

I confess to not remembering all the details of that first flight. As I had done many times before, I concentrated on trying to master the aircraft, and I worked pretty hard just to stay ahead of the jet. A list of what stands out is as follows.

1. It was surprisingly easy to fly the F-16. It handled beautifully; if you were getting off airspeed, a small adjustment to the throttle quickly made things right. The engine was incredibly responsive; you could get yourself into a PIO (Pilot-Induced Oscillation) chasing the airspeed if you got too heavy-handed with the throttle. Again, the side stick, almost static in the right console, felt perfectly natural. The fly-by-wire flight controls allowed you to take your hands off the stick, and the jet would mostly stay in the same attitude—a very nice, very smooth, very stable platform.

2. Cockpit visibility was amazing. The bubble canopy didn't have any rails, and sitting way out front of the wings, it felt like you were zooming through the sky on your own. You could literally

look over your left shoulder and see your right wingtip.

3. A 9-G bat turn was all pain. Coming from a Tweet background where we didn't even wear a G-suit, I had never pulled more than about 6 Gs, and then for only a few seconds. If you got the Block 5 A-model F-16 up past 450 knots, you could snap the jet into a 9-G turn almost instantaneously. I thought my G-suit was going to cut me in half as it inflated then stayed inflated for longer than I anticipated. I was ready for the onset, so I didn't grey out, but it was a definite physical challenge operating in that environment. It provided a sobering example of why we had already lost so many pilots due to G-LOC (G-induced Loss Of Consciousness) in those early years of flying the F-16, before the arrival of the Combat Edge systems we used later.

4. The FLCS limiter was a surprise. I was used to max-performing the T-37 or T-38 by feeling the wings shudder at the edge of a stall. The F-16 FLCS limiter prohibited that from happening; it wouldn't allow the aircraft to stall, so The Viper didn't talk to you in the same way other jets did at slow speeds and high angles of attack. You could feel like you were pulling the stick off the console, but your nose wouldn't track any faster—no cats dancing on the wings.

5. It was easy to get mesmerized by the green stuff—the avionics systems that constituted the HUD, the REO, and the RWR. I tried working the radar, but I started to fixate on radar returns, to the detriment of aircraft control. I quickly began to concentrate solely on flying the jet, which was all we were supposed to do on these first few sorties. As I flew the mission, I saw the cursor on the radar locking on prospective targets—my IP was working the radar from the rear cockpit.

6. The SFO pattern was unlike anything I had ever experienced before. It required performing a nearly vertical climb at the end of the runway up to around 10,000 feet, circling over the runway, pulling the throttle to idle, and BFMing the runway to arrive on speed over the overrun, simulating you had lost your engine and were making a dead stick landing. It was actually easier than I anticipated, but it felt like Mr. Toad's Wild Ride at Disneyland.

7. Landing the F-16 with style and finesse was harder than I would have thought. Takeoff speed is generally lower than landing speed in the F-16, so you almost have to fly the jet onto the runway. Once on the runway, it wants to takeoff again. If you have ever seen an F-16 land, you might see slight gyrations from the wings as it gently dances down the runway. That is the jet trying to get airborne, and you have to lean into the stick to hold it down, yet still keep the nose up to help reduce speed until you are slow enough for the NWS (Nose Wheel Steering) to become effective. Also, the F-16 will float on you forever; I would pull the throttle to idle about halfway through the overrun and end up floating down the runway for another 2,000 feet before my wheels touched down. All of my initial landing attempts were long and hot as a result.

All in all, it was a pretty good first ride, and my second sortie was similar to the first. I got 2 grades on both missions, and Hooter was okay. He talked me through most of the maneuvers, provided some useful techniques, and while his generally abusive demeanor persisted, we got along well enough. I started to feel a little better about the program and about myself. Heck—I had flown the F-16!

The third mission was an instrument/qual (I/Q) ride. It would essentially duplicate our initial F-16 I/Q Checkride from Stan-Eval, which would occur shortly after we soloed out, and would mark the end of the conversion phase. I was pretty confident going into this sortie; if there was one thing I had learned in my years as a FAIP, it was how to fly instruments. The area work went fine, and we were proceeding to the initial holding fix at 300 knots. Three minutes prior to arrival at the holding fix, I reduced the throttle and started to slow down.

"What are you doing?" asked Hooter from the rear cockpit.

"Slowing to holding speed," I replied. Holding airspeed was 250 knots.

"It's way too early," he barked.

"No, it isn't," I said. "51-37 allows you to start reducing speed three minutes from the holding fix."

"Are you sure?" he sneered. I could tell from his tone of voice that he didn't think I was correct.

"Of course. I taught this stuff for three years, man." That was probably a mistake—I let my ego get the better of me, as I tried to put Hooter in his place.

"Well, push it back up. We don't wanna be out here all day— you can slow down when we get closer." By that time, we were about two minutes from the fix, but I pushed the power back up to 300 knots as directed.

I continued preparing for the TACAN approach and holding, made a few radio calls, and as we hit the holding fix and I initiated the turn, I heard Hooter say, "check airspeed!" Yep—I was still at 300 knots.

Muttering to myself, I jerked the throttle to idle, quickly slowed to the 250-knot maximum holding airspeed, and from there rather clumsily completed the TACAN approach. We made a few more approaches, then proceeded back to Luke for more traffic pattern work.

The rest of the ride went fine with only a few momentary deviations, although my landings still tended to be long and hot.

After the mission and during the debrief, we discussed the ride. Hooter checked Air Force Manual 51-37 to see if I was correct about the "three minutes prior" guidance (I was), then started filling out my gradesheet. When he passed it to me, I was flabbergasted—I got a 1 overall, with a 1 in the Holding and Airspeed Control categories, and a note indicating NE/SNP.

I had failed the ride for lack of proficiency and would have to repeat it. The look in his eyes was one of triumph and delight. "Hey, you would have busted a checkride for holding, so you need to repeat the ride."

I didn't know what to say—I felt it was grossly unfair, and as a former IP myself, wholly inappropriate. However, I didn't want to show any weakness by whining about it. After all, I had, in fact, violated holding airspeed guidance. Despite the circumstances, I was the one flying the jet. The Tweet FAIP had just busted his third training mission.

The next day, my flight commander, a good-natured Major, called me into his office. He didn't mention the bust, but he asked, "How are things going with your IP?"

"This is dangerous territory," I thought to myself. While I desperately wished I had a different IP, to try and blame my evident lack of progress solely on him would be dishonest. "He's a sarcastic S.O.B., but he's okay," is all I could say.

My flight commander looked at me for a moment, then said, "Okay," and that was it. I flew my makeup ride with my flight commander the following day, and things went fine.

I returned to flying with Hooter on the fourth scheduled mission, which would be the ride prior to my initial solo. Neither Hooter nor I mentioned the busted ride or the makeup; the briefing was normal, except when he was going through the motherhood items on transfer of aircraft control.

"I'll let you know when I've got the jet. But after all, I'm a sarcastic S.O.B., aren't I?" He wasn't smiling.

I tried to make light of it. "Well, you are!" I laughed, "and you know it!"

He finally grinned but didn't say anything else. We flew the mission, and I did well enough. No surprises this time.

The fourth sortie was the last ride before our initial solo. It would involve some basic formation flying since the IP would be chasing us in his own F-16. Another student and I flew out to the operating area with our IPs in the rear cockpit, switched leads a few times to allow both of us an opportunity to get some wing time, then split up to fly the rest of the mission separately. Again, I was impressed by how smoothly the F-16 performed in formation flying. Little wonder it was selected as the jet the Thunderbirds flew. I felt I was improving slowly but surely, and with 8.0 hours in the jet, Hooter cleared me for solo on the gradesheet.

With anticipation, I looked forward to properly flying a single-seat F-16 without the GIB (Guy In Back). The mission called for us to do a standard profile in preparation for our I/Q checks. I would takeoff, fly the departure route to my assigned working area, perform a series of acrobatic maneuvers, then proceed to the TACAN holding fix. I would perform one turn in holding, then execute the TACAN approach, followed by vectors for a PAR (Precision Approach Radar) and an ILS (Instrument Landing System approach). We would then proceed back to Luke for overhead traffic pattern work, to include a few SFOs.

Hooter would be in trail with me the entire time, flying close enough to me to assess my performance, without being in actual fingertip formation. I was told to be aware of his location, but to fly my jet first and foremost. At the conclusion of the briefing, Hooter looked me in the eye and said, "You know, you don't look like you enjoy flying. I have never seen you just take the jet and horse it around the sky for the fun of it. This is the best jet on the planet! Are you sure you want to be here?"

Again, this was dangerous territory. I wanted to say, "Well, it's not a lot of fun trying to learn how to fly the best jet on the planet with a raving a##hole as your IP," but I knew better.

Then it dawned on me; I realized he just wanted me to let loose in the operating area so he could have some fun chasing me around the sky before the relatively benign instrument and pattern work.

So, I said, "Okay, since you're giving me the green light, I'll put the jet through its paces before we head to the holding fix."

We signed out at the duty desk, got our tail numbers, and received our final step brief. As usual, it was a clear-in-a-million day in Arizona. Our jets were located right next to each other, so the IP could monitor what was going on with his initial solo student.

I saluted and shook hands with the crew chief, checked the 781 forms, and started the exterior inspection. The ILS antenna on the Block 5 F-16s was located under the nose directly in front of the nose gear. As I bent down to check out the gear, I pranged my cranium on the ILS antenna, creating a nice slice on the top left of my skull. It started bleeding fairly heavily, and I muttered a few expletives as I stood up to continue the walk-around. The crew chief noticed right away. "Holy crap, sir—you better get that taken care of."

However, there was no way I was going to let a little scratch interfere with my initial solo, so I smiled and said, "Ah, I'll be alright," and continued around the jet, making sure Hooter didn't notice. By the time I was strapped in the cockpit, it was still bleeding.

The chief gave me a paper towel to clean up some of the gore, I put my helmet on and just forgot about it. The rest of the mission went as advertised. After we finished our area work, I flew the jet as requested for a few minutes, performing a few high-G turns, loops, barrel rolls, and an Immelman transition into a Split-S. It was wonderful flying solo for the first time, even if I was being chased. No heavy breathing or complaining from the back seat, just me and The Viper. Glorious.

After I landed, taxied back in, and shut down the engine, I saw Hooter waiting for me at the bottom of the ladder. When I took my helmet off, I saw his face turn white with horror. "What the heck happened to you!!??" he yelled.

Blood was everywhere, probably aggravated by the Gs and fluctuating cockpit pressure. I sheepishly explained how I obtained my injury. He said, "Well, that's one beauty of a Viper Bite. You better get yourself to the Flight Surgeon right away."

I turned my gear into Life Support, made a pit stop in the bathroom to wash up a bit, and headed over to the hospital. As I sat in the waiting room waiting to be checked over, Wendy, of all people, walked by and saw me. She was there picking up some prescriptions. It took a lot of explaining to convince her that everything was okay, and no, my IP nor the jet had tried to kill me.

It took even more convincing talking to the flight surgeon, who was not happy. "We have had enough LOC incidents in the

F-16 without some fool trying to fly who just cut his head open!" he said as he sewed me up with a couple of stitches.

I received the same stern warning and admonition from my flight commander when I got back to the squadron. However, within a few days, the episode brought forth a few chuckles. I guess I was lucky RTU squadrons didn't hand out call signs to students—who knows what name I would have ended up with (Skull? IronHead? NoBrains)?

After the initial solo, we had two more rides before the I/Q check—one dedicated instrument ride in the D-Model, and one more solo ride with the IP in chase. They went fine; I still had momentary deviations in my instrument work and persisted with my tendency for long and hot landings, but my performance was essentially correct, and I recognized and corrected errors. As we finished the debriefing on the last sortie before my checkride, Hooter gave me a 2, and with a smirk said, "There you go, good luck."

I said, "Thanks. I'll be alright."

He replied, "No, you won't. I think you're gonna wash out."

I was stunned. If he thought I was going to wash out, why allow me to proceed to my I/Q check? An essential part of an IP's job is to try and inspire, encourage, and motivate a student to be the best he or she can be. Some were better at that than others, but this was something else entirely. It was almost as if he was hoping I would bust the checkride. I could barely believe what I was hearing, and I didn't quite know how to respond. So, I just picked up my checklists and walked out, highly confused, and my confidence again badly shaken.

I had two days to stew and think about what he had said, and to prepare for the check. I guess I could have spoken to my flight commander, but I didn't say anything to anyone, not even Wendy. My fragile ego wouldn't allow me to confess my doubts in myself, or to try and deflect my problems on to Hooter or anyone else. Somehow, I needed to put this crisis of insecurity aside and get on with the program.

On the morning of the checkride, I left our apartment as the sun was coming up and headed for the base. I had chair-flown the mission over and over and was as prepared as I was going to be. Shortly after turning onto Glendale Avenue and heading west towards Luke, I looked into my rearview mirror and saw the flashing lights of a cop car. Sure enough, I was being pulled over. I had no idea why I was being stopped, but this was no way to start the day. The officer approached my window, asked for my license and registration, and informed me that one of my rear lights was burned out. He let me off with a warning, but this was not what I needed to curb my nerves.

As it turned out, the checkride went well. Standard all the way—I flew the mission with the evaluator in chase, just as we had practiced in the rides before. I earned a Q-No Hits, meaning I had passed this first F-16 checkride completely without a need for additional training. I was immensely relieved, and Wendy and I celebrated at the Duck and Decanter Deli and Restaurant that evening.

I never flew with Hooter again. I don't know why—I don't know if he requested it, or if it was a decision made by my flight commander or the squadron commander, knowing that I had struggled somewhat through the conversion phase. We never even spoke to one another, even though we passed each other in the halls of the squadron nearly every day. He never congratulated me on passing my checkride, and I never thanked him for getting me there. But this much was certain; although I had passed the initial I/Q check, I had already earned a reputation for being one of the weaker students, if not the weakest, in the class.

> FLYING TRAINING SUMMARY—CONVERSION:
> Captain White completed the conversion phase in an average manner. After some initial problems with his instrument crosscheck and overhead patterns, he met course standards.

Our entire class passed the I/Q check, and we all started to lighten up a little. Three of the bachelor lieutenants rented a house with a pool in nearby Goodyear; it became party central for our class.

About a third of us were married. We would all meet up at the Officer's Club on Friday after the last flight, and invariably trundle over to the Goodyear Bachelor Pad afterward. Late-night poker games on the weekends, softball games, and pot luck dinners were part of our lives.

The wives all grew close and did a myriad of things together—day trips to Prescott, Sedona, Tucson, or Nogales in Mexico, meeting for lunch and shopping somewhere unique, or just enjoying an afternoon at the pool on base.

In addition to her classes at Glendale Community College, Wendy took a self-defense course, for which I served as her live practice dummy, and stayed busy exploring the Phoenix area for hidden treasures.

The end of the conversion phase also signified the time for us to submit our new Dream Sheets with our requests for which F-16 base we would be assigned following graduation from RTU.

In 1984, the F-16 force was new and still growing, so the choices were few: Hill AFB in Utah, Shaw AFB in South Carolina, and Nellis AFB in Nevada stateside; Hahn Air Base and Torrejon Air Base in Europe; and Kunsan Air Base in South Korea. Naturally, Wendy and I wanted to return to Germany at Hahn, if at all possible, so I loaded up my Dream Sheet with every rationale we could think of.

Both Wendy and I had lived in Germany for many years, graduated from high school there, and had a working knowledge of the language and culture. I had flown with and taught German Air Force pilots at Sheppard AFB as a T-37 IP, and I had a master's degree in Political Science as if that mattered. We put Torrejon and Nellis as our second and third choices, but we had all our hopes on Hahn. It would be several weeks before the announcement of our assignments, and we were on pins and needles with anticipation.

Everyone in our class couldn't wait to get started in the air-to-air phase of our training. The F-16 had already earned a reputation for being the most deadly fighter in the sky in a visual BFM contest. If you were in a close-in, eyeball-to-eyeball knife fight in a phone booth, you wanted to be in The Viper. Its 9-G capability and incredible thrust-to-weight ratio made it the best in the world in 1984. We would finally be taking real concrete steps in our transformation to U.S. Air Force F-16 fighter pilots.

Aerial combat is by far the most difficult aspect of flight for the fighter pilot to understand and master. It is an arena where equations and theories are dynamic and where experience and understanding of basic fighter maneuvers are the keys to success. The skills used in aerial combat are learned over time, and the interest, desire, and personal discipline of a pilot are important factors in speeding up this learning process. AF MCM 3-3 Vol V, "Fighter Fundamentals-F-16"

The air-to-air phase was structured with one Aircraft Handling Characteristics (AHC) flight, five offensive BFM flights, four defensive BFM flights, three neutral BFM flights, three Air Combat Maneuvers (ACM) flights, and five intercept flights. We would also have the opportunity to live-fire shoot the DART aerial gunnery target. Finally, we would be introduced to air-to-air refueling (AAR). It looked to be a fun, yet demanding syllabus.

The AHC sortie was designed primarily to get us familiar with flying in a high-G environment and develop a feel for maneuvering the F-16 in a low speed/high AOA regime with the effects of the FLCS limiter.

The incredible maneuverability of the F-16 at its corner velocity range of 330 to 440 knots could help a pilot recover from many mistakes. All things being equal, you could pull about 7 Gs at 330 knots, and get your full 9-G pull at 440 knots. However, once you got increasingly slower, you could be a sitting duck—speed is life!—if you weren't careful, as the FLCS limiter dominated your inputs.

As a force, we were still learning about the impacts of the F-16's 9-G capability, and as mentioned earlier, the Air Force had lost several pilots who blacked out under the stress of an F-16 high-G break turn and never woke up. There were no Combat Edge systems, which later provided F-16 pilots with a G-vest to go with the G-suit, inflated bladders in the helmet, and forced oxygen into the mask to prevent G-induced Loss-Of-Consciousness (G-LOC).

In those days, the squadron didn't have weight rooms, nor did fighter pilots have physical training requirements to help strengthen their bodies. Requirements to execute a G-warm up maneuver at the beginning of an air-to-air engagement also didn't exist. We continued to learn some hard lessons over the years, and nearly every 80's-era F-16 jock I know has lost several comrades due to G-LOC. Both my AHC ride and first offensive BFM sortie really developed my appreciation and respect for the F-16. It was a beast.

The G-LOC threat made TAC wary of those first introductory BFM training sorties, so the first two were scheduled in the D-model with the IP in the rear cockpit. Thankfully, we had only a few rides scheduled in the two-seat family model.

On my second offensive BFM sortie, I was in position on my offensive perch when the "fight's on!" call was made. I dumped the nose and had selected full afterburner. We heard a loud BANG, and it felt like the jet had been swatted by the hand of God. My feet were literally knocked off the rudder pedals, and both IPs, the one out front as my practice adversary and the one in the rear cockpit, shouted "Knock It Off!!" on the radios.

My IP in the backseat thought we had been hit by something, but the IP in the other jet told us he had seen fireballs shooting out both the front of the intake and the tailpipe. We quickly deduced we had had an AB Blowout when I selected the afterburner.

We had been continuously warned about the susceptibility of the F-16 Pratt & Whitney engines to afterburner blowouts. Instructions taught us to select AB steadily and smoothly to allow the different stages to light off sequentially. If you ham-handed the throttle—which I obviously had done—you could expect the afterburner to cough. As a force, as we continued to learn more about the F-16, these AB blowouts became almost commonplace, no big deal. You still had to terminate the sortie and return to the base after declaring a Precautionary, but you didn't even have to return via the SFO pattern as a safety contingency unless you really felt you needed to.

However, perhaps since this was the first blowout my IP had experienced, we declared a full-up Emergency, and the IP directed me to activate the Emergency Power Unit (EPU) as a backup should the engine fail. We selected 100% oxygen in accordance with the inflight checklist, and I turned the EPU on. The EPU is used during an emergency to augment the engine, electric, and hydraulic systems during a multiple generator failure, dual hydraulic failure, or engine flameout. It uses a combination of engine bleed air and hydrazine, a toxic, hot ammonia-based chemical, to operate. Landing the jet with the EPU running requires a response from the Hydrazine Response Team, decked out in protective gear, in addition to Fire Department personnel. After landing, you had to taxi to a pre-designated isolated area until the Hydrazine Response Team could deal with the activated EPU. Cranking up the EPU was generally something you wanted to avoid, if at all possible.

After landing and taxiing to the hydrazine area, we were finally cleared by the Fire Chief to shut down and exit the aircraft. We were surrounded by fire trucks, crew vans—and the white-roofed sedan of the Wing Commander. As soon as we climbed down the ladder, the Wing Commander got out of his car and walked up to my IP. "What happened?" he asked.

"Sir, it looks like we had an AB Blowout," replied my IP.

"Why did you activate the EPU?" the Wing Commander angrily countered.

"Just as a precautionary, sir," my IP sheepishly said.

With that, the Wing Commander wheeled around, stomped off, got back in his car, and left.

I felt bad for my IP. While it may have been unnecessary to activate the EPU and generate all that emergency response, it was still his call to make. He was almost as new to the F-16 as I was. Still, it was a good lesson learned for me. As opposed to ATC, there seemed to be a million more ways to get yourself in trouble in TAC.

I progressed through the remaining offensive BFM rides without incident, and I made steady progress. On my fifth and final offensive BFM ride, I was all over the IP and achieved several gun kills. Walking back to the squadron after engine shutdown, I was grinning like a Cheshire cat.

"Don't get cocky!" he laughed.

I was really starting to enjoy the program and take joy in flying The Viper.

My first defensive BFM ride watered my eyes, however. The task is simple on paper. Your adversary is trying to solve problems in range, aspect, and overtake, so you are merely trying to create problems for him in those areas, right?

Once airborne, we set up for my first engagement. The IP was on the perch to my left, about 40 degrees offset and about a mile-and-a-half out. We were both at around 440 knots. "One's Ready. Two's Ready. Check Camera's On—Fight's On!"

I steadily pushed the throttle forward to AB, leaned forward a little to keep him in sight as he jinked right towards my lag corner, and I snapped the jet into a left break as hard as I could. I wasn't ready for it—my head immediately slammed between my knees from the acceleration of the G-forces, and I was eyeball-to-eyeball with the radar console. I didn't want to let up too much on the Gs, but I had to release a little back pressure to get my head back up where I could see the IP.

There he was! I snapped the jet back into another hard break, and my head plummeted down once again into the radar. With my left hand grasping the left handrail of the canopy, I struggled myself back up one more time, having no clue where the IP was when I heard, "That's a guns kill," over my headset. Lose sight, lose the fight.

We had a few more engagements, but I was already physically drained from that first fight and didn't have much G-tolerance left in me.

After landing and during the debrief, the playback of my videotape was revealing. I am breathing heavily, and as I strain to get on top of the Gs during that first break, my heavy breathing turns to panting as I struggle to get my head back up from between my knees. When I initiate the second break, my panting turns into whimpering and groaning, and you can tell I have absolutely no idea where the IP is.

My remaining defensive BFM rides went much better as I learned to brace myself more efficiently for the high G-forces, position my head and neck, and keep the IP in sight. Neck and back problems are occupational hazards for F-16 pilots, mostly earned from defensive BFM engagements flying against another equally maneuverable F-16. Learning how to move your body and physically perform a good anti-G straining maneuver—sort of like having a challenging bowel movement—were acts of survival.

Our aerial gunnery DART ride was scheduled as we were completing the BFM phase. This flight was a big deal; you had to get a DART hit to complete the program, and you only got two chances. It would also be our first experience in live-firing the gun, so we were nervous and pumped-up over the opportunity.

The flight consisted of a 4-ship, with three of us in D-models with our IPs in the rear cockpit. The flight lead was an IP in a single-seat C-model. He would orchestrate the sequence and score the hits we were all hoping to get. Our task was to fly out to one of the areas over Goldwater Range, clear the area below to ensure there weren't any unauthorized folks that might get hit by debris, perform our weapons systems checks, and meet up with a Korean War-era F-86 towing the DART, flown by a private contractor.

The DART itself was, of course, shaped like a dart. It was about 20 feet long and made of shiny, reflective aluminum and wood. The aluminum surface allowed you to lock on and track the DART with your radar. The F-86 met us in the area, and after we all had him in sight and were ready to begin the sequence, released the DART, which was mounted on his right wing. The DART was attached by a steel cable about 1,500 feet long, and the four of us circled over the top of him, safely out of the way in case the DART snapped off on its own or started behaving erratically. The tow pilot could cut the cable at any time in the flight, and after we all completed our guns passes, he would release the DART, which would safely fall to earth and eventually be retrieved by range personnel.

During the flight brief, we were cautioned about locking onto the DART and allowing the radar to automatically transfer to the bigger F-86 with the larger radar cross-section. The F-86 pilot was naturally concerned with the prospect of inexperienced F-16 pilots pointing a live gun at him, so offset angle and nose position was critical as you set up your passes.

At the "fight's on" call, the F-86 would enter a right descending, 450 knot, 3-4G spiral. You wanted to enter from high-to-low with about 30-40 degrees angle off, work your angle down to about 10-20 degrees, close in to about 1,000 feet, pull a little lead, fly the DART to the Lead Computing Optical Sight (LCOS) pipper, and let 'er rip.

You didn't want to have less than 10 degrees offset, in case you shot the DART off the cable and it came flying back into your face. Plus, chances were that if you had that little offset, the F-86 was probably in your HUD field-of-view as well, and that was an absolute no-no.

After each burst, you would pull off, reposition, and work yourself back in for another pass. If you were lucky, you might get two or three firing passes at the DART before you ran out of ammo, but you wanted to take good, long bursts to ensure you had a fair chance of hitting the thing.

After each one of us had completed our passes, the flight lead would fly up next to the DART and visually count the holes in it to confirm a good hit. Sometimes, the F-86 tow pilot could call out a hit if he felt the DART shake from the impact of the rounds striking the DART, or you could see sparkles coming from the aluminum as the bullets passed through.

All in all, it was a pretty primitive way of conducting aerial gunnery training, especially when compared to the Aerial Gunnery Targeting Systems (AGTS) we had later, but it nevertheless had been proven effective for decades.

I was the second shooter in sequence and was able to complete three pretty good passes. I was relieved to hear the flight lead confirm hits over the radio, especially after the third shooter ended up shooting the DART off the cable.

Flying intercepts was a different kind of challenge. Performing the first several intercept missions in the simulator, it seemed to me to be a much more procedural, step-by-step process, almost like flying an instrument approach. It was like working a geometry problem on the radar screen.

However, even in the Block 5 A-Model F-16s, the radar display provided enough clues for you to perform a classic baseline, or single-side offset intercept, assuming you were engaging a target head-on/high aspect and wanted to acquire some turning room to complete a conversion turn to the target's beam or stern six. The sequence essentially went like this:

1. Lock the target with your radar, hopefully outside 20 miles
2. Put the target on the Collision Antenna Train Angle (CATA) cross on the radar screen, which provided the geometry to the quickest intercept/collision/visual with the target
3. Get some offset at 20 miles—to allow you some turning room for a conversion turn to the target's beam or stern
4. Get a speed advantage—the radar provided the target's estimated speed
5. Monitor aspect—to ensure the target wasn't trying to evade you
6. Go Single Target Track (STT) at 10 miles, to help ensure the chances of retaining a radar lock through the conversion turn maneuvers
7. Go pure pursuit—put the Threat Detector (TD) box in the HUD at 120 degrees aspect, which normally happens at 6–8 miles on a high aspect target—essentially, point your nose at the target
8. Visually acquire the target and work your way into missile range
9. Kill him

Later, I would execute intercepts virtually without a thought, but in those early training days, it was an intricate procedure to be memorized.

The learning process is similar to learning how to parallel park a car when you first learn to drive. The How to Parallel Park guide in a local DMV pamphlet describes a 415-word, 8-step sequence, but after you become an experienced driver, you parallel park naturally and without much mental effort.

Former USAF Chief of Staff Merrill McPeak explains this transition from initially learning to executing with experience in his book, *Hangar Flying*, "Craftsmanship in flying develops along two pathways. In the beginning, we fly the same way we first managed to ride a bike or drive a car, using the conscious part of the brain to process commands serially. Over time, we store results that ripen into habit patterns, memories and skills kept in the subconscious, a parallel processor solving simultaneous problems at much greater speed. When the pathways finally merge, we fly the airplane without thinking about it, our conscious mind now a sentinel—alert, keeping watch."

While I sometimes tended to get mesmerized with the radar while working through the sequence, occasionally to the detriment of aircraft control, I did alright with baseline intercepts. However, my biggest problem came when performing vertical intercepts, which involved trying to get vertical turning room on a target that was coming straight-down-the-snot-locker and pointed at you purely nose-to-nose.

The procedure called for your trying to get vertical turning room—8,000 feet or more desired—and performing a Split S high-to-low or Immelmann low-to-high conversion to the target's rear at 3nm. The problem with the high-to-low conversion was the target tended to disappear underneath the nose at about six miles, so you needed to have acquired him visually by then, as the radar tended to break lock as it flew beneath your radar scan. If your radar broke lock and you didn't have him visually, you frantically rocked the jet on its side, trying to see directly below you to try and find the target with your eyeballs.

On my fourth mission in the intercept phase, I failed on two attempts at a pure high-aspect vertical intercept and busted the ride. It was my second bust. However, while I was frustrated with myself, I had enough confidence to feel like I could figure it out, and wasn't yet in panic mode.

My flight commander gave me an X ride the next day to provide me an opportunity to practice my vertical intercepts before re-attempting the sortie again. I was in a D-Model with the Assistant Flight Commander, who happened to be a Danish exchange pilot, in the rear cockpit.

On the first engagement, it all happened again—pure vertical, target beneath the nose, radar breaking lock, me not being able to acquire the target visually. As we set up for another attempt, my IP said, "You need to offset him a few degrees left or right, so he doesn't fly directly under your nose.

That way, you can keep sight of him all the way until you are ready to pull to his six."

Wow—I didn't know you could do that. I thought you had to keep him pure high aspect all the way.

"No!" my IP laughed. "We just want you to demonstrate the ability to complete a simple vertical intercept!"

Well, heck—that's easy! Accordingly, my next several intercepts were successful, and I went on to fly my final intercept rides without any problems. I wish that someone had told me this before, but I felt like a real dunderhead for not getting it on my own. I realized that my entire thought process was in error. I was trying to complete a step-by-step mathematical procedure rather than analyzing a tactical problem and flying the jet to a successful resolution. I made it harder than it needed to be.

We flew our first aerial refueling (AAR) missions during the intercept phase, and it wasn't nearly as difficult as I anticipated. We were basically flying formation with a big, lumbering KC-135; the trick was relaxing while you were on the boom, and not having a death grip on the stick, possibly over-controlling as a result. The pre-flight agreement was that it would cost a case of beer for anyone who fell off the boom, but we didn't have any buyers that day.

There really wasn't much to these introductory AAR rides in RTU. I later learned the nuances, hazards, and style points of the fighter turn-on intercept to the tanker, how dependent you were on a talented and proficient boom operator, and how much a skilled tanker aircraft commander with situation awareness could make or break a successful refueling.

Much later, someone asked me if I was ever nervous flying combat missions over Iraq. I said, "No. Trying to find a tanker—in the weather, at night, when everyone is low on gas, and you are running out of divert options—that's what made me nervous." God bless our tanker crews.

Our final missions in the air-to-air phase were Air Combat Maneuvers or ACM missions. Here was our chance to put it all together. A pilot and a flight lead would go 2 versus 1 against an adversary. As a wingman, we supported the flight lead as he engaged the bandit, looking for opportunities to enter the fight and achieve a quick kill with style. It was all about teamwork and effective communication.

There were only three ACM sorties, one offensive, one defensive, and one flying intercepts to an engagement. We were fortunate at Luke to be stationed at the same base with an F-15 wing, so our final ACM mission, and the final sortie in the air-to-air phase, would be dissimilar, flown against an F-15 IP from across the ramp.

As noted before, the F-16 was still relatively new to the Air Force in 1984, but the mostly-but-not-always friendly rivalry with our F-15 comrades was already alive and well. The F-15 was the premier air superiority fighter aircraft in the world, but we considered our little multi-role Viper Jet to be a pretty good dogfightin' machine.

At the Officer's Club on Friday nights, we pretty much kept to ourselves; the F-15 guys stayed on their side of the bar, and we tended to stay on ours. The final sortie, would be our first opportunity to experience and compare our F-16 with another fighter, and we all looked forward to our ACM-3 rides with relish.

Now, to be fair, the F-15 was a training platform on the mission, and there was only one of him and two of us. But I was shocked how easy it was to outmaneuver and quickly kill the F-15 in a visual heaters-and-guns fight.

We had been taught in our academic classes that to attack an adversary without becoming the prey yourself effectively, you must get inside his turn circle, and get there with an energy advantage as soon as possible. Kill and survive. Up until now, we had been fighting another F-16 with the same maneuvering capability, and getting and staying inside the turn circle could be a challenge. However, getting inside the F-15's turn circle was a piece of cake.

It didn't matter from what aspect—offensive, defensive, or neutral—we clearly had a significant advantage. It was a total revelation, and more than ever made me glad that I had elected to list the F-16 over the F-15 on my Dream Sheet. As my IP later chortled during the debrief, "It was like whupping baby seals!"

Inside the turn circle was where you wanted to be.

FLYING TRAINING SUMMARY—AIR-TO-AIR:
Overall, progression during this phase was average. Captain White had the normal problems with controlling angles and overtake offensively but made good progress. Defensively, he initially was unable to reacquire a lost tally-ho but improved steadily throughout the phase.

Completion of the air-to-air phase also coincided with our finally getting our operational assignments.

The announcement came out of the blue. At the start of academics one morning, we were told we would meet in the mass briefing room at end of the day after flying to be issued our assignments. I didn't have a flight that day, so I spent the afternoon preparing for the next day's mission and trying not to be too nervous.

I called Wendy at home and told her to get prepared. We both still badly wanted Hahn and a return to Germany, but we were prepared for any alternative.

There was no ceremony, no elaborate announcement, and since it was Wednesday, no big celebration planned. The squadron commander arrived, and with that ever-present half-smile on his face, he simply read out the assignments. There was no cheering or hollering as he called out the names and bases, just some muttered acknowledgments and high-fives.

He went through the class roster alphabetically, so I was last on the list. One other guy had gotten a Hahn assignment; I was praying there would be at least one more. When he finally said, "P.K. White, Hahn!" I felt like yelling, "YEAH, BABY!!" Instead, I just grinned and nodded as I got a few pats on the back. Everyone in the class seemed happy with the base they had received, so it was smiles all around.

On the way home, I bought a bouquet from the darkly suntanned lady who sold flowers at a stoplight on Glendale Avenue. I passed her nearly every day and rarely stopped. That day, however, I left her a big tip and said with a laugh that it was going to be an evening to celebrate with my wife. I flew in the front door, grabbed Wendy, and said, "It's Hahn!"

We both whooped, laughed, and rejoiced in our good fortune. We were so happy together, I was surviving RTU, and we were going back home to Germany. We called our parents with the good news and started making plans.

Wendy immediately joined a German–American Club in an effort to improve and refresh her German language capabilities as we sought to reacquaint ourselves with the German culture. We started to seriously plan for the move: do we sell the cars? Should we live on or off base? What should we do with the cat? We were both excited and full of optimism. Life was glorious.

I really looked forward to the air-to-ground phase. I felt that this was finally going to be my time to shine. This final phase involved low-level formation flying, nuclear and conventional attacks on a controlled range, and surface attack missions on a tactical range. I had done well with the air-to-ground sorties at LIFT and felt confident that I would finish the program with high marks.

Academically, we were beginning to study air and ground threats, classified intelligence on potential adversaries throughout the world, and political-related topics that I had studied previously and felt were my strengths. Throughout the program so far, I had never received a grade above a 2 in the simulator or in the air, and it was time to elevate my game.

> *The surface attack mission is the bread-and-butter mission of the F-16. Hauling iron is a challenging mission that requires complete knowledge of your aircraft systems, handling characteristics, and ordnance. Given current threats (surface-to-air, air-to-air, and the ground), the surface attack role is highly demanding.* AF MCM 3-3 Vol V, "Fighter Fundamentals-F-16"

Flying The Viper at low level, with all the information provided in the HUD through the onboard computers, sensors, and INS made timing tasks much simpler. It was so much easier than hacking the clock and flying off the map, as I had done in the T-37. You still did those things as a backup and for situation awareness, but the onboard systems allowed you to more efficiently fly the jet and clear for potential threats for you and your wingman.

We started on the controlled ranges with canned conventional attacks from the curve pattern, 10/20/30/45 degree attacks using the death dot Continuously Computed Impact Point (CCIP) pipper, and low-level strafe. Everything seemed much easier than my brief experience on the ranges flying the AT-38 at Holloman; my pattern work was okay, and my scores were generally counters.

When we began Dive Toss (DTOS) attacks, allowing a standoff capability for weapons delivery, I had a few more challenges. I tended to get into a slew PIO (Pilot-Induced Oscillation) trying to stabilize and finesse the TD box in the HUD, and threw a fair share of bombs out before I started to get the hang of it.

Strafing was exhilarating and fun. But I tended to have a death grip on the stick going that fast, 450 knots, while hurling myself towards the strafe panels, and it took me a while to be able to settle down and stabilize the strafe pipper comfortably.

Performing pop-up attacks, flying low and then aggressively pulling up to curve attack parameters, was another exciting new experience but wasn't particularly difficult.

In the debriefs, we were exposed to the standard bet for the first time. Each bomb pass was scored with a quarter going to the winner. Strafe quarters were scored from total hits on the strafe rag. Since we normally flew on the controlled range in 4-ships, you could walk away from a day at the range with a pocketful of change if it was your day. I tended to break even, so while I wasn't excelling in quite the way I thought I would, I was holding my own, and maintaining my standard 2 grades. Everyone in the class was doing well, growing in confidence and cockiness as the graduation date grew nearer.

Then, near-disaster struck. I was on my seventh controlled range sortie, single-ship in a D-model with an IP in the back. For some reason, I simply was not having a good day. My patterns were a little sloppy, my pipper placement erratic, and my bomb scores mediocre. My IP that day was an attached pilot from the academics squadron. We had flown together several times before, and I could tell by his silence that he was somewhat frustrated with my evident lack of progress, as was I.

On my first strafe pass of the day, I saw the foul line rapidly approaching and fired a short burst—and kept going. It was a split-second case of target fixation. Instantly realizing the danger, both my IP and I simultaneously snatched the stick back to recover and climb out, but as we pulled, I actually saw the bullets strike the dirt near the strafe rag. I had almost killed us both.

My IP cursed loudly, then transmitted on the range frequency, "Ranger, was that a dangerous pass?"

To which we heard the reply, "Almost!"

I recognized the voice of my flight commander in the range tower. As we pulled up to downwind, we looked down; the strafe pits were totally obscured by dust from the effects of our tailpipe exhaust as we initiated the climb. I had come that close to augering in and pancaking us onto the desert floor.

"Safe 'em up—you're done!" my IP growled from the rear.

Silence was our companion on the way back to Luke. Both of us were badly shaken. I had no idea why it happened, or what could have caused me to freeze up that way. I flew one overhead full-stop and taxied back in, still numb and somewhat in shock. Even the debrief was quiet and subdued. When we got my bomb scores faxed in from the range, we were both surprised that I wasn't even issued a foul on the pass, but we both knew how close we had come to dying.

We were the last flight of the day, and the only ones left in the squadron by the time we finished the debrief. The IP took my gradebook, turned out the lights, and I watched him slowly walk out of the building with his head down, hearing his footsteps echo down the hallway as he left. I just sat there in the dark for a while before gathering myself and heading out the door.

When I got home, all I could do was tell Wendy that I had busted another ride. I couldn't tell her the details; I didn't want to scare her.

When I arrived in the squadron the next day, I immediately checked in with my flight commander. He shut the door to his office and showed me my gradesheet. I was issued a o for the ride for a lack of ability, and the sheet was bordered in red, due to my *Dangerous* strafe pass. I had no answers for my flight commander, and no excuses to offer. It was decided that I would fly an X ride with the squadron commander, and while it wasn't verbally stated, I knew it was to determine my suitability to continue the program. He gave me two days to prepare and think about it.

By the time the day of the mission arrived, word had spread through the squadron, both to the IPs and to my classmates. I freely offered up the story to anyone who wanted to hear it; I had no reason to try and hide it, with X ride posted on the flying schedule anyway.

The mission followed the same sequence as the one I busted. As usual, the squadron commander was cool as a cucumber. As a Misty FAC, he had faced hazards a million times greater than a Tweet FAIP in danger of washing out of the program. We briefed the mission together, that same half-smile never leaving his face. He never specifically mentioned the busted ride or the dangerous strafe pass; he simply briefed the mission as if it were business as usual.

Amazingly, the mission went great. The squadron commander hardly uttered a word from the rear cockpit, and for some reason, I flew better than I had flown in a while. All my scores were counters, and even my strafe passes and scores were respectable.

The debrief was quick and without drama; he didn't give any special words of encouragement or admonishment, no advice or particular criticism. I received a 2 overall, and my flight commander told me to prepare to resume the program. However, I knew things had changed. With three busted rides, of which one was considered dangerous, I was suddenly on the razor's edge for completing F-16 RTU.

After we finished our ten conventional range sorties, which included one night range mission, we were scheduled for six nuclear range sorties. It would be important for me to become proficient in nukes since that was one of Hahn's primary Designated Operational Commitments (DOCs). The nuke mission required far more switchology and green stuff avionics and took additional study and mission preparation.

We practiced radar and visual laydowns and lofts, using the Continuously Computed Release Point (CCRP) and Low Angle Drogue Delivery (LADD) functions. We practiced INS system updates and exercised the Permissive Action Link (PAL) enable procedure to complete the complex process of actually arming a nuclear weapon should the situation be required.

I tended to get behind the aircraft occasionally with these additional switch inputs, but nevertheless, was doing okay until my fourth nuke ride.

I was in a D-model again, with another IP I had flown with several times before. He was the only IP in the squadron who had flown the A-10, and he was typical of the type—a huge guy with a big voice and a big personality.

About halfway through the mission, as we were coming in for a radar loft delivery on one of the nuke targets, I noticed the TD box in the HUD, indicating where the INS thought the target was, above the horizon and suspended in the sky. Confused, I tried to slew the TD box back towards the target, but it wouldn't move.

"What the f@*k is going on up there?!!" my IP shouted.

I didn't know. I couldn't figure it out. So I went through dry. On downwind, we tried to figure out what was wrong, with the IP screaming expletives and quizzing me on my systems knowledge. Between that, trying to solve the puzzle, flying the jet, and making the radio calls, I went through dry a second time.

I thought the IP was going to climb through the rear cockpit and strangle me. "G*&^#$n it, P.K., you better figure this out, or I'm going to bust your ass!!" he yelled.

I finally compared my lineup card data with the inputs on the Fire Control Navigation Panel (FCNP) and saw that I had typed in the wrong system altitude for that particular target. We were then able to complete the attack and the mission, but my IP was absolutely livid. He screamed abuse all the way back to Luke, and after we had shut down, he stomped his way back into the squadron without saying a word. I was angry, scared, humiliated, and I had had enough.

He was waiting for me in the flight commander's office. He started in right away. "What the f*&k is wrong with you?!!" He continued as my flight commander simply sat and listened.

Finally, I held up my hand. "Stop. Just. Stop." I paused for a moment, then said, "I don't know if I can do this."

And I truly didn't know. I thought back to Hooter, who had told me he didn't think Tweet FAIPs belonged in the program, and he didn't think I would finish RTU. He could be a jerk, for sure, but maybe he was right after all, and I certainly couldn't blame my current problems on him. I was stumbling through the air-to-ground phase, and it looked like I was about to bust my fourth ride—my second bust in twelve days.

There was a moment of silence, then both of them erupted simultaneously, "Oh, no, you've come too far to quit now!"

I don't remember much more of the conversation, but it was decided that I would pass the ride and that the IP was going to take me under his wing and help get me through the program. Strangely enough, I never flew with that IP again, a decision made, I assume, by my flight commander.

However, I left the squadron that day utterly unsure of my future in the F-16. When I got home to Wendy, I fell into her arms, and we held each other for a long time. I told her about the ride, about the discussion in the flight commander's office, and sincerely asked her what she thought about me flying C-130s if it came to that. I was at the lowest point in my Air Force career up to that point, and it was nobody's fault but mine. I just wasn't hacking it.

The very next day, the Assistant Flight Commander and Danish exchange pilot I had flown the intercept X ride with said, "Hey, P.K., let's go to the O'Club and have a beer."

I replied, "Okay." I was sure he wanted to talk to me about my flying issues, but I liked him, and I certainly didn't have anything to lose.

After we had gotten our beers, he came right to the point. "So, what do you think is the cause of your problems? You come to the flights more prepared than anyone it seems. Your mission planning is great, your maps and lineup cards are excellent, you always have a positive attitude, but you always manage to do something stupid."

I had to chuckle at that; of course, he was right, but I certainly didn't have any answers. We continued to chat, and he essentially told me to relax and to think about the big picture of each mission instead of getting wrapped around the axle on the small details. He then told me that the IPs were all pulling for me. I wasn't sure about that, but I really appreciated his reaching out to me and taking the time to try and talk me through my current crisis.

At that point, I had 14 rides left in the program, eight of which would be Surface Attack Tactics (SAT) rides on one of the tactical ranges, whereby various tactical targets—airfields, aircraft parked in the open, vehicles, anti-aircraft sites, surface-to-air missile mockups, etc.—were set up in different locations. Somehow, I bounced back and didn't have any genuine difficulties with any of the remaining sorties.

I enjoyed flying over the tactics ranges, simulating engaging real enemy threats and targets. On my third SAT mission, my IP was one of the older IPs, a grizzled major who had seen it all, and who I liked and respected. After the mission debrief, he gave me my gradesheet. I was given a 3 grade for the first time.

"Wow," I stammered. "That's the first 3 I've gotten."

Without looking up, he said, "Well, you should have gotten a lot more by now if you ask me," and left the room.

I didn't quite know what to say, how to take that comment, or what he meant by it. There were only seven rides left in the program, including the Sea Cactus final mass force exercise. I started to think I was actually going to graduate.

And suddenly—lo, and behold—I started to get 3 grades on all my rides. Maybe it was because the ice had finally broken with that first 3 grade, maybe because the program was almost over and the IPs were in a good mood, or maybe they just felt sorry for me. I didn't know, and I didn't care.

My entire class did well on the Sea Cactus exercise, and I flew my final mission in RTU with the newly-appointed 311th Squadron Commander, who had just taken over from the former Misty FAC. I received a 3 and a congratulations handshake. I had made it through F-16 RTU by the skin of my teeth.

FLYING TRAINING SUMMARY—AIR-TO-SURFACE:
Captain White completed the air-to-surface phase below average. While he quickly qualified in bombing events, he had some tracking problems during low angle strafe. Initially, he paid too much attention to the avionics at the expense of basic aircraft control. This caused problems in both the Surface Attack and Nuclear modules. These problems were overcome, and by the end of the Tactics module, he was performing well.

END OF COURSE SUMMARY:
Captain White completed the F-16 training course in a slightly below average manner. He put forth an outstanding amount of effort during the course and continually tried to improve. Captain White has a tendency to become overly concerned with avionics operations if they are not as preplanned. With good continuity and more experience, he should progress well.

The official graduation was still a week away, so that last week life at Luke was leisurely and enjoyable. We had time to sell the Celica, pack our household goods, check out of our apartment, and move into the TLQ on base for a few days. My report date to Hahn wasn't until the end of August.

I had plenty of leave saved up, so we flew my Mom out to Phoenix for the graduation ceremony. Our plan was to slowly make our way to Charleston AFB, our port of call to Germany, in Wendy's Le Sabre with my mom and Etcetera, our cat, with stops in Denver to visit some of my family members, Dallas and San Antonio to visit Wendy's family, and Titus, Alabama, where we would drop Mom and Etcetera off.

We would fly to Charleston from Montgomery, and leave Etcetera with my Mom and Dad until we found a home in Hahn; they could then ship Etcetera to us. We would also leave the Le Sabre with Mom and Dad as they graciously agreed to sell it for us.

Graduation was a formal affair, held in one of the fancy hotels in Scottsdale. We graduates wore our summer white mess dress uniforms, and the ladies were decked out in their finest.

Just before the program was about to begin, one of the IPs called all of our class together and gave us a cranium's up. At some point, he was going to call all of us up to eat a raw egg, shell and all, as part of our initiation into the U.S. fighter pilot force. You may remember from my initial solo episode as an IP at Sheppard that I am allergic to eggs, but there was no way I was going to not down that egg with the rest of my comrades.

Unfortunately, Wendy overheard the conversation; she told the IP in no uncertain terms that I would end up in the hospital if I ate a raw egg, and that it just wasn't going to happen. So, shortly after the program began, we were all called up together as a class, and each of us was given a raw egg except me. I stood there rather awkwardly as the rest of my classmates popped the eggs into their mouths to much laughter and applause.

Later, as each flight commander came forward to say a few words about our class, my flight commander had this to say about me, "I tell you what. P.K. White is a fighter pilot and deserves to be here just as much as anyone!"

My classmates hooted, hollered, and applauded loudly—the reaction from some of the IPs was a little less enthusiastic. I was horrified. I know my flight commander was just trying to be gracious, but it highlighted the fact that I had barely made it through the program. From my viewpoint, the night was an absolute disaster, somewhat befitting my F-16 RTU experience.

I had started the program on 16 February and finished on 31 July with nearly 80 F-16 hours. In a class of 14, I had finished dead last; since leaving Sheppard and Holloman, I had gone from first to worst. Wendy and I were finally on our way to Germany, a dream we both shared from the first night we met.

However, I was heading out with some doubts in my own mind as to how good a fighter pilot I could be. And a fighter pilot without confidence... ain't no fighter pilot.

CHAPTER FIVE

FIGHTER PILOT

Hahn Air Base, West Germany

1984–1988

You can't come here, groundling. I dwell in space so foreign that even though you stare at it, you will never taste it. While you are simpering over your greasy eggs, I am climbing out at a hundred percent, in burner, nose boring through the cold, blue-black air while you shave. I make the sun rise and set again with a touch of my gloved fist on the stick. I can't see you down there, locked inexorably in the twisting mosaic beneath my wing. You can't see me up here; you don't tread among the gods. This is a closed shop. Only those that hack it are allowed. And even those who dare had better press it; for my purpose transcends aesthetics—I am here to flame something. When I am on the ground - reluctantly - I seek the company of others who live beyond the edge. If I seem haughty, call it honest arrogance.

—Marshall Lefavor

INITIAL CHECK OUT

On final approach into Rhein-Main Air Base in Frankfurt, Wendy and I stared out the window of our DC-10 cabin in awe. We had finally broken through the clouds on short final, and Germany opened up before our eyes. With huge grins on both our faces, I grabbed Wendy's hand and gave her a quick kiss.

After a ten year absence, we had finally returned home, together.

The nearly 9-hour flight from Charleston had been largely uneventful. The MAC-chartered transport jet, crammed with active duty military and dependents bound for Europe, was a strictly no-frills affair—no movie, no inflight radio, and nothing much else to offer except a couple of meals and lots of conversation with seatmates. However, nearly the entire passenger manifest was excited about the grand European adventures to come with new assignments, new bases, new friends, and new challenges.

A few weeks earlier, I had received a Welcome to Hahn packet in the mail from our squadron sponsor. Everyone was assigned a sponsor to aid in the transition to a new assignment. In it, we received letters from the Wing Commander and my new Squadron Commander, in addition to several information packets about Germany, Hahn Air Base, and the local community. We also received a personal letter from my new Flight Commander, who informed us that a major Operational Readiness Inspection, or TACEVAL would be in progress when we arrived and that his wife would be picking us up at the airport. We offloaded, processed through customs, collected our luggage, and found our Flight Commander's wife in the welcome crowd holding a "Capt White" sign.

The first thing I noticed was the smell of being back in Europe; it just smelled differently, and it wasn't the JP-4 from the flightline. It was diesel fuel, and again, smelled like the Germany I remembered. We had left Charleston in 94-degree heat and 94% humidity, to arrive to cool, green mid-70s temps; it was fantastic.

Driving to Hahn on the autobahn, we were amazed at how fast everyone drove, and couldn't help but ooohh and ahhhh over nearly everything we saw. The smiles and grins never left our faces; the Flight Commander's wife probably thought we were a couple of mindless idiots.

We checked into billeting on base, and as per the standard, were told we could stay for 30 days while we searched for permanent quarters off base.

Our little room shared a bathroom with the neighbors next door, and kitchen facilities were down the hall and shared by everyone on the floor, as were the washer and dryer. One of the first things we did was turn on the TV and watch a tired re-run on the good ol' Armed Forces Network; we truly felt like we had returned to our days of adolescence.

However, we quickly learned that our neighbors were not used to having a couple share their facilities. We heard the husband enter the bathroom without locking the door on our side, joking with his wife, as we listened in shock as he loudly passed gas in rhythm, singing a rousing version of Tchaikovsky's "1812 Overture"—dahdahdahdahdahdah-dat-dat-dah...PHRHARRTT!!! dahdahdahdahdahdah-dat-dat-dah... PHRHARRTT!!!

Wendy and I nearly passed out while trying to control our laughter. Later, whenever I passed them in the hallway, I'd hum the "1812 Overture" under my breath. I don't think they ever got it.

After we recovered from what sounded like a true Napoleonic battle, I called my Flight Commander at the squadron and told him we had arrived. He told us to lay low for the next 3-4 days until the TACEVAL was complete. That worked great for us since it allowed us time to find a car, find a house to rent, and get to know the surrounding area. But, first and foremost, it gave us a chance to reacclimate to Germany after being gone for a decade. We couldn't wait to get started.

The main gate for Hahn Air Base was located in the tiny village of Lautzenhausen in the Hunsrück region of Germany, a low-mountainous area not far from the Mosel River. The base was established in 1951 and was the smallest and most remote of the German USAFE fighter bases, which included Ramstein, Bitburg, Spangdahlem, Sembach, and Zweibrücken.

Chuck Yeager commanded one of the fighter squadrons at Hahn in the late Fifties. It was home to the 50th Tactical Fighter Wing, and the first base in USAFE to receive the F-16, which had been operational there for a little more than two years.

Due to its relatively high elevation of over 1,600 feet, Hahn was often socked in by fog and statistically had the worst flying weather of any fighter base in the entire Air Force. The Wing was tasked with the nuclear strike mission against potential Warsaw Pact foes, with secondary and tertiary roles in surface attack and air defense. It was a true, multi-role combat wing, with the newest, coolest fighter jet in the world set in a quaint, picture-postcard European location. Wendy and I thought it was the best assignment in the Air Force.

There were three fighter squadrons—the 313th, the 10th, and the 496th, to which I was assigned. Due to their distinctive patches, the 313th was called The Lucky Puppies, the 10th The Gay Blades, although they much preferred The Fightin' Tenth, or Blue Zoo, and the 496th was dubbed Electric Chickens.

The 496th had won the coveted Hughes Trophy in the late fifties, which designated the squadron as the world's finest air interceptor squadron. Subsequently, the words World's Finest were sewn into the 496th patch, which depicted a hooded hunting falcon with lightning bolts, hence Electric Chicken.

Billeting was in easy walking distance from the main gate, so we decided to have our first meal in Germany off base somewhere. We were delighted to find a Walter's Futterkrippe barely 50 yards from the gate. Walter's was a fast-food restaurant that primarily served wurst and pommes frites. The original restaurant was in Wiesbaden, located across the street from the American Amelia Earhart hotel near Lindsey Air Station when we were kids. We couldn't believe they had a Walter's in Hahn as well and went rushing in for a never-forgotten taste of Germany.

As we chowed down in ecstasy, we heard a large group of people marching towards the main gate. We went outside to see what caused the commotion and saw about 30 mostly younger folks chanting something about America, and it didn't sound complimentary. We then saw them hurl water balloons filled with red dye at the Welcome To Hahn Air Base sign, clearly meant to represent blood. Later someone explained to us that they marched like this about once a month or so to protest the neither confirmed nor denied presence of nuclear weapons on the base.

My sweet wife went ballistic. "Hey!!" Wendy yelled. "You better be glad we've been here defending you for the past 40 years!!!! What's the matter with you people!!"

I grabbed her and hustled her back inside Walter's, trying to calm her down and not make a scene while several in the crowd eyed us suspiciously.

The protestors dispersed in short order, and we eventually finished our meal, but it was clear that some things had changed in Germany while we were away.

But at the end of Day 1, back in our little room fighting jet lag, we went to bed that night as happy as any couple could be.

With the free time allotted us, we set our priorities of first finding a car, and second finding a house. Even though most of the base was under inspection, Housing Referral and Driver's Testing were open in the no-play areas, so we were able to visit both offices.

We had been sent a study guide for German driving rules and traffic signs while still at Luke, so we passed the test and received our licenses without difficulty.

Housing Referral had a long list of approved houses for rent at different towns and villages in the area and offered us a sense of what was available at what price. The dollar was still strong, nearly four Deutsch marks to the dollar, so the money we saved went a long way.

To my relative dismay, there was a Toyota dealership, Ruedinger's, within walking distance of the main gate. I had sold my beloved Celica at Luke because I thought there was no way Japanese cars would be popular in Germany, and I was afraid I wouldn't be able to get it serviced anywhere. Boy, was I wrong! We saw more Toyotas and Hondas flying down the autobahn than we did Mercedes and Volkswagens.

We bought a new Toyota Corolla for Wendy and a used Toyota Tercel for me and set about driving through the surrounding countryside. Everything about Hahn had a small-town feel to it, and we absolutely adored it.

Base housing, mostly stairwell living like we grew up with was no concern of ours since we wanted to live in a small town somewhere and immerse ourselves in the German language and culture.

As soon as the TACEVAL was over, one of the guys from the 496th, Ziggy—destined to be a lifelong friend, contacted us and told us about a newly-remodeled house in the little village of Reich where he and his wife lived. He made arrangements for us to meet the landlord, and we drove out early on a Friday morning.

Reich was about 25 minutes from the base, a little farther than we wanted, but we fell in love with it instantly. It was a tiny, picturesque town with a small population of about 300, including four other American families. It was located off a local road, with only two streets that formed a loop, Ringstrasse, through the town. You could completely walk around it in 10 minutes.

Accompanied by Ziggy, who was fluent in German, we met our landlord at the newly-remodeled house. It was only a 2-bedroom, but it had a large walk-in closet, kitchen cabinets, and a huge storage area. We found out that the building used to be the old village dance hall, and the storage area was where the dancing took place. It had a beautiful brick patio overlooking a valley into the nearby village of Biebern, where a medieval church spire highlighted the horizon.

It was perfect. We tried to put our new landlord at ease by speaking our elementary-level German, and immediately committed to a year-long lease. This house became our home for the next four years.

With the TACEVAL successfully finished, the Wing had declared a no-work holiday that Friday. So, our first introduction to the squadron was a Saturday gathering in the town of Bernkastel-Keus on the Mosel, where the squadron victory celebration coincided with an annual wine festival and fireworks display held every first week in September.

Everyone in the squadron, from the commander on down, welcomed us and made Wendy and I feel part of the family. They were ecstatic that the highly-demanding inspection had come to a successful conclusion, and this being Germany, the wine was flowing, and everyone on the street was jollier, friendlier, and happier as the day went on.

The celebration concluded with fireworks shot over the castle ruins overlooking Bernkastel and the Mosel River.

Monday would be my first real introduction to the 496th and the beginning of my transition to mission-ready status in the F-16. Given my less-than-mediocre performance at RTU at Luke, I was more than a little nervous with anticipation, but for now, our first few days at Hahn could not have gone better.

One of the first things I learned when I reported to the squadron that Monday was that they were due to ship out to Incirlik Air Base in Turkey in two weeks and would be gone for over a month, not scheduled to return until late October.

This news made the start of my Mission Ready check-out program complicated. Since the primary mission of the 50th Tactical Fighter Wing was nuclear strike, the first task of a newly-assigned pilot was to certify before a formal board made up of several subject experts. This process required approximately two weeks of intensive study in the secure, classified vaults in the squadron before you were ready to face the board.

Following that, you were given five low-level strike (LLS) rides, followed by a Mission Qualification (MQ) nuke-strike checkride. Once you had completed the Cert and the Mission Qual check, you were declared Mission Ready (MR).

I was informed that with the 496th packing up and preparing to deploy, I could anticipate a couple of simulator rides and a basic local familiarization ride before the squadron departed. I would then be attached to the 313th squadron for study, preparation, and completion of my Initial Nuke Cert, an annual requirement.

Following successful board certification, I would travel to Incirlik AB on a MAC-hop, rejoin the 496th, and hopefully complete the five LLS rides and MQ check before returning to Hahn with the rest of the squadron.

Obviously, this wasn't an ideal way to begin, but that's the way it had to be. Wendy would have to do a lot of the settling and moving into our off-base home on her own.

The 496th was great. All of the guys seemed loose, happy, friendly, and full of bravado. The comparison in atmosphere between the training squadron at Luke and this operational squadron at Hahn was striking. I had a couple of simulator rides right off the bat just to get me used to the F-16 again after having not flown in almost a month, but both the sims and my local orientation sortie, flown in a B-Model with an IP in the rear cockpit, went well.

Despite my poor performance at Luke, suddenly, I didn't feel as stressed as I had been, partly because of the team feeling so evident in the 496th and the fact that I understood this was an opportunity for me to start over.

I hated seeing everyone depart for Incirlik without me. On top of that, working and studying in a different squadron so soon felt a little awkward, but I knuckled down and began to prepare for the Initial Nuke Cert with the Lucky Puppies.

Part of the initial training program to become MR and nuke certified was a tour of the Victor Alert Compound, or VAC. Victor Alert was an alert status whereby pilots had 15 minutes from a scramble notification to get to the jet, start the engine, copy a valid tasking message from the Command Post, and be airborne, screaming east at treetop-level for pre-designated Warsaw Pact targets. The 50th TFW at Hahn kept jets on nuke-strike alert 24/7, and the pilots, crew chiefs, and jets were all maintained in the segregated VAC.

It looked like the movie set of *Stalag 17* with several layered fences of high barbed wire, a metal and stone gate at the entry point, and heavily armed security forces and sentry dogs on patrol. Inside the hardened VAC was a dayroom and TV with a large VHS tape collection, individual closet-sized rooms where the pilots and crew chiefs slept, showers, a small cafeteria that served three square meals a day, and an intelligence-planning area that provided all of the maps, photos, charts, and pre-planned mission packages for the specific line target you were assigned.

We were then taken out to one of the hardened aircraft shelters (HAS) to see a fully-armed F-16 on alert status, to include the B-61 nuclear weapon strapped underneath one of the wings, with more kiloton power than the bombs we dropped on Hiroshima and Nagasaki. Victor tours were divided into three segments of two, two, and three days a week, and you could expect to pull a tour at least once a month. It was a sobering introduction to the wing's mission and the reality of nuclear warfare.

I learned a few more things during this introduction that hadn't been revealed to us in detail during academics at Luke. All of our primary nuclear deliveries would be planned via a Radar Loft (RLOFT) or Radar Lay Down (RLD). Our final target runs would be at 500 feet, or lower, and at 540 knots, or faster. The RLOFT was designed for an above-ground detonation so that you would make your run-in, and at a computed distance from the target, initiate a steady climb to a similarly computed altitude. You would then auto-release, loft the weapon, quickly do a 4-G slice down and 120 degrees away from the target, and descend back down to low altitude. The whole philosophy here was to outrun the nuke blast, and Escape Distance Actual (EDA) versus Escape Distance Required (EDR) were numbers you had to be aware of.

The RLD was designed for a ground-level detonation; the weapon had a chute and timer attached to it, and after you released it, it would float down to the target, lie on the ground for a few seconds, then explode after the time expired. In theory, this gave you time to keep going straight ahead, fast and low, away from the target, and outrun the effects of the blast. The nature of the target determined whether you did an RLOFT or RLD delivery.

Simple enough, right? Well, you would also do this with only one eye; you were encouraged to wear an eye patch, supplied in your target package, over one eye, so if you were flash-blinded from the nuclear blast, you would possibly have at least one good eye with which to get back. At 500-ish feet. At 600 mph. Single-ship. Dodging SAMs, AAA, and enemy fighters. With other nuclear blasts in your target area. No sweat. And hopefully, you had enough gas to get back home in the first place. Depending on your target, sometimes you did, and sometimes you didn't. When I look back on those days, I wonder what the heck were we thinking? The scenario was right out of *Dr. Strangelove*, but we were absolutely certain we would prevail.

We FNGs, "Funny" New Guys, were also invited to be part of the audience watching the annually required formal Mission Certification for nuke-certified pilots. The Cert Board was chaired by the Wing Director of Operations (DO) or his designated representative and accompanied by Plans, Intelligence, Operations, Weapons & Tactics, Command Post, and Life Support experts.

The examinee had been issued a real-world mission package, and the certification would be based on how he planned to execute that mission successfully. Each Mission Cert began roughly the same way, with the examinee reciting a standard introductory, "For purposes of this board certification, I have assumed Victor Alert status, and I am either in the Victor Alert Compound or have expanded to my squadron. Upon hearing Scramble-Scramble-Scramble or Klaxon-Klaxon-Klaxon on the loudspeaker or on my radio, my crew chief and I will respond immediately to my aircraft. Upon approaching the Hardened Aircraft Shelter, I will return the classified Number-of-the-Day signal to the Security Personnel on duty. He or she will open the HAS doors at that point, and I will proceed inside the shelter. While I am donning my g-suit and harness, my crew chief will open the cockpit. After he or she places the ladder on the rails, I will enter the aircraft, strap in, turn the radios on, and prepare to copy the message from Command Post. Sir, I am ready to copy the message at this time."

At that point, the Command Post rep read a code-encrypted message which the examinee copied on the appropriate message encoding sheet. He then quickly reviewed the message, opened the sealed cookie code envelope to verify tasking for his particular mission, and recited the following verbiage, "Sir, I have copied a valid message, my mission is tasked, and I can make the Time-Over-Target as planned."

The examinee then spent the next thirty minutes or so explaining how he intended to execute the pre-planned mission, followed by, "Sir, this concludes my briefing, and I am ready to take your questions at this time."

For about the next hour, he was fair game, as each subject expert quizzed him on his knowledge in their specific area. Once he had completed this round of Stump-the-Dummy, the DO had one last round of general questions, concluding with, "Do you have any hesitation or reservations about conducting this mission?"

To which the examinee replied, "No, sir."

He was then sent out of the room while the Board discussed his fate. Shortly thereafter, he was called back in, and each subject matter expert addressed his strong and weak areas, concluded by the DO rendering the Board's decision. Congratulations!

The entire process seemed stressful beyond any academic endeavor I had ever experienced. I had no idea how I was going to learn all of that stuff in two weeks.

It may seem fairly trivial today, now that the USSR is no more and the Soviet threat has been negated, but in the 80s, we took that threat very seriously. We knew we were being watched and monitored, and our Top Secret clearances were no joke. One of the stories told to me during my Cert Academics was enlightening.

As the legend goes, a captain and his family decided to drive to Berlin. A few highways transited through East Germany to reach the destination, but drivers were required to submit itineraries to the East German state tourist office up to nine weeks in advance. Fuel must be purchased from specially approved gas stations, and the designated route must be followed. Naturally, drivers were subject to being stopped and inspected by the East German police at any point. Somewhere along the route, the captain was stopped by the police, who asked for his passport and ID card, which he willingly surrendered. The police went back to their car, leaving the captain and his family waiting with nervous anticipation. After about 20 minutes, the policemen returned. "Have a safe trip, enjoy your stay, and congratulations on your promotion to Major." The major's list hadn't been released yet—the captain had no idea he had been promoted.

Now, I don't know if I believe that tale or not, but it's an example of the cloak-and-dagger environment in the Cold War days being stationed near the Iron Curtain.

The guys in the 313th were friendly enough, but I was new, and I wasn't one of them. The weapons guys back in the vault were helpful, but I wasn't even quite sure what kind of questions to ask in some cases.

I studied hard, rehearsed my narrative, and the day before my scheduled Cert, the 313th Operations Officer set up a Murder

Board consisting of himself and other pilots from the squadron to allow me to go through a practice certification. I muddled through okay, but I was clearly not going to impress anyone. At the conclusion of the question-and-answer period, the Ops O said, "You are not ready. What time is your Cert tomorrow?"

I gulped, "11:00, sir."

He stared at me for a few seconds, then said, "Fine. I will meet you here in my office tomorrow at 7:00 AM. Just me and you. We'll rehearse it until you get it right."

With that, I studied through that evening in the areas I was weakest, went back to billeting for a few hours sleep, then reported back the next morning to the Ops O in the 313th. We went over my Cert presentation a few times, and he continued to pepper me with questions. Finally, at about 9:00, he said, "Okay. I think you're ready. Go get some breakfast, and I'll see you at the Cert."

When I arrived there, I noticed him in the audience. I passed without a hitch—piece of cake.

I will always remember the kindness and generosity of that 313th Ops Officer, call sign Big Guy. I wasn't even in his squadron, yet he took extra time with me, personal time out of his crazy-busy schedule, to ensure I received a fair chance to pass that initial nuke cert. I will always be grateful to him. To no one's surprise, he later went on to earn general's rank.

While I had been immersed in Cert prep, Wendy occupied herself with learning how to get things done on base, and how to get around the local area. Her German, always much better than mine, was improving rapidly, and she was starting to feel right at home. She drove me to Rhein-Main AB, then left knowing she needed to check out of billeting, move into the new house, accept our household goods, unpack, pick up Etcetera, the cat, at Frankfurt International Airport, and make those all-important first-impression contacts with the people of our small village on her own.

It would not be the last time she would take on those types of tasks while I was deployed elsewhere. I regretfully kissed her goodbye and boarded the C-141 for Incirlik, knowing she was going to do great, but feeling a little guilty all the same.

After about a four-hour flight, we touched down in Incirlik, and some of the guys from the 496th B Flight, to which I belonged, met me once I cleared customs. The new guy-feeling rapidly melted away as they updated me on what was going on, checked me into my room, and drove me to squadron ops down by the flightline.

I got a brief outline of the plan to get me Mission Ready-qualified before returning to Hahn. I would have two weeks to successfully complete a local orientation ride, five LLS rides, and my Mission Qual check. If all went smoothly, I would get my first flight checking out in Chemical Warfare gear as well. I had ten flying days to complete at least seven rides, a pretty quick pace for a rookie, but with no other distractions, it seemed perfectly reasonable. However, I learned that one new guy who had arrived a few weeks before me had already busted his Mission Qual check, and another was struggling through his LLS rides.

This was the typical battle rhythm for squadrons stationed in Central Europe, but especially for Hahn. Training requirements needed to be accomplished during every six-month cycle. Yet the weather was generally so poor at Hahn and on the various bombing ranges in Germany and the Netherlands that the squadrons deployed elsewhere for 4-5 weeks for a Weapons Training Deployment (WTD), as these trips were called. In the fall, we'd rotate to Incirlik, Turkey, and its range at Konya, and in the winter to Zaragoza, Spain, and its range at Bardenas-Reales.

It was extremely difficult completing bomb training squares without the deployments, and as a result, the bulk of the sorties were dedicated range rides. We would return to Hahn by the middle of October but would deploy again to Zaragoza in January. I hadn't known we would be on the road quite so much, but it sounded like it was going to be an awesome experience, with an outstanding group of guys.

The flying in Turkey was fantastic. You could fly just about anywhere you wanted within a 50-mile circle around Incirlik Air Base, which we shared with the Turkish Air Force. You could plan your own surface attack missions against a variety of targets within the circle, and fly as low as 500 feet. Outside the

50-mile circle, you had to remain within a choice of several low-level corridors, where you could fly as low as 250 feet on your way to the bombing range at Konya, which was about 150 miles from Incirlik.

The population was pretty sparse along the routes, but there were enough roads, buildings, and geographical points to allow you reliable INS updates. As you approached the range at Konya, the terrain was high-desert, relatively flat, and there were plenty of easy-to-identify ground radar returns, including the Efes Beer plant on long final, where you could plot radar offset aim points (OAPs) for your RLOFTs and RLDs.

The most welcome surprise was that my performance in the air was consistently solid. Here is an excerpt from a letter I wrote Wendy, "Wendy, the past week has been the best five flying days of my career! I can't understand it, I keep waiting for the inevitable bad ride, but it just hasn't happened! I hope I'm not saving it for my checkride. But my bombs have all been on time, on target, no problems with the radar, formation, landing, or anything. I'm getting good grades; it's so unlike me! It's been great—flying 500 feet over mountains 12,000 feet high, down low through Alexander's Pass where Alexander the Great marched his legions and cut the Gordian Knot, over rooftops made of mud and stone in the middle of a landscape that looks like the surface of the moon. It has truly been the best and most satisfying flying I've ever experienced."

On one of my first flights to Konya, I was inbound low level with my IP in chase when a MiG-21 Fishbed flew low and off to our left side. Breaking radio protocol, I blurted, "Did you see that??!!" on my victor radio.

My IP quickly replied, "Don't ask!"

Being a good student, I never asked or brought it up again. But that was a real eye-opener; keep your cranium on a swivel, and prepare for the unexpected.

My Mission Qual check was planned, as anticipated, as an RLOFT first-run strike against the nuke circle target at Konya. I was provided a mission scenario to include simulated air and ground threats in the target area and along the route, to which I would have to react. I planned the sortie, put together all the mission materials, and briefed my Stan-Eval IP on how I was going to successfully attack the target at the designated TOT (Time-Over-Target) he had given me the night before.

I planned the timing using real time just as I had done in Luke, and had done on the five LLS rides leading up to the check. However, the IP, with whom I had never flown, wanted me to change the timing plan from real time to elapsed time, setting the TOT at 0:00 and running the route timing back from there.

I confessed I had never done it that way before, so he gave me a quick tutorial. I wasn't real keen on having to change such an important habit pattern a couple of hours before takeoff, but I wanted to excel on this ride of all rides, and agreed to give it a shot.

Ground ops, start, taxi, and takeoff were all uneventful. As I was setting up holding over the first navigation point preparing for an on-time push down the route toward Konya Range, I tried to reset the timing to elapsed time as the Eval IP had instructed.

I don't know what I did wrong, but I totally screwed it up. As I looked at my watch, I noted it was time to go, with no time to make any corrections, so I thought to heck with it and started down the route, using only the watch on my wrist to calculate and adjust time. Generally, the INS and on-board computer would provide an arrow in the HUD to tell you exactly what speed to fly to exactly meet your TOT, but this was not available to me now. However, I wasn't really worried. I had instructed many low-level navigation sorties in the Tweet with just a map and a watch, and I didn't think it would be that big a deal to adjust to a faster speed.

We planned our low levels in the F-16 at 480 knots, or 2 miles in 15 seconds, and the IP-to-Target run at 540 knots, or 2 miles in 13 seconds. There was also the rough technique of increasing/decreasing your ground speed by 1/6 (for instance, for 480 knots, change by 80 knots) for every 10 seconds you are off time, or some variation thereof (40 knots for 20 seconds). I had to get a scoreable bomb within 30 seconds to pass the ride, so I just pressed on. I still had my INS and navigation steering, so it didn't feel like a big deal.

With the IP in chase, I flew the route, reacted to the simulated threats he called out, adjusted my speed and timing referencing my wristwatch and map, and made my first run RLOFT attack on the range.

"6 meters at 12," I heard the ranger reply with my score—well within the minimum hit criteria for an RLOFT. I quickly glanced at my watch, and I was definitely inside 30 seconds. The rest of the range work went well, and all of my bombs were within hit criteria.

As we were going Arm Safe exiting the range, the Range Control Officer said, "Congratulations, PK."

That gave me more confidence as we returned to Incirlik, shot a few patterns, and landed.

During the debrief, we were watching the film of my bomb passes and my IP noticed that I didn't have any time, real or elapsed, in my HUD. He asked why, and I told him how I had fouled the FCC up converting from real time to elapsed time, and didn't feel I had time to sort it out, so I just pressed and made adjustments on the fly.

He laughed and said, "Well, you got a 6-meter bomb within 3 seconds of your TOT—not bad, man!" I had passed my Mission Qual check, and even earned a Commendable for route and timing maintenance.

That night at the Incirlik O'Club, the squadron celebrated its newest Mission Ready fighter pilot. I received congratulation handshakes and backslaps from the guys, and I couldn't help but marvel at how completely things had turned around. Few really knew how poorly I had performed at RTU; they just knew how great I was doing here and now.

To this day, I can't explain the dramatic change in my flying execution. Maybe I finally started to make the conscious to subconscious transition described earlier by McPeak. I knew I had a long way to go to be the fighter pilot I wanted to be, but my old swagger was coming back, and it felt really, really good.

Incirlik Air Base, located near Adana, was fairly small, but it had an O'Club with a bartender named Mike who had been there forever, a small BX, and a small commissary. The base was built primarily to be a U.S. staging base for training and other operations in the Near and Middle East. Most of the permanent party members assigned to Incirlik were there on 1-year remote tours, but a limited amount of accompanied 2-year tours were available for those who wanted to bring their families.

Just off base was The Alley, a long-strip of assorted shops catering to U.S. servicemen. A shopping-list of must-haves went hand-in-hand with a visit to Incirlik. The most-desired items to bring home included carpets, leather jackets, copper pots, gold cartouches, harem pants—later called MC Hammer pants—and bags of salted pistachios, which eventually gave us all sore thumbnails as we pried open the shells.

I had never been to Turkey before, or in any Muslim-dominated country, for that matter, but it was great. The Turkish people were friendly and helpful, with few traces of anti-Americanism. The store owners were smiling and outgoing, as were the taxi drivers who ferried us on and off base.

The food was delicious. Gastro-intestinal problems were an ever-present threat, but even if you came down with Ataturk's Revenge, the flight surgeon had a plentiful supply of thick, horrible tasting goop to stop you up. Most guys swore they got sick more often from eating the salad at the O'Club than from eating or drinking anything off base. Our favorite restaurant off base was at a British-Petroleum gas station just off the main gate, where they served killer doner kebabs and flat tread bread.

We were told—warned—that Kamal Ataturk was like George Washington, Benjamin Franklin, and Abraham Lincoln rolled into one, and any perceived insult to him would result in jail time, or worse, (*Midnight Express*, anyone)? The weather was warm and humid, the flying was awesome, the billets okay, and it was a great place for a WTD.

Since I was the newest member of the squadron and the last to arrive, I was also scheduled to be one of the last to return to Hahn with a couple of other guys, and I helped pack everything up and fly back on the C-141 with all of our gear. Our F-16s had flown home the day before, and my flight commander called Wendy and told her we were expected to arrive around 11:00 PM.

As we neared Hahn, we were informed by the pilot that Hahn was enshrouded in fog, and we would have to divert to Rhein-Main. I felt bad for Wendy and hoped someone was keeping her and the other spouses informed. However, halfway to Rhein-Main, the pilot announced that Rhein-Main had gone down as well, and we would make another try at Hahn.

I had no idea what to expect from Wendy, but the fog lifted just enough for us to land around midnight in some of the thickest schmeeze I had ever seen. As we stepped off the airplane, there was Wendy, with two young security policemen—her new best friends.

It turns out when she arrived on base she didn't really know what to do or where to go, so she waved down a Security Police truck to see if they knew. The guys were aware of the inbound C-141, which had been delayed for a few hours, so they told Wendy to hop in the truck. They drove all around Hahn in the fog until we arrived, probably to some secure areas where civilians shouldn't have been, and the guys treated Wendy like a homecoming queen.

After I collected my bags, she drove us to our new home, which she had set up beautifully in my absence. Etcetera and I had a happy reunion as well, as she followed us around the house yowling and purring while Wendy gave me the grand tour. Six weeks after our arrival in-country, we were settled in.

SQUADRON LIFE

Even though I was certified and mission-ready in the 50th's primary DOC on nuke-strike, I still had to check out as a wingman in the other roles of Surface Attack Tactics (SAT) and Air Defense (Air-to-Air). My flight commander informed me that the goal was to have me completely checked out by the time we completed our Zaragoza WTD in January. Assuming the weather cooperated, this was doable. The squadron pretty much left me alone as far as additional duties were concerned, so I concentrated solely on flying and getting to know rules and procedures for raging around Central Europe.

The airspace in Germany in the Eighties was a fighter pilot's dream. For air-to-air training, there was Temporary Reserved Airspace (TRAs) from 10,000 feet up to about 35,000 feet. U.S.

jets tended to be assigned TRA 204 north of Hahn, or 205E/205W to the south. Below 10,000 feet, you could fly VFR virtually anywhere, weather and restricted airspace (airfields, ranges, etc.) permitting. You could fly as low as 500 feet, except in several low fly areas (Low Fly 7 to the south, Low Fly 1 and 3 to the north) that allowed you to descend as low as 250 feet.

There was a standing agreement between neighboring NATO countries that if you squawked 0033 on your IFF, you were transmitting to the world that you were willing to engage and take on all comers. So, you could be conducting a SAT mission with your 4-ship and be randomly attacked by U.S. F-15s, German F-4s, Belgian Mirages, Canadian F-18s, Dutch F-5s, or any NATO fighters out looking for some action.

We carried 1:500,000 maps in our cockpits—one for Northern Germany, and one for Southern Germany, that had pre-designated and plotted geographic references for our VFR planning. We had target photos of Nike sites, Hawk batteries, weapons storage facilities, communication power stations, and any number of practice targets that we could use for our SAT missions.

During annual U.S. Army exercises like Reforger, Return-of-Forces-to-Germany, we had plenty of targets of opportunity (tanks, trucks, APCs) to attack. Several controlled ranges—Siegenburg to the south, Nordhorn to the north, Helchteren in Belgium, Suippes in France, and Vliehors/Noordvaarder in the Netherlands—were available so we could work on our bomb squares. However, getting range time could be a challenge, with all the fighter bases in Central Europe needing the same requirements. You could take off in your 4-ship, fly a SAT mission against a real-world target or targets, threat react to numerous dissimilar fighter adversaries, and return home never having flown above 500 feet or talking to any outside controlling agency.

We were flying Block 10 and Block 15 F-16s at Hahn when I first arrived, so the Data Transfer Cartridges (DTCs) and detailed computerized mission planning assets that came with the conversion to F-16C model jets had not yet occurred. Mission planning was accomplished with our own hands and craniums, and we could rip and strip a fullblown SAT mission faster and nearly as efficiently as we would do with the high tech mission planning equipment provided later.

Using the pre-plotted geographic references on our 1:500,000 maps, the wingmen would plan and make the maps for the route of flight, and complete the lineup card with heading, distance, time and fuel calculations. The flight and element leads would plan and provide the 1:50,000 maps for the actual SAT attack, and prepare the mission briefing. During our local exercises, called Salty Nation, the mission planning area would be a crowded flurry of maps, razor blades, and scribbles. Later I sheared off the fingertip of my left pinky with a razor while cutting down maps during speed-planning. As I was driven to the hospital, one of my comrades, Foosh, found the piece of my finger on the floor and taped it into the squadron Hog Log for posterity—see Appendix: Culture, Customs, and Craziness.

In the days before Desert Storm, when the Warsaw Pact was our primary focus, we were a low-level Air Force, especially with the weather in Central Europe and the weapons we had available at the time. The F-16 of the early-mid Eighties was still similar to the low cost, light-weight fighter originally envisioned by much-revered airpower theorist, Col John Boyd.

All of our SAT missions were planned low level, as were all of our nuke strike sorties. The classic attack, which every F-16 pilot at Hahn could execute at a moment's notice, was a 10/20 Hi attack, allowing the flight lead to bomb the target while the wingman did the same, but at an altitude that allowed him to stay above the lead jet's bomb frag pattern. The need for low altitude attacks led our Fighter Weapons School graduates at Hahn to develop a Low Level Low Drag (LLLD) attack.

We had a limited number of high-drag weapons that would allow you to overfly your target at low altitude, but we needed a shallow, 2-to-5 degree attack that allowed you to stay below the low cloud ceilings in Central Europe with low drag, or slick munitions. In the LLLD attack, you attacked your target with slick ordinance, and upon weapon release, you would perform a 4-G pull 120 degrees away from the target, similar to a LOFT recovery, but at low altitude. You would actually fly inside the bomb fragmentation pattern, but (hopefully) outrun the bomb frag during your egress.

To my knowledge, we never flew this attack in actual combat as it was not needed during our Desert Wars in Iraq and Afghanistan; however, it was part of our bread and butter at Hahn. Even our air defense missions, either for base defense or SAT package escort, were planned for low altitude. We were heaters-and-guns only in our Air Defense configuration, with the AIM 9-L/M Sidewinder heat-seeking missile giving us a short-range front aspect capability. We had no IFF interrogator, so we had to visually identify any threat before firing on it. It was gutsy work; fast and low, violent, up close and personal, and it was fabulous.

One of the nicknames for the F-16 in those days was Lawn Dart, due to the high number of crashes we experienced. In addition to the Loss-of-Consciousness episodes already mentioned, we had a fairly high incidence of losses during SAT missions. Anytime you spend 80% of your flying life at 500 feet or lower and 500 mph in a single-seat jet, it doesn't take but a few seconds of inattention to cost you your life. To this day, after learning I flew Vipers, if someone, while trying to be funny, alludes to the jets as Lawn Darts, I educate them if they are civilians, and I challenge them if they are flyers. Them's fighting words.

I got a hard reality check for flying in Central Europe on my first SAT ride after our return from Incirlik, with the squadron Operations Officer, Hugo. Frankly, I was amazed that we could just fly wherever we wanted, at 500 feet, and attack targets at random. I thought to myself, "Really? We can do that?"

As we were setting up for a re-attack on a radar site we had selected during mission planning, I was flying tactical line abreast when I saw a German F-4 coasting up behind Hugo's jet. I didn't quite know how to react. During our training at Luke, we were never attacked while performing our air-to-ground missions, and all of my threat reactions during the MR checkout in Incirlik had been simulated. I couldn't believe what I was seeing. Does that F-4 see my flight lead? Is he in some kind of difficulty? Or—is he getting some quality gun camera film on a Hahn F-16?

I finally blurted out "F-4, closing on you, six o'clock," but by then, the F-4 was happily pulling away. Too late! I had not called out the threat quickly enough.

"Fine! Just fine!" Hugo spit out over the radio. After landing and in the debrief, he ripped me a new one. "Don't ever—EVER—let anyone get an unobserved kill!" on your flight lead.

It was superb training for real world mutual support, and forced us to perform one of the most important duties a wingman has to fulfill. We would typically do a formation takeoff, accelerate to our standard low-level airspeed of 480 knots, perform a tac-split as we departed the airfield, and start checking six as soon as possible. I soon learned that our friendly neighborhood F-15s from Bitburg would often circle overhead on top of Hahn airspace and attack us within minutes of takeoff. Again—great training and overall great fun.

Flying VFR whenever possible, it was wise to memorize the TACAN stations for most of the primary air bases in the area, both U.S. and German, to help ensure you knew where you were at all times and to keep from trespassing into controlled airspace and airfield boundaries.

Each pilot also tended to keep their own separate collection of approach plates on their lapboard. With the weather as poor as it generally was, and with most airfields consisting of a single 8,000-foot long runway, the chances of quickly having to divert to another base were ever-present. Like most of my comrades, it wasn't long before I had about twenty TACAN stations and Initial Approach Fix (IAF) radial/DME locations memorized.

Flying in Central Europe quickly developed your instrument flying skills. Having been a FAIP in Arizona and Texas, I had trained and flown many instrument sorties, but rarely did I fly an actual instrument approach in weather anywhere close to minimums.

When you first arrived in USAFE, you were limited to taking off and/or landing in weather with at least a 700 feet ceiling and 2 miles visibility. Depending on the time of year, that meant you might not get to fly much, due to the always-lousy weather. After you were fully checked out as a wingman, your pilot weather category was reduced to 500 feet and 1 1/2 miles visibility. Later, after you had accrued a certain number of hours based on your experience, your category was further reduced to 300 feet and 1 mile.

The difference at Hahn was as soon as the weather even approached minimums, we launched the fleet. Weather was typically so bad, so often, that we took advantage of any opportunity to get jets in the air. One of the things we did prior to returning to base after a successful mission was to call back to the Supervisor of Flying (SOF) and inquire about the current weather conditions.

If you heard 300 and 1, ragged, you knew you were in for an interesting landing experience. We generally carried a little extra fuel above-and-beyond standard divert requirements with the knowledge that we might have to go missed approach at Hahn and join any number of jets short on gas trying to find a place where the weather was good enough to land.

Over the course of the next four years, Wendy got used to receiving a call from me, letting her know I would be spending the night somewhere else, having diverted to another base, usually Spangdahlem or Bitburg, due to poor weather back home.

However, even having to execute a missed approach and divert was good training. Years later, as the 51st Operations Group Commander at Osan Air Base in Korea, I maintained that same philosophy of launching at minimums. Based on my experiences at Hahn, I believed that even if the jets were likely to divert, or the pilots had to fly numerous instrument approaches because the weather was too poor to do anything else, they could gain something of value. The squadron commanders of the two fighter squadrons at Osan took to calling 300/1 ceiling/visibility conditions "Colonel White Weather."

At the same time, I was adjusting to flying in Germany, both Wendy and I were getting acclimated to living in our new home. Our neighbors in Reich were welcoming and friendly towards us. Most of them spoke very little English, so our limited knowledge of German was useful and appreciated. Evidently, few of them had seen a Siamese cat and seemed to think

Etcetera was a feline breed, both exotic and expensive, "sehr teuer, ja?"

Wendy stayed busy, and trips to the base—commissary, BX, bank, shoppette, video store, etc.—generally took the better part of a day. She became familiar with the neighboring towns and villages and quickly discerned the best shops for purchasing items on the economy that we couldn't find on base. The 496th squadron wives were active and supportive of each other. Day trips to the French Commissary just across the border, the big BX at Ramstein Air Base, local vegetable and flower markets, indoor swimming pools and spas, and other attractions were organized weekly. Wendy also decided to continue work toward finishing her bachelor's degree and began taking night classes at the University of Maryland Extension office on base with other spouses and enlisted personnel.

Most of the villages couldn't receive the AFN-TV signal, so the video store on base was extremely popular. Wendy's mom did a great job religiously videotaping our favorite shows, *Night Court*, *Designing Women*, *Family Ties*, *The Cosby Show*, *A Different World*, *Cheers*, and sending them to us in the mail. My mom tended to tape special events, like the Olympics, or mini-series like *North and South* and *Peter the Great*. It was cause for great excitement whenever we received a new package.

After viewing, we passed them on to friends, who would, in turn, share what their parents stateside may have sent them. When visiting someone's home, one of the first things everyone did was to take a look at their video collection and borrow anything not yet seen. The entire swap-and-barter system of VHS movies and TV shows was a virtual culture unto itself.

One of the greatest things about being in a fighter squadron is the closeness and camaraderie that occurs, especially if you are stationed at an overseas fighter unit where there are fewer distractions outside the squadron family. Hahn, being a small base and fairly isolated, magnified that spirit of closeness, with the spouses as well as the pilots. You could count on a party or some kind of social event nearly every weekend—the annual Halloween party at Ziggy and his wife's home was legendary. We worked hard, but we played hard, too. Everyone seemed to get along with everyone else and genuinely enjoy each other's companionship.

Approaching Christmas, Germany came alive with holiday decorations and the smell of roasted chestnuts and gluhwein as we strolled the Kriskindlemarkts nibbling on lebkuchen and other assorted goodies. The mayor of Reich informed us customarily each family trekked into the forest nearby and cut down one tree for Christmas, so one Saturday, he took us and the other Americans living in town out to select and bring home our first Christmas tree. Having spent our first Christmas in a tiny BOQ room at Holloman, this was really our first family Christmas in our own home, and Wendy made the most of buying traditional German-style decorations from Kaefer's in nearby Sohren.

The squadron threw a family Christmas party, and Santa Claus arrived taxiing in the back seat of an F-16B to pass out gifts to the kids. The Officer's Club threw a huge New Year's Eve party, and the first considerable snow of the season started just before midnight. We carefully drove home in a swirling white-out of blowing snow and fog to welcome 1985.

The squadron departed for Zaragoza Air Base (ZAB) in northern Spain on January 5th. I flew one of the 18 jets we deployed, my first cross-country in the F-16. With wing and centerline fuel tanks, we reached ZAB, crossing through France and into Spain, without needing a tanker.

Zaragoza was much like Incirlik in terms of its mission, serving primarily as a Weapons Training Deployment location for fighter squadrons based in Northern Europe. Flying in Spain was more restrictive than flying in Turkey, but the Bardenas-Reales Aerial Gunnery Range near Tudela was superb, with a wide variety of tactical targets (airplanes, buildings, trucks, etc.) as well as standard nuke and conventional range pylons. The range was only about 60 miles from ZAB, but we were restricted to remaining within VR routes in our coming and going; there was no free-play 50-mile circle like there was in Incirlik.

However, the billets were nicer and more modern than they were at Incirlik, and the O'Club was located well within crawling distance, about 40 yards away. Jesus and Maria tended bar at the O'Club, serving the best sangria and Bloody Marys I have sampled to date. Jesus kept his homemade elixirs in plastic jugs, and he refused to divulge the recipes. With numerous deployments to ZAB in my time at Hahn, I always returned home thinking I had figured out the secret, "It's gotta be lemon juice!" But in all my attempts, I never made sangria or Bloody Marys anywhere equal to those at the O'Club at ZAB.

One of the traditions for any fighter squadron deploying to Zaragoza was a Saturday evening excursion to Los Tubos, or The Tubes. The Tubes was a long, cramped alley in downtown Zaragoza lined with tapas bars that provided a vast variety of food and drink. Each bar had its specialty; fried garlic and onions, scotch and cigars, squid in its own ink, the coldest beer in town, the Tinto-in-the-bota-bag, the famous Bar Texas, etc.

Still being the rookie, I was unaware of the initiation required for a first-time visit to The Tubes, with each fighter squadron probably having its own individual ceremony. For us, it was downing shots of Ponche Cabellero at each tapas stop. Ponche was a Spanish orange brandy, also known as Silver Bullet, because of the bottle, which looked like a cross between a gaudy Christmas ornament and a B-61 nuclear bomb. At our first stop in The Tubes, the calls for Ponche ensued for the FNGs. I'd never been a big drinker, so when the shot was thrust at me, I muttered, "I ain't drinkin' no Ponche!"

Hugo overheard me and yelled, "Oh, yes, you are!"

So, as demanded, I hammered it down. It was horrible—and unfortunately for me, many times repeated as we staggered our way down the assorted tapas bars in The Tubes.

At one stop in The Tubes, the tapas bar offered what looked like a just-out-of-its-shell baby bird soaking in vinegar and olive oil, more akin to what I had heard about the delicacies in the Philippines than in Spain. Thankfully, one of the other FNGs was challenged by one of the squadron veterans to, "Chow that bird! Chow that bird!" To his credit, the rookie tried but failed, vomiting the not-nearly-digested baby fowl onto the much-trod-upon concrete floor.

In silence, the vet calmly scooped up the dripping, gooey remains, and to a growing crescendo of encouraging shouts from the gallery said, "Well, I guess you aren't ready to join us yet." He popped it into his mouth and looked the horrified FNG in the eye as he chewed away and swallowed with an audible gulp. Much more challenging than downing a raw egg in its shell, I thought at the time.

Downtown Zaragoza was a wonderful surprise. I guess I was expecting Spain to be like the border towns in Mexico for some illogical reason, perhaps reinforced by the large flocks of sheep running freely on base, and the bullfighter kitsch available at the gift store next to the BX. But Zaragoza was more like Rome or Paris than it was Juarez or Nogales. Beautiful old Euro-classical buildings and cathedrals, mixed with modern shopping centers, museums, parks, promenades, all spotless and clean.

Additionally, pound-for-pound, the Spanish people were the most attractive people I had ever seen; both men and women stylishly dressed, with an air of sophistication. I started to have a better appreciation of why so many loved their assignments to Torrejon AB near Madrid.

Another tradition at Zaragoza involved the F-86 static display located near the main gate. Squadrons arriving for their WTDs typically put their squadron zaps, or decals, on the cockpit glass of the F-86. This took some doing. Since it was elevated off the ground by quite a few feet, it took real team effort to hoist someone high enough to zap the cockpit without being caught by the Security Police. Accordingly, it was a major hassle for base clean-up crews to remove the zaps. During our orientation briefing on our initial arrival, we were warned that zapping the static display would be met with serious consequences. Of course, this was a challenge that could not be ignored; we FNGs had it zapped in less than 24 hours.

By this time, I was fully submerged into the fighter pilot culture. The work hard, play hard bordering-on-reckless-or-unlawful reputation the fighter pilot community had—and continues to have to a lesser degree—is mostly built on those times when you are away from your home base and away from the prying eyes of your Wing Commander or spouse.

After the end of a hard week of flying, the lads tended to let off steam at the O'Club on Friday nights. While some of the activities might routinely occur at home at Hahn, they tended to be magnified when we were on a WTD to Incirlik, or especially Zaragoza. Some of the wilder episodes seemed to happen at Zaragoza, perhaps because the O'Club was close enough to the billets to allow for a quick escape if things got out of hand, which they often did—see Appendix: Culture, Customs, and Craziness for some examples.

The weather in Zaragoza wasn't consistently as good as it was in Incirlik, especially in January, so you still had to be on your toes. ZAB was located in a valley, so it wasn't unusual to encounter high surface winds, or in the absence of wind, pea-soup-thick fog. Weather recalls for wind or fog were not uncommon, and the Spanish air traffic controllers had little concern for a pilot declaration of minimum fuel, meaning that if there were continued further delays for clearance to begin an instrument approach to land, an emergency declaration might result. With everyone airborne simultaneously trying to get home, the Spanish controllers would direct you to a holding fix and seemingly forget about you, "You hold, I call you back! You no like it, you go to Torrejon!" As a result, we put more than a few jets in Torrejon during mass weather recalls.

We flew a more aggressive schedule in Zaragoza than we did in Incirlik, probably because the range was so much closer to the base, and we were one unrefueled hop away from returning to Hahn if a jet needed extensive maintenance. The 496th was a 24 PAA (Primary Assigned Aircraft) squadron, as were most fighter squadrons in the Air Force, and deploying with 18 jets allowed us to do a lot of flying.

We tended to fly a three-go day, 14 x 14 x 12, with the first two goes flown by the same pilots. The schedule allowed for two spare jets and two for routine hangar maintenance. Often we would hot pit refuel after landing and prior to engine shutdown, meaning we would refuel with the engine running, allowing the maintenance crews to more quickly turn the aircraft and prepare it for the next launch.

On Wednesdays, we would surge to a 14 x 14 x 12 x 10, generally as a hot pit-and-go, meaning we would land from the first mission, refuel via the hot pits, and immediately takeoff again for the second mission. We then spent the afternoon debriefing both missions and preparing for the next day while other pilots flew the two afternoon goes.

Every mission was a dedicated upgrade of some kind; new instructor checkout, flight lead upgrade, annual instrument or mission evaluation, or DOC certification in SAT or ACT for new guys like me. I was breezed through the program without any problems and returned to Hahn as a fully certified wingman.

About a week before we were scheduled to fly back home, Wendy and one of the squadron wives boarded a train at Kaiserslautern. They traveled to Madrid for a sightseeing jaunt that included The Rastro open flea market before railing back up to join us for a few days in Zaragoza. We spent a fun reunion weekend in one of the older, elegant hotels downtown. Before heading back home to Germany, the girls dropped off their purchases for us to pack and fly back with us. So, in my travel pod on the flight home to Hahn, I stuffed a disassembled suit of armor, several used priest robes, and an assortment of other Spanish treasures.

G-AWARENESS TRAINING

With the high fatality rates in the F-16 due to G-LOC, the Air Force realized that Viper pilots needed additional training to fly the world's first 9-G jet safely. Shortly after returning from Zaragoza, in March 1985, I was sent to Soesterberg in the Netherlands to NATO's primary test centrifuge to evaluate my ability and tolerance to withstand flight in a high-G environment. This was an entirely new program, but every NATO-based U.S. F-16 pilot was required to participate. I had not been in the Netherlands since living there in 1965, so I looked forward to a return, and of course, took Wendy with me to combine some leave/vacation time in Amsterdam with business.

Centrifuge training, currently conducted at Brooks Air Force City-Base in San Antonio, is today required of every U.S. fighter pilot-designee. However, in the mid-Eighties, it was only scheduled for F-16 pilots, and the pass/fail criteria was to stay conscious for at least 10 seconds in a 9-G sustained environment. This is much harder than it sounds. When you are in a dogfight in the air, the 9-G duration is generally only about

3-4 seconds maximum; this allows you to recover from the pain and physical exertion resulting from the G-forces, and to evaluate how your maneuver has impacted your adversary. The centrifuge is rather humorously depicted in the James Bond movie *Moonraker*, where Bond, preparing for space flight, is subjected to increasingly higher-G forces by a villain in the centrifuge control booth. Bond was shaken, not stirred—what a wimp!—but heck, this was our playground, and I thought it would be a simple walk in the park. Wrong.

When we arrived at the centrifuge center, we were given a cursory physical exam to ensure we were up for the test, then briefed on the procedure. The cockpit was configured similarly to an F-16, and you would indeed have control of the centrifuge in that you had to actually yank back on the stick to continue the acceleration sequence; that way, if you lost consciousness, the centrifuge would automatically shut down.

However, the sequence itself was going to be an unexpected challenge. It wouldn't be a simple ramp up to 9-Gs, decelerate, and call it a day. Oh, no! The program consisted of a slow build to 4-5 Gs—pause—then a continued increase to 9 Gs—then a deceleration back to 6-7 Gs—pause—then a return to 9 Gs, and finally ending with a slow deceleration to conclude the test. As a result, we would be under sustained heavy G-forces for about 30 seconds—again, something that most likely would never actually happen in a dogfight. It would be a real test of our physical endurance, and Wendy would get to watch the entire event.

We were given some academics on physiology and anti-G straining-maneuver techniques, followed by a video showing guys who had passed out during the centrifuge test; our own tests would be videotaped. It was sobering to see the eyes roll to the back of the head, the slumping over, then the thrashing and convulsions when the centrifuge stopped, and the individual regained consciousness. What was most interesting was the disorientation even after regaining consciousness; most of the pilots didn't even realize they had passed out, and many had a hard time even knowing where they were at first. It did much to explain why we had lost so many guys to G-LOC. Even if you regained consciousness, you might still ride it in due to massive disorientation. Another touch-and-go on Reality Runway.

Four of us would be tested, and as usual, I volunteered to go first. To get to the centrifuge, you had to walk down a flight of steel stairs, at the base of which was a leather recliner, "Strange place for a recliner," I thought to myself. I strapped in, got a final briefing in my headset from the evaluator in the control booth, and off we went.

What followed was perhaps the longest 30 seconds of my life. I was doing fine, getting on top of the Gs as they increased, getting to the 4-5 G pause, doing my anti-G straining maneuver, listening to the evaluator coach prep me as we increased to 9 Gs. I really bore down on it then, doing fine, everything under control, then came the gradual decrease back to 6-7 Gs. That's where I ran out of gas.

Thirty seconds may not seem like a long time to you, so try this simple exercise. Right where you are, bear down and tense up every muscle in your body—toes, legs, butt, stomach, arms, hands, chest, neck—as hard as you can. Harder! That's right! See what I mean? Thirty seconds is a long time under that kind of physical stress, eh?

So as we began the ramp up back to 9-Gs, I had nothing left. I tensed my legs as much as I could, but I was out of breath, out of stamina, and simply rode on panting and gasping for air as we started the acceleration back up to 9-Gs with the evaluator screaming in my headset, "Get on it! Don't let up!"

As we hit 9-Gs again, I felt my vision start tunneling and turning grey on the periphery, but I hung in there. Finally, I felt the centrifuge begin its final deceleration and heard the evaluator say, "Stay on it. Almost done. Good job."

I had passed, and I had not passed out.

When we came to a halt, a member of the staff hurried down the stairs, helped me unstrap, and assisted me in getting out of the cockpit. My legs were like rubber, and I couldn't have made it out without his assistance. As I stumbled over to the stairs, I realized the purpose of the leather recliner. I wasn't going to make it back up the stairs anytime soon, so I flopped down in the recliner and tried to recover.

After a few minutes, I felt Wendy beside me. "Wow!" she laughed. "Now I know what you are going to look like as an old man!" She helped me up the stairs, and the team played back the video of my test.

As we hit 9-Gs, it looked like my face had turned to putty, eyelids sagging, jowls drooping—it really did look like I had aged 50 years. Sort of like I look like now.

We spent a fun few days in Amsterdam, doing all the touristy-things and visiting some of the places we had both seen as kids. We took a side trip one day to the small village I had lived in when I was nine, then called Hamersveld, now called Leusden. We drove to the house we had lived in back then, and I posed for a few photos in front to send back to Mom and Dad.

While Wendy happily snapped away, a man came storming out of the house, yelling at us in Dutch and angrily waving his hands at us. I was stunned to recognize our old landlord. I quickly apologized, explained who I was, when we had lived in the house, and why we were taking pictures. His demeanor changed immediately; he apologized in return and told us he thought we were lawyers representing his recently-divorced wife. He claimed not to remember my parents or me as he rented the house to a rotating number of American servicemen and their families over the years. Still, he kindly invited us into the house for coffee and cake. The house had changed drastically, having been remodeled several times, but it was an enjoyable trip down memory lane.

SAFETY SCHOOL

Now that I was a fully-certified wingman, it was time for me to be assigned my primary additional duty. Many people think that all pilots do is fly. Not so. There is a myriad of duties and responsibilities that must be fulfilled when you are not in the air or planning for it. A partial list includes scheduling, weapons and tactics, flight commander, assistant operations officer, or even Squadron Snacko—the highly-demanding job of keeping the squadron snack bar, coffee pot, and beer kegs stocked.

Immediately I was assigned the role of Assistant Squadron Safety Officer, which required little effort on my part since I was merely the assistant. I had been the Squadron Safety Officer for my squadron at Sheppard, so I was familiar with the responsibilities; conducting spot checks for ground and weapons safety, conducting weekly flying safety briefings, and keeping the squadron safety bulletin board up to speed.

Shortly after our return from Amsterdam, I was informed that I would be attending the Aircraft Accident Investigation (AAI)) course, conducted by the University of Southern California, at Norton AFB, which started at the end of April. The course was hosted by the Air Force Inspection and Safety Center at Norton, and would take a full eight weeks.

I wasn't excited at all about being separated from Wendy and flying for two months, but a flying wing always needs at least two or three AAI-trained officers so they can fulfill roles as Mishap Investigation Officers in the case of an aircraft mishap involving one of the Wing's jets. Most wings wanted their AAI-graduated safety officers to have some previous flying experience, so as a FAIP and former squadron safety officer, I was a natural choice. I resigned myself to the gig and tried to look on the bright side.

Norton AFB was located near San Bernadino, and served primarily as a MAC base, flying C-141s. There were about 30 students in the class, larger than I had imagined. Of those thirty, there were only four fighter pilots, one who flew F-16s with the Air National Guard, one F-111 driver, and one Saudi pilot who flew F-15s.

We naturally gravitated to each other and spent the next two months in each other's company. The Saudi pilot was one of the many princes in the Saudi Royal Family; unlike the rest of us who stayed in the VOQ, he had a luxury apartment off base with a butler, chef, and bodyguard. He was a nice friend to have, and we spent a lot of time at the Norton Officers Club after classes debating the obvious superiority of the F-16 with him.

The course itself was no cakewalk. There were tests after each module, and yes, you could fail the course and be sent home in disgrace. Studies included Aerodynamics, Metallurgy, Human Factors, Biomedical Issues, Field Investigation

Techniques and Procedures, Media Relations, Technical Assistance, Analysis & Reports, and other related areas. Since I, for the most part, was stranded on base without a car, I didn't have much else to do but study, and so I passed all the tests fairly easily.

Weekends were often boring, so I generally teamed up with the other F-16 pilot to hire a Rent-A-Wreck and explore Los Angeles. We had a great time; a day in Disneyland, a Highland Games Festival at the Rose Bowl, viewing the grand opening of the James Bond film *View To A Kill* in Grauman's Chinese Theater—heck, we even went to see *Cats* performed at the Los Angeles Theater. I also got to meet up with one of my best friends from high school, the bass player from Uhuru, now serving in the Navy, and his future wife. Nevertheless, I was itching to get back to Germany, Wendy, and the cockpit.

Meanwhile, Wendy was having a wonderful time in my absence. Her mother came to visit for a few weeks, and they traveled Europe together, revisiting many of the places they had seen when they lived in Wiesbaden ten years earlier. After her mother departed, Wendy flew to London to visit one of her friends from college who was working for Reuters. In addition to experiencing the gorgeous German spring weather, she managed to survive just fine without me for those two months.

This pattern became part of our routine; whenever I would be sent TDY, Wendy would take advantage of being in Europe and go touring with friends, family, or the other squadron wives. In my absence, she visited Prague, Vienna, Istanbul, Dubrovnik, Budapest, Berlin, Munich, Paris, and other locations that always made an assignment to Europe so unique. However, I wasn't always pleased with her carefree traveling ways.

Once, on a trip to a nearby sauna with the squadron wives, they were all in the pool, taking advantage of the natural hot springs. In typical European fashion, they were all au natural, naked co-ed saunas being no big deal for most Europeans. Wendy got out of the hot sauna and stepped into a shower stall by the pool.

Much to her surprise, a slightly older stark naked man jumped into the shower stall with her. He took the shower nozzle from her, and in German carefully explained to her that she had to be cautious transitioning from the hot sauna water to the cool shower; she might have a heart attack!

He demonstrated on himself how to use the showerhead to prevent such a calamity. Then, to make sure Wendy understood, he very gently—and with great attention to detail—hosed her down, grabbing her arms and slowly spraying her from hand to shoulder, turning her around, spraying her even slower from foot to butt, making soothing remarks all the way. Wendy was too shocked to say anything, so she just stood there and let him administer his much-too-kind assistance.

The squadron wives watched the whole episode and nearly had heart attacks themselves from suppressed laughter. I had to establish a new rule whereby there would be no more naked co-ed saunas unless I was present.

Within a few days of my return to Hahn from AAI, the squadron held a big 4th of July party at the local castle, Reichsburg Cochem, on the Mosel River. It's a gorgeous, picturesque town, with the castle on a hill overlooking the river—one of our favorite locations in all of Germany. The event was a medieval dinner with jugglers, musicians, and costumed wait staff.

Part of the event was a competition to see who would be worthy of becoming a knight, Ritter, of the castle. Having been absent for two months, I was almost an FNG again, so the squadron commander selected one of our old, crusty majors and me to compete for the honor of being knighted by the Queen— the squadron commander's wife. Both the major and I suspected this was an opportunity for much humiliation for the entertainment of the crowd, but we didn't have much choice.

The first contest involved serenading the Queen with a love song. I was first up. Luckily, Wendy and I had been listening to a Joan Jett cassette in the car on the way there, so I leeringly sang "Do You Wanna Touch Me" and threw in a few gigolo dance moves for good measure. The major declined to follow that act, so I won the round.

The second contest challenged us to see who could saw through a foot-thick wooden log the quickest with a two-handed crosscut saw. The major was an old southern country boy; he cut through that log like it was butter, and I lost the round big-time.

The final event was a beer chugging contest, a stein of beer for me, and for the non-drinking major, a stein of cola. It wasn't much of a challenge; I downed my beer quickly and won the contest.

Kneeling before the Queen, the commander's wife knighted me by pouring a goblet of wine over my head—must have been the song. I got a nifty certificate as an official Ritter of Reichsburg Cochem, but more than that, I felt warmly welcomed back by my squadron mates.

Towards the end of July, only a few weeks after I returned from the Aircraft Accident Investigation course, one of our guys had just initiated afterburner for takeoff when the whole jet exploded, right there on the runway. He ejected immediately, and luckily, wasn't sucked back into the fireball.

Within a few hours, I was named the Interim Mishap Investigation Officer. My primary role was to preserve and document evidence to be used by the formal Class A Mishap Investigation Board that would be appointed and arriving at Hahn within a couple of days. We closed the runway for about 36 hours while most of the other squadron safety officers and I photographed and charted pieces of the wreckage until we felt there was enough material for the Mishap Board to conduct their investigation. I was only involved with the process for about a week, but it was an early indicator of how being AAI-trained would impact the rest of my Air Force career.

UPGRADES

In mid-September, after having been at Hahn for a year, minus the two months stateside for AAI, I entered the flight lead upgrade program. Over the course of a fighter pilot's career, everyone begins life as a wingman. As your skill level progresses, you sequentially upgrade to 2-ship Flight Lead, 4-ship Flight Lead, Instructor (IP), Standardization-Evaluation Flight Examiner (SEFE), then finally, large-force (12 jets or more) Mission Commander.

Each program has a specific syllabus and a set number of scheduled rides, followed by a final checkride usually given in-house by the Squadron Commander, Operations Officer, or Squadron Weapons Instructor, a graduate of the extremely demanding Air Force Fighter Weapons Instructor Course at Nellis AFB.

The 2-ship Flight Lead program was pretty simple; only four rides consisting of Surface Attack (SA) to a controlled range, Surface Attack Tactics (SAT) off-range, a day or night intercept mission, and a Basic Fighter Maneuvers (BFM) sortie. The final checkride could be any one of those four. Upgrading someone to 2-ship Flight Lead allowed you to take baby steps as you later approached becoming a full-up 4-ship Flight Lead, and provided the squadron scheduling shop more flexibility. You could be #3 in a 4-ship mission, and you could lead simple 2-ship sorties on those rare occasions when the schedule allowed. Finally, it allowed the squadron leadership to see what you were made of. Were you going to be a good flight lead or just an average one? My upgrade coincided with our annual Fall WTD to Incirlik.

The flying part of the 2-ship upgrade was not overly challenging. Most flight leads and instructors routinely allowed their wingmen opportunities to lead portions of a flight, usually during the return-to-base and landing phase, so leading in the air was something not wholly unfamiliar. The real focus in this first test of your abilities as a flight lead was in the briefing and debriefing—an activity that tended to separate the men from the boys.

As wingmen, we observed that the best flight leads also tended to be the ones with the best briefing and debriefing skills. You could usually tell how well a flight was going to go by the quality of the pre-flight brief. Does this guy know what he's doing? Is he confident? Is he applying a realistic tactical scenario to the mission? Does he truly understand the specific Rules of Engagement (ROE)? Does he provide adequate guidance? Has he considered all of the possible contingencies? The same applied to the debrief; how good was this guy's situation awareness? Did he note all the mistakes? How good were his drawing skills on the whiteboard? Was he honest with himself?

I breezed through the 2-ship program quickly, concluding with a checkride from the squadron commander, Razor, who was on his last WTD before turning the squadron over to the operations officer, Hugo. My pre-flight briefings and inflight performance tended to be strong, but my debriefs were mediocre, especially the BFM debrief.

Utilizing the inflight video recording helped, but I would sometimes develop amnesia when trying to illustrate all of the twists and turns of an average F-16 dogfight. My artistic skills on the whiteboard also needed work; I tended to draw the engagements too small, not always to scale, and my turn circle depictions were sloppy. "Draw with your whole arm, not just with your hand attached to your wrist!" one IP told me.

I bought a miniature whiteboard when I returned to Hahn, and practiced drawing turn circle entries and the standard symbols for depicting the vertical maneuvers and extensions of a standard dogfight until they improved.

I also developed the habit inflight, just before the fight's on call, of writing down the basic heading and what side the offensive jet was on prior to the first break turn. Immediately after the knock it off call, I would write down the swirl sequence—left break, left turn, reverse right, guns—to better help reconstruct the engagement during the debrief.

Throughout my career, I was never great at BFM debriefs, but with a lot of practice, they eventually became fairly decent. I came to believe that being good at air-to-ground was largely procedural—something you could study, learn, and commit as a process to a successful outcome, while much of air-to-air was purely instinctual. Air-to-Air was an art; Air-to-Ground was a science. I had to work hard at both.

One of the best things about becoming a flight lead was that you finally got to have your own call sign, and a squadron-assigned inflight call sign is usually different than the nickname you may earn at a Nameage ceremony—see Appendix: Culture, Customs, and Craziness. In USAFE, each squadron was assigned a set number of call signs it could use inflight, and to add or subtract to the list took an act of God.

After you became a flight lead, you had to select a call sign from the list that was remaining at that time. When a pilot left the squadron, his call sign would be added back to the list of availables. I didn't have much to choose from, but Orca was on the list. How cool, I thought. Orca—like a killer whale—means Bringer of Death in Latin. They hunt in packs. Yes!

So, I became Orca for flying purposes, and I took to somewhat pretentiously writing ORCA - BRINGER OF DEATH on the whiteboard for my pre-flight briefings.

I soon learned that taking the Orca call sign resulted in some unintended consequences. For some reason, Orca was difficult for German flight controllers to pronounce, but they could say Okra without any problem.

I tried to correct them. "ORCA," I would transmit with authority.

"OKRA" they would repeat.

"ORCA!!" I would shout.

"OKRA!" they would reply.

After a while, I was pretty sure the flight controllers were putting me on. What was worse, after I had finished putting up my pre-briefing whiteboard, someone invariably would sneak in, erase ORCA - BRINGER OF DEATH, and write OKRA - BRINGER OF SLIMY GREEN VEGETABLES or something of that nature. It was a joke that continued for the nearly three years I had left at Hahn. So, so funny. Sigh.

We spent that Christmas of 1985 in Kenya. Along with two other couples from the squadron, we booked ten days in Mombasa, staying at a hotel on the beach, followed by a photo safari in the Masai Mara. Everything was arranged by the African Safari Club, a German vacation charter group.

While we enjoyed the sunny beaches of Mombasa after several months in the foggy Hunsrück gloom, the highlight was our time in the Masai Mara, camping out by a river, eating our gourmet-picnic meals, and getting the opportunity to see lions, elephants, rhinos, water buffalo, hippos, and the entire host of animals in their natural habitat.

One evening, sitting around a fire after dinner, we were conversing with several of the Germans who were also on the trip when I spied a guitar supplied by the Safari Club, typically brought out for just such occasions. I started playing some blues, and one of the ladies asked if I knew any country and western songs. Ha! Little did she know my parents raised me on country, so I played a few oldies that, surprisingly, many of the Germans knew quite well and were able to sing along. Suddenly, a young Masai breathlessly came running up, carrying a djembe drum.

"Sir! I am very much liking the songs of Kenny Rogers and Charlie Pride!" He sat himself down beside me, put the drum between his legs, and looked at me with expectation.

So, I started strumming and singing softly, "On a warm summer's evening, on a train bound for nowhere..."

The kid started banging his djembe and loudly took up the song, "I met up with a gambler; we were both too tired to sleep..." His voice was barely in tune and heavily accented, but so beautiful. His eyes closed, he passionately sang with everything he had. He was one of the guards that protected us from animal incursions at night, and we spent the next few hours singing all the Kenny Rogers and Charley Pride songs I knew. I will never forget jamming with a young Masai warrior by firelight under the huge starry skies of the African plains.

When we returned to Zaragoza in January 1986, I successfully completed the 4-ship Flight Lead program. Being a 4-ship Flight Lead was a bigger deal; you could lead all the missions for which the squadron was tasked, and 4-ship Flight Leads are the essential bread-and-butter of fighter squadron operations. My skills as a fighter pilot continued to improve, and I was enjoying everything about the lifestyle. However, somebody somewhere decided to make me one of two squadron AGTS-tow pilots for the Aerial Gunnery Target System (AGTS).

The AGTS was relatively new to the fighter force in 1986. Instead of a DART towed by an F-86, as we had used at Luke AFB during RTU, the AGTS was attached to a pod under the wing of the F-16. You could take off with the AGTS pod, fly to the operating area, then deploy the AGTS. It would extend out from the wing on a cable about 1,500 feet long, and functioned just like the DART, except that the target looked more like a giant fishing lure than a large aluminum arrowhead. The other difference was that instead of requiring an IP to fly alongside the DART after a hot pass to count the holes in the target to assess whether or not you had got any hits on it, the AGTS was equipped with an acoustic scoring system. It would provide real-time results on the number of hits on a digital panel attached to the console on the rear right side of the cockpit.

After the conclusion of the live-fire event, you would then fly back to home base, and release the cable onto the infield of the runway, allowing maintenance crews to retrieve the AGTS target and reload it on the pod again for another mission.

Later AGTS systems allowed you to reel the cable and target back in while airborne, but in those days, you had to fly all the way back to base with the cable and target trailing behind you and cut the cable just prior to landing. Somehow, someone convinced me that being an AGTS-tow pilot and allowing my squadron mates to shoot live 20MM rounds just off my tail was a good idea. I agreed to the checkout.

We used one of the dual-seated B-models as our AGTS-tow jet, so on my familiarization ride, I sat in the back, watched, and listened. Our live-fire working area was over the Mediterranean Sea just off the coast of Valencia, so it was a fairly long trek, about 200 miles. As a result, unless we had a KC-135 available for inflight refueling, which we did for several days, fuel conservation was an issue, especially with the drag the AGTS target imposed on the jet as you flew the long-ish distance back home with it trailing behind you. The four shooters didn't have much time to setup, sequence in, and sequence out before we had reached bingo fuel and had to return to ZAB.

I learned that the biggest challenge was continuing a steady, right descending 4-G spiral and sustained airspeed to allow the shooters a stable platform for their passes. I took to placing my left hand under my chin to give my neck some support for the relentless Gs; 4-Gs isn't very much initially, but after several passes, it could be tiring. As you made your way back home, the four shooters would fly a loose trail behind you to monitor the AGTS target. The most fun was cutting the cable over the infield, and trying to precisely place the target only a few feet from the maintenance truck and crew there waiting to retrieve it.

During my first mission as an AGTS-tow, we had just completed the first pass, and the second shooter was cleared to engage. I was maintaining my 4-G spiral and glancing down at the digital acoustic scorer when I saw it register hits. "Cease fire!" I announced on the radio and started to transmit the number of hits.

"Er, Orca, I haven't fired yet," came the response. We learned that based on the winds aloft, you could sometimes get false readings from the scoring mechanism. It caused some occasional delays but didn't prove to be too much of a problem in the long run. The goal was to cycle the entire squadron through aerial gunnery qualification, and with us two AGTS pilots flying one sortie per day each, we were able to finish in about five days. Not my favorite thing to do, but it was a unique experience.

FERRY FLIGHT

A few months after returning from our annual January WTD to Zaragoza, the 496th began shuffling us back to Luke AFB for training as Hahn transitioned to the new F-16C/D. There had been upgrades to the F-16A/B through the Block 20 versions, but these were primarily cockpit and avionics improvements to our A/Bs already on station. However, the F-16C/D was an entirely new jet.

The new C/D introduced substantial improvements in cockpit avionics, including improved fire control and stores management computers, an Up-Front Controls (UFC) integrated data control panel, Multifunction Displays (MFD), radar altimeter options, and many other changes. One of the biggest improvements was the addition of Data-Transfer Equipment (DTE), which allowed you to input all of your now-computerized mission planning data onto Data Transfer Cartridges (DTC) instead of having to manually type the data onto the Fire Control Navigation Panel (FCNP).

Now, after starting the jet, you could simply activate the DTC and relax instead of frantically having to manually type in all of your mission planning data prior to the designated taxi time. They were also equipped with General Electric engines, which we all considered superior to the Pratt-and-Whitney engines.

We were all excited to make the transition to the newest improved jet in the Air Force.

The changes were significant enough to require a specific transition training program back at Luke, so off we went in the middle of March. The checkout was scheduled for about two weeks. In addition to academics classes and a few simulator rides, there was a six-ride familiarization syllabus consisting of basic instruments and patterns, air-to-air (intercepts and BFM), and air-to-ground (both controlled and uncontrolled tactical ranges).

Many of us had gone through RTU at Luke, so it was a homecoming of sorts. The first event we engineered was a trip to La Perla's restaurant on Glendale Avenue for some genuine Mexican food, something we sorely missed back in Germany. Sadly, La Perla's has since closed, but for many years, it was my favorite Mexican restaurant on the planet.

One of the requirements, of course, in transitioning to the C/D models was to ferry our A/Bs back stateside and fly the new-off-the-assembly-line C/Ds back to Hahn.

Only a couple of weeks after completing the upgrade program at Luke, a group of us flew commercially to the General Dynamics plant at Carswell AFB in Fort Worth to ferry eight jets to their new homes in Germany. This would be an entirely new experience for me; a flight estimated to endure approximately ten hours, numerous air-to-air rendezvous and refuelings, my first real use of go/no-go pills, my first time wearing a poopy suit—an airtight, form-fitting, waterproof anti-exposure flight suit to temporarily protect you from the icy waters of the North Atlantic in case you had to bail out—and, for me, at least, the inevitable first-time use of the piddle pack.

The piddle-pack was a heavy, funnel-shaped vinyl bag about four inches by ten inches. Inside the bag was a compressed dry sponge; it looked like thin cardboard when dry, but would expand to full size when immersed in bodily fluids. After you were done, you twisted the open-end closed and clamped it shut with heavy plastic twist ties. Crew chiefs called it the lemon sandwich, and wisely would not touch it while helping the pilot retrieve all of the mission materials after a flight.

Most of us always had a piddle pack in our helmet bags in the cockpit in case nature called, but I had not had to use one at this point in my career. After 6+ years of flying, my bladder had trained itself to a mission duration of 1.3 to 1.7 hours, so this was going to be an entirely different experience.

My Aunt Vicki and her husband Robert lived in Dallas, and we arranged to meet up at our hotel located near General Dynamics. As I was walking through the foyer to meet them, I was flabbergasted to see my Mom and Dad, my Uncle Lloyd, and a cousin there as well. They had set up a little surprise reunion, and since I hadn't seen my parents in nearly two years, it was an added bonus to the trip. I was the swaggering, steely-eyed killer fighter pilot son and nephew now, and we had a great evening together telling stories and a few tall tales.

Since crew rest waivers were required for the trip, we had to ensure that we landed in daylight back in Germany, so the first few hours of the journey would be at night, as well as our first tanker rejoin and refueling. Our route would take us from Dallas to Charleston, up the East Coast all the way to Newfoundland, crossing the ocean before hitting landfall over Ireland, then England, and then on into Hahn.

Everything was going great; the sunrise was spectacular, the guys were all loose and having fun with plenty of radio chatter, nibbling away at our high-protein box lunches, standard bets with anyone falling off the boom during refueling, just a thoroughly enjoyable flight. Then nature finally called.

Let me explain the physiological challenge of employing a piddle-pack in the relatively confined spaces of an F-16 cockpit. First off, as discussed earlier, the smallish F-16 cockpit tends to fit you like a glove, so there is not a lot of room to maneuver in the best of circumstances. You are also in a 30-degree reclined seat, so everything is pointed uphill, if you get my drift. To further complicate matters, the poopy suit is an added layer of zippers and materiel one must circumnavigate to eventually gain access to the problem at hand, so to speak.

To successfully accomplish the maneuver, intense and precise prior planning is required—"Prior Planning Prevents Piss Poor Performance," as they say. To complete the sequence, one had first to inform the members of the flight that he was conducting Operation Race Horse, so they knew that said pilot would be temporarily limited in aircraft mobility, the real use of the auto-pilot function in The Viper.

Then, said pilot would have to unstrap the seat belt (yikes!), carefully reposition his feet around the rudder pedals, and raise the seat to its highest level to allow a downhill flow into the piddle pack (are you still with me?) At that point, the unzipping and maneuvering of numerous layers of flight suit, poopy suit, and under-garments would commence. Finally, one would grab the piddle pack and complete the task, in which, if you had failed to complete any of the above actions, it was far too late to try and interrupt the sequence, as we all understand.

Sadly, one of the gibes at the F-16 community is that we have lost two jets, to my knowledge, at least, with pilots in the process of completing Operation Race Horse. With the F-16 control stick on the right side of the ejection seat, if you were not careful after you unstrapped and began to raise your seat, the right seat buckle could get jammed between the seat and the control stick, sending the jet into a continuous right aileron roll. Can you imagine? You are not strapped in, you are unzipped and potentially already in the process, and you begin an uncontrollable right aileron roll with urine floating everywhere to further distract you as you flail around the cockpit. Happily, both pilots successfully ejected and survived, but we lost two jets and gained a warning in the Dash 1.

Bottom line, using the piddle pack in the air in an F-16 was an activity not to be taken lightly. I was mildly intimidated.

So anyway, I inform the boys that I'm conducting a Racehorse operation and carry out the steps as described. Everything is going great until the actual urination sequence; I had put it off as long as possible, so I really had to go badly. Once I started piddling, I found, to my horror, that the piddle pack has a smaller funnel within the overall pack—for which purpose I still don't understand—about two inches into the bag, with drain holes on each side. This creates an overflow situation if you are not careful; I later learned that you need to basically separate the smaller funnel apart with your fingers first to allow for a full free-flow later. This is pretty dang complicated, eh? Well, due to my first-time ignorance, I didn't do that and had a case of overflow *in extremis*. In other words, I pee'd myself. Not badly, but enough to have that wonderful urine-soaked feeling all the way across the Atlantic. Lesson learned. Live to fight another day.

TACTICAL LEADERSHIP PROGRAM (TLP)
While we were in Fort Worth preparing for the ferry flight, the squadron commander informed us that our squadron had been selected to fulfill two slots for the Allied Air Forces Central Europe (AAFCE) Tactical Leadership Program, or TLP, for the May '86 course. AAFCE-TLP had been created in 1979 out of a desire for Euro-NATO Central Region Air Forces to, "...develop and improve tactics, techniques, and procedures which would enhance multinational interoperability in tactical air operations."

Participants at this stage were primarily the U.S., Britain, Netherlands, Germany, Denmark, and Belgium. The TLP flying course was located at Jever Air Base in Northern Germany, typically had between 14 and 18 jets/crews enrolled for each course, and the month-long curriculum consisted of 15 large package missions. Attendees were specifically designated in the air-to-ground or air defense role. TLP was AAFCE's version of the USAF Fighter Weapons School on a much-reduced scale, but graduates were entitled to wear a coveted TLP patch. Hahn generally had only two TLP slots annually, and the 496th hadn't had a slot in a few years. I was genuinely surprised when I was informed that I was going to be one of the two lucky guys selected to attend the course.

The other guy selected to attend TLP with me was Packer, one of my best friends in the squadron. Packer had been a T-38 FAIP, had arrived in the squadron shortly after I did, and is one of the best fighter pilots I have ever flown with. He later became the USAFE F-16 Demo Pilot and went on to earn 2-Star rank in the Air National Guard.

I admit to being a tad daunted at the prospect of attending the demanding TLP course and representing Hahn's 50th TFW before a multinational audience of fighter pilots. On top of that, we soon learned that we would be flying in the air defense role, which was our tertiary DOC, and not really my forte. There were more than a few guys in the 496th, like Packer, whose flying skills were superior to mine. It was an honor to be chosen, but I knew I had to bring my A-game.

Shortly before we were scheduled to arrive for TLP, the world received news of El Dorado Canyon on April 15th—our airstrikes against Libya and Muammar Gaddafi in retaliation for the West Berlin discotheque terrorist bombing ten days earlier, which killed three people, one a U.S. serviceman, and injured 229 others.

The attack comprised eighteen F-111F strike aircraft of the 48th TFW from RAF Lakenheath, supported by four EF-111A Ravens of the 20th TFW from RAF Upper Heyford, in conjunction with fifteen A-6, A-7, F/A-18 and EA-6B Prowler Electronic Warfare jets from aircraft carriers on station in the Gulf of Sidra.

We were denied overflight rights by France, Spain, and Italy, as well as the use of European continental bases, forcing the Air Force portion of the operation to be flown around France and Spain, over Portugal and through the Straits of Gibraltar, adding 1,300 miles each way and requiring multiple aerial refuelings. The French refusal alone added nearly 1,700 miles to the entire journey.

We lost one F-111 and two airmen in the attack. It once again hammered home the seriousness of our profession and added a touch of animosity and contempt for some of our allies.

Packer and I flew up to Jever on a Friday afternoon, giving ourselves an orientation of the Low Fly 1 area on the way, since we didn't fly that far north very often, and would no doubt fly many of our missions there. A team of crew chiefs and maintainers from the 496th AMU drove up to meet us; they would be deployed for the month just as we were.

We were in our brand-spankin'-new F-16Cs. My jet, tail #310, newly-painted with my name on the side of the canopy, had less than 30 hours of flying time on it, and the cockpit smelled like a brand new car. On top of the large force missions, TLP would also give us an opportunity to experience the new C-Model jet and improved systems—Multi-Target Track!—in a demanding tactical environment.

That evening at the TLP bar, Packer and I got to meet most of the rest of the class. Serving in the air defense role would be us in our F-16Cs armed with AIM-9Ms, two Dutch F-16As from Leeuwarden Air Base armed with AIM-9Ls, and two U.S. F-15Cs from Bitburg armed with AIM-7s and AIM-9Ms. In the air-to-ground role were the crews of two U.S. F-4G Wild Weasels from Spangdahlem, four German F-4s, and four British Tornados.

Our TLP sorties planned over the next four weeks would consist of this 16-ship package, flying low level missions in Warsaw Pact-type scenarios, against an undetermined number and type of adversaries from other NATO bases throughout Central Europe.

Bragging rights began immediately that night at the TLP bar, with Packer and I becoming good buds with the Weasel guys right away. Packer, who played rugby at the Air Force Academy, and The Flyin' Hawaiian from the Weasel contingent, led the bar in the singing of songs until the wee hours of the morning. At that point in my career, I hadn't a clue that I would later become the commander of an F-16 Wild Weasel squadron, but that would be a few years in the future.

Room and board at Jever was pretty spartan, at least by U.S. standards. We were housed in a German barracks, and while we had our own rooms, the rooms came equipped with only a military-style single cot, a small metal-and-plastic table, and a lamp—that's it. Latrines and showers were open-bay down the hall, and the showers were the push-the-lever-for-ten-seconds-of-water-flow type, so you constantly had to push the shower lever to get a decent shower. The mess hall served simple but hearty German fare and did the job well enough.

For the first time, rather than jogging, I took to running ten forty-yard sprints every morning in an effort to improve my short-burst stamina and G-tolerance.

The daily routine was fairly standard; report to Ops for a mass briefing at 7:30, receive the mission order of the day, mission plan and brief, takeoff around 11:30, fly, land, lunch, assess videotape and debrief within your flight, followed by a mass debrief. The day was generally over by around 4:30, followed by an adjournment to the TLP bar, dinner at the mess hall, and another quick trip to the bar before lights out. Jever

Pils is a well-known beer in Germany and was always available on tap.

Being the first time that I had ever really escorted a large air-to-ground package in the air defense role, I was struck by how little mission planning was required of us. Packer and I had already flown together many times before, and our flight lead/wingman squadron standards eliminated much of the planning and briefing tasks.

In terms of defending the air-to-ground package from other air threats, we really only needed to know where the A-G mission commander wanted us; did he want us flying combat air patrol (CAP) over the target area, did he want us out in front of the package flying sweep, or did he want us embedded within the package itself? Generally, it was some kind of combination of the three. Once that determination was made, it was a simple matter of getting together with our fellow air defenders and making maximum use of the weapons and capabilities on board.

We obviously wanted to take advantage of the F-15s, with their superior radar and AIM-7s, so we generally had them flying higher above the package, searching for threats. At the same time, we F-16s tended to stay low level with the package, since we felt comfortable flying in that regime anyway, being primarily surface attackers ourselves.

One of the fun aspects of TLP was that we never really knew who our dedicated adversaries were going to be. On top of that, given the free-wheeling nature of flying fighters in Central Europe, we might be attacked by any number of fighters simply looking for action and having stumbled upon this large low-level package.

Later, after Packer and I returned to Hahn, if we were on the flying schedule together, we would usually head north in search of a TLP package, just to kick the hornet's nest.

The biggest challenge for us was running out of ammo; we were limited to four AIM-9Ms (simulated) each, and would often bingo out before the package had cleared the designated target area. We Viper Drivers came to envy the everyday lifestyle of our Bitburg F-15 comrades; as air defenders, we would complete our mission planning and be drinking a relaxing third cup of coffee while the air-to-grounders continued frantically planning the route, timing, making maps, devising attacks in the target area, deconflicting etc. We had a blast.

The F-15 pilots and the Dutch F-16 pilots were all majors, so Packer and I were the young whipper-snappers of the bunch, both being captains. The F-15 guys, in particular, carried themselves with an always-serious mature mentality, while Packer and I tended to be loose, joking around, and thoroughly enjoying ourselves. One day, however, that perspective changed.

About halfway through the course, we were observing the F-15s takeoff in front of us as we took the runway. We watched in horror as one of the F-15s attempted an aileron roll shortly after bringing up his landing gear near the departure end. At that still-relatively-slow speed, it looked more like a sloppy barrel roll than an aileron roll, and he almost bottomed out, maybe clearing the earth by about 100 feet.

"P.K., did you see that??!!" Packer exclaimed.

After the mission, that F-15 driver was still white as a ghost. To my knowledge, he wasn't punished for that stunt, but he certainly didn't attempt it again.

The three weekends we spent at Jever were full of activity. On the first weekend, Wendy and Packer's wife drove up on Friday and spent the weekend with us. Jever is just a few miles south of the North Sea coast, and about a two-hour drive west of Hamburg. We rented a hotel for the weekend, did some local sightseeing and shopping, and went dancing at night.

On the second weekend, the TLP staff set up an over-night road trip to Hamburg. We departed on mid-day Saturday, and the bus unceremoniously dropped us off at the Reeperbahn, the infamous entertainment district of Hamburg. We were told that the bus would return at noon on Sunday, and we were on our own.

My main desire was to spend most of the evening in the Star Club, where the Beatles had cut their chops before making it big. Much to my disappointment, the Star Club had long since closed, but there was a memorial plaque outside the building where the Star Club used to be. Packer, the Weasel guys, and I

FIGHTER PILOT

spent the rest of the night stumbling in the cold North German weather from club to club, paying way too much for beer and bar food. As the sun rose, we were happy to find a cafe and spent most of the morning drinking hot chocolate and drowsing until the bus picked us up.

On our last weekend, the TLP staff hosted an all-day Long Bullets or Irish Road Bowling competition. Though the day was drizzly, we warmed ourselves with the flow of libations, required as part of the rules. The evening concluded with a pre-graduation party in the TLP bar, and I think we all needed the entire day Sunday to recover and prepare for the last few missions in the program.

Our last mission at TLP is still remembered as The Battle of Ahlhorn. Our target area was located near the Luftwaffe base at Ahlhorn Air Base, which also served as a Forward Operating Location (FOL) for our A-10s based out of Bentwaters AB in England. Engaged in the target area, we soon learned that our adversaries were four German F-4s—so not only was there a giant swirl of activity, we had to determine who were the friendly German F-4s and who were the bad guys.

At any rate, as the swirl continued, we ended up at near-tree-top level right over the top of Ahlhorn and received a stern warning, "This is Ahlhorn tower on guard. Please vacate our airspace immediately. I repeat..."

However, no one was willing to give up turning room, so the fight continued. After landing, we were mildly chastised, but we all acknowledged it was an outstanding last sortie. We all had a laugh at our Dutch F-16 compadres; they decided on this last mission that they would have belt-fed AIM-9Ls, as they each must have fired off around eight missiles each, and claimed kills on each one.

We ended up flying thirteen TLP sorties, with two missions being weather-canceled. It was an outstanding experience for me and did much to shape my tactical awareness of air warfare in Central Europe against a Warsaw Pact adversary.

The Tactical Leadership Program has since been moved to Albacete Air Base in Spain, where the terrain is more similar to our operations in the Middle East AORs than Northern Germany. TLP has expanded to include all of our Euro-NATO allies, and there are various academic courses included now, in addition to the flying course. It remains one of the premier training opportunities in the Air Force.

R-B-DOUBLE-A-BRAVOS

This summer of '86 also saw the birth of the R-B-Double-A Bravos; "Red-Blooded All American Boys," taken from one of the many songs written by fighter pilot singer Dick Jonas.

Tex, the operations officer and later squadron commander of the 496th, had been a bass singer in church and gospel groups most of his life, and his wife was an outstanding piano player. As a lark, Tex, his wife, and another officer active in the base chapel decided to convert the Dick Jonas version into a gospel barbershop-type song with four-part harmonies, slightly altered to reflect life in the 496th.

Tex then started investigating who within the squadron had any background in singing in church or chorale groups. He ultimately came up with Skull singing baritone, Rev singing lead, and me singing tenor.

What started as strictly a squadron fun-thing-to-do quickly became a demand at most of the 50th Wing functions. As popularity continued to grow, the next two years saw us performing at various military functions, balls, and parties throughout USAFE. We had a list of a mix of patriotic, religious, and comedy songs we typically performed, but by far, the most popular was our version of the Dick Jonas song, "R-B-Double-A-Bravo"

> *Well, I'm an R-B-Double-A-Bravo, and I fly the F-16!*
> *It's better than sex and mom's apple pie,*
> *It's the meanest little jet you've ever seen.*
> *It'll kick the hell out of Fishbeds, Foxbats, Floggers and the F-15*
> *I'm an R-B-Double-A-Bravo, and I fly the F-16.*
>
> *I once trapped at six an F-5 Echo at 17,000 feet*
> *He was loaded down with 20 millimeter and AIM-9*
> *J and Pete*

FIGHTER PILOT

Well, I laid a bat-turn down his throat, and I shot him in his two front teeth
And I heard him shout from the fireball, "Damn it, I just can't stand the heat!"

Well, I've got a friend in Bitburg, and he flies the Eagle Jet
He called me up and said "Come on down - you ain't seen nothin' yet."
So I kicked the tires and lit the fires, and over the Rhine we met
And in 22 seconds he called me up and said he wanted to change the bet.

There's a squadron at Hahn called the 4-9-6 the World's Finest is their name
Flyin' and fightin' and drinkin' and singin' and KILLIN' is their game.
They fly real fast, and they'll kick your ass, and they put them all to shame.
With their deadly skill and their iron will, they'll send them down in flames!

Well, if Ivan ever decides to fight, and I kinda think he'll try,
The 50th's (Wing Commander) will teach those commies how to die (those assholes!)
Us and the Lima and the 'Lectric Jet will more than fit the bill.
We'll chase him down from hell to breakfast and kick his ass for grill.

Well, I'm an R-B-Double-A-Bravo, and I fly the F-16!
It's better than sex and mom's apple pie,
It's the meanest little jet you've ever seen.
It'll kick the hell out of Fishbeds, Foxbats, Floggers, and the F-15 (ptoooey!!)
I'm an R-B-Double-A-Bravo, and I fly the F-16.

We're R-B-Double-A-Bravos, and we fly the F-16 (Hooaah!!)

One extremely early Saturday morning, while we were at Zaragoza for another WTD, I got a knock on my door. It was Tex. "Get your flight suit on NOW. CINC-SAC is in and refueling his jet on the ramp, has heard about the 'R-Bs,' and wants us to come sing for him."

So, the ZAB wing commander met the four of us out front of the VOQ in his sedan and drove us out to the flightline where we boarded the 4-Star commander of Strategic Air Command's personal jet. We walked in, made our introductions, and a colonel brought me a cup of coffee—cream and sugar? What the heck??!! After some small talk, we sang the song. Word had gotten around. We became semi-famous in USAFE, and had a great time spreading the news until new assignments eventually split us up by early 1988.

WING STAFF

At the beginning of that summer of '86, I received some news I had been expecting; I was going to be the Wing Chief of Flying Safety on the wing staff. Every school-trained flying safety officer eventually spends time on the wing staff, so while it was inevitable, I was nevertheless not looking forward to leaving the 496th.

I would still be attached to the squadron for flying purposes, but my office would be at wing headquarters. By this time, Tex had been named the 496th squadron commander, and he assured me it was his plan for me to serve at the wing for only about six months, at which time he would bring me back as a flight commander in the squadron. I was delighted at that prospect; most every captain in a fighter squadron wants to be a flight commander, so I packed up and headed for the wing, trying to remain optimistic.

As it turned out, it wasn't so bad. All of the folks on the Wing Safety staff were top-notch, and my flying schedule wasn't impacted to the degree I feared. I continued flying about as much as I did when I was in the squadron; the only difference was I wasn't spending all of my time in the squadron. Of the three squadrons in the wing, the 496th was the only one located within walking distance of wing headquarters, so my flying duties and staff duties flowed fairly seamlessly. I did all the things Wing Flying Safety officers did—planned and led monthly flying safety meetings, performed inspections, delivered reports to USAFE HQ, wrote articles for safety magazines, etc. Two incidents stand out, however, with my time at the Wing—both including Wendy.

Since I was now on the wing staff and officially designated Mission Support (MS) instead of Mission Ready (MR), I thought this would be a perfect time to have my wisdom teeth removed. They had been bothering me for a while, and since now I didn't have quite as many flying squares to complete as a Mission Support pilot, the time seemed right.

So, there I was, or so I am told, drugged out of my mind, still in the dentist's chair, wisdom teeth having just been removed when the dentist called in Wendy—she'd been loyally standing by in the waiting room so she could drive me home. She walked in, took one look at me as I stared blankly at her and mumbled something inaudible, and she fainted, slowly sliding to the floor as the dentist frantically tried to grab her and ease her down.

After she quickly came to, the first words out of her mouth were, "What did you do, give him a lobotomy??!!" She later explained she had never seen me that way before; lips moving, eyes glazed, and nobody home. Which leads us to our next episode.

Wendy was in London, visiting her best friend from college, Linda, who was now a writer for Reuters. I was going to stay behind for a week, then join them in London for a week of leave.

However, during that time, we lost a jet, though the pilot ejected successfully. I called Linda and asked her to tell Wendy that, unfortunately, I was not going to be able to join them in London, being tasked with the interim Mishap Investigation Board. Linda caught up with her, shopping at Herrod's department store:

Linda: "Wendy! Did you hear about the F-16 crash?"
Wendy: "No....???"

Linda: "Oh, Wendy! I'm so sorry!" At which point, Wendy's knees buckled, and it was her turn to look like she had a lobotomy.

Linda recognized what had happened immediately. "No! No! It's not PK! He's okay. He just can't join us here!"

Military wives, and now Linda, quickly learned how and how NOT to deliver bad news.

FLIGHT COMMANDER

That fall of '86, despite being on the Wing Staff, I was able to travel to Zaragoza with the squadron for an entire month for another WTD. I upgraded to Instructor Pilot (IP) while there, a big step in preparation for my return to the 496th as a flight commander.

As a Company Grade Officer and fighter pilot, being a flight commander in a fighter squadron was the job most everyone hoped to achieve. It's a position that has to be earned, by serving your time successfully in other jobs like scheduling, training, safety, weapons, or making good coffee (don't underestimate the kudos one can get from being a great Snacko), earning respect and trust of your comrades, and perhaps more importantly, proving yourself capable in the air. When it was finally announced in January '87 that I was leaving the Wing Staff and assuming duties as the B Flight Commander, I couldn't have been happier.

As a flight commander, your job is to be responsible for the monitoring, scheduling, and training of the 8-10 squadron pilots assigned to your flight, there generally being four flights per squadron. It's really the first opportunity a fighter pilot has for command; molding the members of your flight into a combat-ready team that is the best they can be, in the air and on the ground. In addition, you are also assigned several senior officers for scheduling and ensuring they get their training squares accomplished; this could be anyone from an Assistant Operations Officer to the Wing Commander.

Filling out the schedule for the next week's training is usually held on a Thursday evening after flying is complete. The schedulers fill out the shell—the number of sorties scheduled for a particular day, the configuration of the jets—air-to-air or air-to-ground—for each launch, what range periods are available, etc. The four flight commanders do their homework, determining which pilot needs what kind of sortie for their upgrades or routine training requirements, and come to the meeting ready to defend their priorities.

These scheduling meetings can be quite contentious while the flight commanders jostle for their flight members' needs, but the process is the heart-and-soul of the daily activity for the squadron. I always looked forward to Thursdays and doing battle with my fellow flight commanders.

Almost immediately after my return to the squadron, I was selected to checkout as a rear-cockpit (RCP) IP. While the F-16's fighting platform is single-seat, most every squadron has a couple of two-seat models, in theory for training purposes, but in reality, they are used to fly flag officers, distinguished visitors, and provide incentive flights to crew chiefs and award winners.

Accordingly, most squadrons only had 2-3 RCP-qualified IPs, since it added on yet another training requirement that had to be tracked and fulfilled. The checkout was no big deal; just a couple of sorties mostly to learn how to land from the backseat with style.

Being an RCP IP was wrought with challenges, however. On many occasions, I was tasked to fly to 17th Air Force at Sembach Air Base or HQ USAFE at Ramstein Air Base to pick up a general officer and ferry him, from the rear cockpit, to wherever he wanted to go. Certainly, the exposure to the handsome and powerful was an opportunity, but it wasn't always fun.

On one of my first flights, I flew to Ramstein to pick up a 3-Star and fly him to Florennes Air Base in Belgium. As I started the pre-flight briefing, he stopped me after a couple of minutes. "PK, I can save us both a lot of time if I do the briefing. I'll start the jet, do all the ground ops, and do all the flying. You do all the radios and radar work; make all the calls, and just tell me what vector to fly or what altitude to be at. Everything else is standard. Questions?"

Well, okay—fair enough, I guess. Things were going fine until our approach into Florennes, on a typical day in Central

Europe with rain and fog down to the ragged minimums. We were shooting an Instrument Landing System (ILS) to landing, and the general up front was having a fairly rough go of it.

"When's the last time you shot an approach to minimums, General?" I jokingly asked.

"About five years," he muttered.

Yikes. Nevertheless, we found the runway at the last second and made a safe landing. After we parked and shut down, a host of senior officers were standing by to meet and greet him.

He hopped out of the jet without a word to me, got in a limo, and sped off, with everyone else in trail. I was left stranded on the flightline in the rain with a couple of non-English speaking Belgian crew chiefs, with no plan on where I was supposed to wait or even what time we were to plan for our return flight. Eventually, a crew truck took pity on me, picked me up, and took me to Ops, where the general showed up a few hours later.

He later became a military-expert commentator for Fox News, but it was one of those times when I didn't really appreciate the upgrade to RCP IP.

On another occasion, I was tasked to fly a 2-Star to Zaragoza for USAFE's first-ever Excalibur competition—a bombing contest that pitted all of USAFE's fighter wings against each other. This particular general was very comfortable in the air, and was a delight to chat with on the way down.

That night at the Zaragoza bar after the competition results were complete, after more than a few libations, he decided he wanted to play Combat Crud with the lads—see Appendix: Culture, Customs, and Craziness. He gamely held his own for a while, until when trying to interfere with a shot he was body-slammed and vaulted into the wall. Everyone rushed to his aid (game over!), but he shook it off with good humor and said his goodnights.

The next morning when I went to pick him up in his room, he was in obvious pain; it looked to me like he had cracked a few ribs, and perhaps a slight hangover wasn't helping. He refused a trip to the infirmary, so off to the flightline we went. He had to be gingerly helped into the cockpit, and I flew the jet back home. After landing, he couldn't get out without the crew chief unbuckling him and lifting him out of the seat. The guy was a trooper, though. Good times!

Nevertheless, my experiences flying in the rear cockpit with generals convinced me that I never wanted to be a general's aid or exec.

The opportunities to excel kept coming. Shortly after I upgraded to RCP IP, the wing designated me as a TAC-EVAL Augmentee. The NATO TAC-EVAL was USAFE's version of an Operational Readiness Inspection, required of every NATO fighter wing in Central Europe every 2-3 years. In order to equip NATO inspectors with enough personnel and weapons systems experts, the team was augmented by several pilots available from each fighter wing to assist in the evaluations. They desired mostly rear-cockpit qualified pilots, so I was basically selected by default.

During my time as an augmentee, I participated in TAC-EVALs for Torrejon Air Base, conducted at Incirlik in Turkey, Leeuwarden Air Base in the Netherlands, and Bierset Air Base in Belgium. It was a good experience, as it provided a first-hand view of how different wings from different nations conducted their combat operations. As we all suspected, the non-US NATO wings were definitely held to a different standard (lower) than the US wings. To be fair, U.S. fighter wings like Torrejon, Hahn, and a few other US bases had nuclear commitments, so obviously, the standards had to be extremely high; however, one got the distinct impression that the non-US NATO bases just didn't take their combat roles quite as seriously as the US bases.

For example, while conducting the inspection at Leeuwarden, an exercise ALARM RED sounded, which required all personnel to take cover immediately and don their chem masks. I ducked into a bunker and found two young guys, hair down to their shoulders in true Netherlands style, talking on the radios with their hands over their mouths so it sounded like they had their chem masks on, which they certainly did not. When they saw me, they just giggled nervously and continued the charade, apparently not concerned that I had to write them up.

At the risk of hurting the feelings of some of my NATO brethren, it seemed as if the non-US NATO bases realized that if the balloon ever really went up, and Russian tanks came roaring across the Fulda Gap, that the good ol' US would be there to pull everyone's fat out of the fire. Thus there was no need to try too hard with these bothersome TAC-EVALs.

The year 1987 was going to be an extremely busy year for the 496th. We subsequently had T-shirts that read "1987 Big Dog World Tour" with a list of all the planned trips.

In March, we were tasked with a three-week classified deployment, more on this to follow. We were then tasked with a TDY to Decimomannu Air Base in Italy for a couple of weeks fighting the Aggressors in their F-5s. Next was an across-the-ocean TDY to Nellis AFB for the classified Constant Peg exercise, immediately transitioning to Tyndall AFB to take part in the Weapons System Evaluation Program (WSEP), where we would fire live air-to-air missiles. After a short couple of months back home, we were off to Zaragoza AB again for our annual fall WTD. I was tasked to be the Wing Project Officer for the Constant Peg/WSEP trip. It was going to be an epic year, the kind of year fighter pilots relish.

THE MOON

Shortly after the start of the new year 1987, rumors began circulating around the squadron about a classified deployment scheduled for March. We knew the project officer was Trigger—one of the other flight commanders and one of my closest friends—and we knew it would involve eight jets for about three weeks. We also knew that we wouldn't find out the location until it was time to launch.

Plenty of discussion and speculation about this mysterious classified location occurred, mostly based on the current news. Some were betting on Egypt, but most, including me, were betting on Tunisia.

We knew of talk in Air Force circles over the need to establish better relations with some of the Middle East countries. The Tunisians hadn't tried to kill any Americans, not recently, at least. It was near Libya, and there had been some discussion about Tunisia building a bombing range in the middle of the country to serve as a third WTD option, after

Incirlik and Zaragoza, for USAFE combat wings to conduct training.

We all took to calling the deployment The Moon, and even though no one knew where we were going, we all wanted to be in the small group of pilots selected to go.

Remarkably, to my knowledge, there was no crack in the secrecy involved in where exactly The Moon was. No matter how hard we pressed Trigger, plied him with beverages, or tried to trick him into the big reveal, he kept his silence. When my name was placed on the go list, I was ecstatic. All I could tell Wendy was I had to pack as lightly as possible for a three-week TDY, that I didn't know where I was going, that I couldn't write or call her while there, and that I couldn't tell her where I had been or what I was doing when I got back. This veil of secrecy caused a lot of angst among the wives, but we told them where we thought we were going, that it would be no big deal, and not to worry.

On the day of the launch, we learned that we still would not be told where we were going. We were not given access to the flight plan. We were informed that when we each individually hooked on to the boom for the in-flight refueling the SOF on board would inform us of our destination, and that under no circumstances were we to discuss it on the radios.

All of the inflight refueling, which provided at least some hint of our destination, would be conducted comm out. In fact, intriguingly, we were told to retain radio silence to the max extent possible for the entire trip. This was going to be an exciting gig.

After we took off, we initially headed west, crossed into France, turned south, then turned east as we hit the Mediterranean. Yup! Tunisia or Egypt! We rejoined comm out on the tanker and took our turns cycling on to the boom. As soon as I got hooked up, the SOF said, "PK, we're going to Israel."

Now, before I go any further, Juniper Fox, as this classified deployment was designated, was officially declassified sometime in the late '90s, so the narrative that follows is all above board. But on the boom somewhere over the Med in 1987,

I was absolutely stunned that we were headed for Israel, and I know most of my squadron mates were as shocked as I was.

I had never even dreamed of visiting The Holy Land, but I had grown up as a believer and had studied the bible enough to have a fair amount of awareness. The exploits and accomplishments of the Israeli Air Force (IAF) and its pilots were world-renown, especially in fighter pilot circles.

As we approached Israel, we were intercepted by a flight of IAF F-16s who rejoined with us close enough for us to see that they were fully armed to the teeth. Cool! They escorted us into our destination, Ramon Air Base.

The following is an excerpt from Wikipedia: "Constructed by the United States and opened in 1981, Ramon Air Base is located southwest of Beersheba, in the central Negev region in southern Israel. It was built as the result of joint Israeli and US government funding as part of the IAF's redeployment out of its bases in the Sinai after the peninsula was handed over to Egypt following the 1978 Camp David Accords."

One of the first things we noticed as we came in for landing was that Ramon had two long runways, but no HASs or any evidence of jets on the tarmac—because there was no tarmac. In fact, you had to look hard to know there was even a base there. What buildings you could see were all painted Creech brown; even the runways seemed to be painted a tan color to blend in with the barren desert landscape. As we landed and followed the Follow Me trucks, we taxied down underground to our individual parking spots, ushered in with our noses facing out, just like we would park back home, but instead of a team of crew chiefs pushing the jet back into its parking space, they hooked up a cable to the tail-hook and electronically winched the jet back into place. Very exotic, very cool, and very high-tech. We were all quite impressed with this introduction to Israel and the IAF.

After getting unloaded, unstrapped, and taken to our ops building, we were given a welcome orientation briefing by the IAF Wing Commander. There were two IAF F-16 squadrons at Ramon, and he shared some of the history and background of Ramon and the IAF in general with us.

After he departed, our squadron commander, Tex, laid down the law: highly-classified and highly-visible deployment at the highest levels, here to work with the IAF, exchange ideas and tactics, and gain some exposure to flying in this very-volatile part of the world, don't touch the Israeli girls upon pain of death, represent the squadron and good ol' USA with pride and professionalism.

As we were dismissed in preparation to be driven to our quarters, Tex pulled me aside. "PK, one of the requirements for this deployment was to have someone who can speak German to the head of support and logistics here to ensure that everything with billeting, meals, transportation, etc. is handled smoothly. The guy doesn't speak English, but he can speak German. You are our guy."

Gulp. Tex had heard me speak German on a few occasions when we were out and about at Hahn, but I was by no means fluent, and I told him so.

"Don't worry about it—it'll all work out."

Well, great. Just great.

First thing the next day, I was scheduled to meet with the head of support at Ramon. He was an older civilian, and true enough, couldn't speak any English. Luckily, there was a young female interpreter there just in case.

All business, he started rattling off a list of rules and requirements as I tried to comprehend everything he said, take notes, and follow along. Finally, he asked me a question—I asked him to repeat it. He tried again—I smiled, shook my head, and shrugged my shoulders. He then started yelling the same question over and over, pounding on the table, and clearly not happy that this American fighter pilot interpreter couldn't speak German for beans. The Israeli female interpreter then stepped in, and things began to calm down.

He later apologized, still highly frustrated with me, definitely not impressed with his first exposure to our efforts, but resigned to the task at hand. He basically outlined the hours the mess hall would be open, how we were to be transferred to the flight line and our operations workspace, rules on billeting, and other admin areas. We eventually got along fairly well over the course of the deployment, but there were more than a few occasions when he shook his head in disgust.

The billets were pretty spartan, two to a room that basically contained cots and a metal desk. Each floor had communal latrines and showers. Entry into the billets was via coded locks. The three-square meals were also pretty basic, and obviously kosher. We had plenty of salads, fruit, and lots of kool-aid. There was no alcohol available, no bar or Officer's Club. We were segregated from the rest of the base, so we had very little interaction with our IAF hosts.

We were disappointed to learn on Day 1 that we would not be flying with, or against IAF F-16s. We were never really given a reason; it just wasn't going to happen.

Around Day 3, I was tasked to provide a briefing to the IAF pilots on our new F-16C radar system, with multi-target track target identification, and some other new features. I provided about 15 of their pilots a classroom-style briefing, then took them out to let them crawl around our jets for a first-hand look. The guys were cold, asked their questions, and were all business; no friendly fighter-pilot banter or joshing typically common among fighter pilots from different nations.

As they departed, I mentioned that we were looking forward to coming to their squadron and taking a close look at their F-16s as well. "No. That is not possible," was the reply.

Later, we were allowed to visit their squadron ops for a briefing, but we weren't allowed near their jets. We were horrified to find posters from the movie *Iron Eagle*, maybe the most ridiculous movie involving F-16s in the history of cinema, scattered throughout the squadron. The posters were autographed by Louis Gossett Jr and other stars from the movie. The U.S. Air Force had wisely declined to cooperate with the makers of that joke-of-a-film, so it was filmed there in Ramon with the cooperation of the IAF. That movie made the USAF look like a clown show. This was all getting a little weird.

The flying, however, was outstanding. The air-to-air areas were directly overhead the base, so you could takeoff, climb straight up, and start the fight within minutes. The deep blue desert sky was clear-in-a-million every day, so spectators could go outside the ops building with a cup of coffee and watch the progress of the fight taking place overhead. The tactical ranges in the Negev were as good as we had seen anywhere. With plenty of trucks, tanks, airplanes, and other assorted equipment captured during the wars in 1967 and 1973, the target array was impressive.

We dropped live Mk-82s, both Slick and Snakeye, and Mk-84s, a unique opportunity not common for USAFE units. I hadn't dropped live bombs, other than BDU-33s and Mk-106s for training since I had left RTU at Luke. There was also an electronic-warfare portion of the range with real-world emitters, monitors, and cameras that would record in detail any threat reactions you made, including the effectiveness of your ECM pod (electronic counter measures), chaff, and flare. Everything the IAF had was as good as anything we had at our Red Flags at Nellis and was literally within minutes of the base.

Because of the location of Ramon in southern Israel, we were constantly under air traffic control; there was no VFR option available. We were vectored and controlled from the time we took off until we landed.

When we were first briefed this mandate, it raised some eyebrows, since we were all used to the relatively free-wheeling flying we had in Central Europe. However, on the first mission, it was easy to understand why. As you raised your gear, you could look to the west and see Egypt; when you looked to the east, you could see Jordan. Israel is roughly the size of the state of New Jersey. Not a lot of room for error.

Tours in the tower for SOF (Supervisor of Flying) duties were compelling. Most air traffic control duties, including the control tower, were performed by females, and the tower itself was a pseudo-women's barracks. When I reported for my first SOF tour, 4-5 women were manning the tower. Within an hour, a slow parade of women started filling up the tower space, until about 20 mostly young, beautiful Israeli women were staring at U.S Air Force fighter pilots from America.

Over the next few weeks, they continued this routine and eventually opened up enough to where fun and easy-going conversation flowed freely. For the first time in the history of aviation, guys started competing for the opportunity to pull a SOF tour. We learned a lot about the IAF and Israel through them. They told us that the IAF F-16 pilots thought we were a bunch of showoffs. Hello. Fighter Pilot. Duh.

When we took-off, we typically did formation takeoffs, held the jets low, and did a dramatic tac-split at the end of the runway to a max-afterburner climb up to the fighting air space overhead. When we came back in for landing, we usually brought four up in a tight Thunderbird-formation for sequenced breaks over the numbers. The IAF, as indicated, were always strictly business; single-ship takeoffs and straight-in landings were their norm. The IAF women were warm and friendly, but our pilot counterparts wanted nothing to do with us.

Because this was a classified deployment, we were also not permitted to leave the base. Also, flying was not allowed on Saturday, as it was the Jewish Shabbat, so we didn't have much to do with any free time we had.

Towards the end of the second week, the Israeli pilots invited us for a friendly game of basketball, and this was a welcome opportunity. Naturally, most of us hadn't brought much in the way of gym clothes, so we showed up in their gym wearing a ragged collection of jean cut-offs, worn gym shorts, and our sweaty squadron t-shirts. Some of the guys didn't have gym shoes, so they played in their stocking feet.

We should have known something was up when we entered the small gym. The stands were packed with spectators. We were standing around, taking some unorganized and chaotic practice shots when a cheer went up. A team of mostly tall Israelis in beautiful blue and white uniforms came jogging into the gym, took up their side of the court, and started a regimented lineup for practice layups. Then the referees entered, also in uniform. We'd been had. The IAF was set to destroy the Americans in front of most of the base population.

Well. We Americans invented basketball, eh? At the end of the first half, we had been holding our own, only behind by about four points. The crowd cheered hysterically with every shot the IAF guys made and met our scores with relative silence—except for our bench, where I was gratefully riding the pines.

Early in the third quarter, things started to get a bit chippy. Tex, our squadron commander, was a pretty big guy and had played some quarterback at Texas Christian University. He was playing center and maneuvering his way around the key, hounded by the opposing IAF center. The IAF guy started really leaning hard into Tex, who countered Charles Barkley-style with his butt. This went on for a few seconds when the frustrated IAF center took both hands and pushed hard into Tex's back. Tex instinctively threw back his right elbow and caught the guy dead in the jaw. He toppled like a felled oak tree—total silence in the gym, except for the sound of the bouncing basketball that had been dropped to the floor, doink, doink, doink. Uh-oh.

They helped their guy to the bench; no foul was called, and the play resumed more or less under control. The IAF eventually ran away with the game; they had a deep bench, and we had, well, no bench. Still, we felt lucky to get out of there alive. What the heck was up with these guys?

Finally, during our last weekend in Israel, we were allowed off base. Due to our classified status, our excursion off base came in the form of a strictly-organized bus tour, with no permitted free-time. We were told that if a bystander questioned us, we should respond that we were in the U.S. Navy at a port-of-call stopover. Somewhat ominously, we were accompanied by several Uzi-toting bodyguards, one of which was a dark-blonde young lady wearing a black leather jacket and knee-high pirate boots. It felt like we were being escorted by Charlie's Angels.

Our bus departed on a Saturday morning for the ancient mountain fortification of Masada, famous for its epic stand during the First Jewish-Roman War in 73 to 74 CE. As the story is told, after a lengthy siege by the Romans, the Jewish defenders committed suicide rather than surrender. It remains a powerful symbol of Jewish heroism and determination, and many Israeli soldiers hike up the mountain and are sworn in there. It sits on a massive plateau overlooking the Dead Sea, and the view is stunning. We were then driven to Jerusalem for tours of the many religious sites, then spent the night in a fine hotel. We were not permitted to leave the hotel once we checked in, and being Shabbat, many establishments were closed anyway. Thankfully, there was a bar near the lobby where most of us spent the evening.

Sunday night, on our way back to Ramon from Jerusalem, we spent most of the ride singing old Motown songs and telling jokes. We knew we were driving through portions of the West Bank, but there wasn't much to see. Suddenly, while passing through a suburb, our bus was struck with what sounded like a couple of huge bricks. "Everybody down! Now!" shouted one of our bodyguards.

Rather than speeding up, however, the bus stopped and our gun-toting protectors ran out of the bus into the darkness, uzis at the ready, scanning the area. Holy smokes! We kept quiet in our seats, furtively looking out the window to see what was going on. After a few minutes, our bodyguards filed back on the bus. Carry on. No big deal. A stark reality check of daily life in Israel. Despite that episode, the tour of Masada and Jerusalem was something I think we all will remember for the rest of our lives. For me personally, it was a meaningful, heartfelt, spiritual, blessed treasure.

On the Thursday night prior to our Saturday departure back to Hahn, the IAF threw us a farewell party. We were put on a bus and driven out to a cavern in what appeared to be the middle of the Negev. It was one of the coolest places I have ever had the pleasure to enjoy a party; a seemingly endless trail of brightly-lit caves and passageways with open bars, couches, chairs, and a mini-theater. They even had a lounge band playing mostly Sinatra songs.

Then lo and behold—our IAF F-16 counterparts showed up and acted like we were long lost pals. Laughing, joking, back-slapping, tale-telling good times shared between comrades. They played for us a short video they had made about the tortures of being based in the Negev; evidently, the squadrons had once been located near Tel Aviv, where the nightlife is the best in Israel. Now they were in the middle of the desert.

Then, some of the girls from the tower sang a song to us to the tune of Billy Joel's "You May Be Right," where they named every one of us by name or call sign— "You may be White! You may be Grumpy! But for all I know you might be Tex!" In turn, the four of us R-B-Double-A-Bravos got up and sang a few of our tunes to the delight of the crowd.

It turns out Tex was wise in asking Trout and me to bring our guitars and for Rev to bring his saxophone while we packed for this trip—the three of us occasionally played some impromptu blues at parties back at Hahn. Because we had our instruments, we sang and played "Shoeshine Man," a couple of other numbers, and finally concluded with our own hastily improvised version of "Hava Nagila."

Our efforts were well-received, and the IAF showered the squadron with gifts, which included a large menorah with F-16-shaped candle holders. I have always coveted this gift, so if you know where it is, let me know. We ended the night in a drink fest with our newest IAF best friends, slamming gin and tonics with sugar around the glass rims. So good! While we got off to a rough start, we ended as warrior friends and comrades.

When we departed for Hahn, I was #4 of the last departing 4-ship. As I raised my landing gear, I rocked my wings back and forth until the end of the runway as a farewell salute before I turned hard-climbing-right for the rejoin. One of our guys was in the tower doing the required SOF duty, and he said the girls—the tower was packed—burst into applause.

As we landed back home at Hahn, the spouses and wing leadership greeted us. Wendy was extremely curious, as were all the spouses, but we were sworn to silence. All I could tell her was that it was awesome! Several days later, as Wendy washed my clothes, she found a shekel in my pants pocket. Doh! It was my turn to swear her into silence.

Postscript. Wendy and I are active members of a Messianic Jewish synagogue in North Seattle. Invariably, when one of the congregants learns that I am a retired fighter pilot, they remark with a nod and a wink, "So! How about those Israeli fighter pilots, eh?"

I always reply the same way, "Yep. Second-best fighter pilots in the world."

DECIMOMANNU

A month after returning to Hahn, we flew to Decimomannu Air Base on the island of Sardinia for two weeks of dissimilar air combat training (DACT), one of the missions all fighter pilots love. Deci was home to the 7555th Tactical Training Squadron and served as one of NATO's premier training locations for European-based fighter wings.

The main attraction to flying out of Deci was the ACMI; the Air Combat Maneuvering Instrumentation system mating computers, big screens, and aircraft weapons systems that allow pilots to more effectively review and evaluate their air-to-air capabilities. The ACMI recorded and later displayed with computer-generated imagery (CGI) all the aircraft movements during an engagement; it was like looking at a giant video game with you as one of the jets. While there, we would be fighting with and against U.S F-5 Aggressors, U.S. F-15s, and German F-4s. Good times.

While the island of Sardinia is the second-largest in the Mediterranean after Sicily, it is fairly isolated and rustic, so there wasn't much to do off base. The beaches were beautiful, but being April, it was still a little cold to take much advantage of them.

The chow and billets on base were pretty good, but why would you want to eat on base when you can eat some genuine Sardo food? Our favorite bar and restaurant was The Monkey Bar. It served great food, great drinks—they even had fairly decent margaritas, rare for Europe—and yes, there was a large cage near the entrance that was home to a monkey. During this trip I developed a taste for Lambrusco; cheap, sweet wine that went great with pizza.

Ziggy introduced me to it. "Lambrusco! It's like Italian soda pop! I can drink as much as I want, and it don't affect me none!" he would loudly announce while performing a (mostly) fake drunken pratfall. Ah, the unique cultural experiences one can get while defending one's country.

Fighting the Aggressors was always a challenge. They were air-to-air experts, employing Warsaw Pact tactics, and they knew how to fly their jets, and ours, and use their excellent Ground Control Intercept (GCI) controllers to the Ph.D. level. I fought the Aggressors a few times before, and though the F-5 was vastly inferior to the F-16, you had to be patient and not take them for granted.

Fighting F-15s was old hat for us; we fought against the F-15s from Bitburg often. Our main strategy was to do our best to confuse and defeat their outstanding radar and long-range missile (AIM-7 Sparrow) capability. If we could get them in visual range, we could usually have our way with them. That wasn't easy, though; those guys trained in their sole air-to-air mission constantly, and they were generally pretty good. If you were fighting them 4 v 4, you could count on losing a couple pre-merge, but generally, one of us would get in unobserved and kick the eagle's nest.

The F-15 pilots would often accuse our creative attempts to defeat their radars of excessive gamesmanship. "You guys would never do that in a real combat situation!" they would bitterly complain.

Well, maybe not—but if you ain't cheatin', you ain't tryin'.

Fighting the German F-4s was frustrating. The pilots at Deci seemed relatively young and inexperienced and maybe a little lacking in situation awareness. During one of our large-force engagements, I took an F-4 up into the sun and popped flares to defeat a potential heat-seeking AIM-9P. He still called a kill on me (I got a good tone!). In the debrief, looking at his gun film, you couldn't even see my jet; the video was washed out by the sun. I asked him if he saw my flares. "Yes! They were beautiful!" Alrighty, then.

Two engagements stand out in my mind during that Deci trip. On the first, my wingman, Sammie, and I were paired 2 v 2 against F-15s. Per our usual tactic, we did a Thunderbird Bomb Burst, violently separating, changing altitude, and going to the beam to defeat their radar. They both locked onto Sammie, so as he separated out of the fight, I came roaring in high, seemingly unobserved.

Perhaps a bit overly excited, I did a 9-G Split-S conversion to their six and promptly greyed out. It was the worst grey out I had ever experienced; I didn't lose consciousness, but I couldn't see anything either. I let off the G, fairly disoriented, and my eyesight returned within a few seconds. There, magically in front of me and not more than two miles, were both F-15s, co-altitude, and still unaware of my presence. I quickly shot one, then gunned the other before he completed 180 degrees of his break turn. After landing, Sammie was passing their briefing room when he heard one of the F-15 pilots say, "I couldn't believe he got back there so fast!" A kill's a kill; sometimes, it's better to be lucky than good.

On the second engagement, we were 4 v 4 + 2 against the Aggressors. I was #3, with Sammie again as #4. As a 4-ship, we again performed our tactics, trying to defeat the GCI radars and confuse our adversaries. Sammie and I performed a drag maneuver away from the inbound F-5s, trying to lure them onto us and allow #1 and #2 a clean entry into the merge, then pitched back into the fray once the fight started.

As Sammie and I approached the swirling mass of jets, a kill was called on Sammie. I couldn't see where it came from, and so with my own loss of situation awareness, I did like *Monty Python's* Sir Robin; I bravely turned my tail and fled. Heading down to the bottom of the floor, full-afterburner cooking, frantically looking over my shoulder to see if I was being chased, out of my peripheral vision, I saw the island of Sardinia coming off my nose. I looked forward into my HUD, and saw that I was raging at 1.2 Mach. If I hit landfall going Mach+, I would bust a lot of windows with the sonic boom and be in big, big trouble, so I jerked the throttle to idle and opened the speed brakes. The rapid deceleration at that low altitude and high speed was so violent that my cranium slammed forward between my knees, and I cracked my helmet visor on the lower console. Thankfully, we didn't get any noise complaints, but Life Support was not happy with having to equip me with a new, expensive helmet visor. Like I said, good times.

CONSTANT PEG AND WSEP

The 50th FTW had been tasked to participate in two stateside training exercises in June: Constant Peg out of Nellis AFB in Las Vegas, and WSEP, the Weapons Systems Evaluation Program out of Tyndall AFB in Panama City. Constant Peg—a then-highly classified exercise that was declassified by the Air Force in 2006—allowed USAF fighter pilots to actually fly combat scenarios against real MiGs. WSEP provided fighter pilots a rare opportunity to fire live air-to-air missiles against remotely-controlled aircraft drones. Both programs were once-in-a-career opportunities, and there was plenty of competition among the three fighter squadrons to see who would be chosen to go. I was named the Wing Project Officer for the trip, so I was in.

Here is what the National Museum of the U.S. Air Force, located at Wright-Patterson AFB in Ohio, has to say about Constant Peg: "Project Constant Peg was a secret program to train US Air Force, Navy, and Marine Corps fighter aircrews to fly against Soviet-designed aircraft. The USAF's 4477th Test and Evaluation Squadron (TES), nicknamed the "Red Eagles," flew MiG-17 "Fresco," MiG-21 "Fishbed," and MiG-23 "Flogger" aircraft. The Red Eagles gave American aircrews the skills and confidence to defeat these threats in aerial combat."

Established in 1977, Constant Peg applied lessons learned earlier in Southeast Asia. Over North Vietnam, the USAF and USN had faced high losses to enemy aircraft, air-to-air missiles, and surface-to-air missiles. These losses sharply illustrated training shortfalls and a loss of skill in the art of the dogfight.

Between 1972 and 1977, the USAF and USN started several specialized training programs to reinvigorate the fighter force, including establishing the first Aggressor squadrons. These squadrons flew USAF aircraft but employed Soviet tactics and flying techniques to simulate realistic adversaries. Constant Peg improved upon this method of instruction—Red Eagles pilots not only used Soviet fighter tactics but also flew the same MiG aircraft that their students could one day face in combat.

The Red Eagles flew out of a secret airfield located in the Tonopah Range complex known as Dream Land. Red Eagle pilots were selected primarily from the ranks of the Air Force Fighter Weapons School, Navy Fighter Weapons School (Top Gun), and Aggressor squadrons—the best of the best.

During our inbrief and discussion of the fighting airspace and local area, we were instructed in no uncertain terms to fly into the area for the engagements and return back to Nellis along strict black-line routes to ensure we didn't get near enough to Dream Land to see what was going on out there. Later, of course, we learned that we were flying and testing our then-secret F-117 Nighthawk stealth fighters, whose existence had still not been revealed to the world, out of Dream Land.

We were warned that if we crossed into Dream Land airspace, we would be ordered to land there and be debriefed. I always pictured a *Men In Black* scenario where we would be forced to stare into a black wand and have our memories erased. After all, Dream Land was located in close proximity to the infamous Area 51, where we keep all of our captured alien life forms and space ships. Serious business, and enough to make you feel a little paranoid.

For our week with the 4477th, we were each scheduled for three sorties. The first sortie was designed as a simple performance-comparison between the F-16 and a MiG; the second sortie was scheduled as a 1 v 1 Basic Fighter Maneuvers (BFM) mission, and the third and final sortie was a 2 v 2 Air Combat Tactics (ACT) mission. It's hard to explain just how pumped up we were over the opportunity to measure ourselves against our potential Warsaw Pact adversaries.

On my performance-comparison mission, I was briefed by my Red Eagle comrade to just show up in the area and wait. He didn't tell me what kind of aircraft he would be flying; he just told me he would enter the area, rejoin on me, and we would start the mission, which essentially involved acceleration capabilities, turn rate comparisons, and energy sustainment demonstrations. When a MiG-23 Flogger rejoined on my left wing, I could hardly believe it—it was so cool to have an opportunity to do this finally!

As we knew, the turn rate and energy sustainment of the Flogger was vastly inferior to the F-16. However, we had always been told that the Flogger had outstanding acceleration capabilities, that in an air-to-air engagement, count on the Flogger to try and not turn with you but to get a quick fleeting shot and accelerate away.

To demonstrate, I flew side-by-side with the Flogger as we accelerated together. My F-16 kept up with the Flogger until we hit Mach airspeed, at which point the Flogger started to accelerate away slowly. Still, in a turning fight, we wouldn't be flying at Mach airspeeds, so the sortie left me with a huge amount of confidence if I ever had to fight a Flogger, confidence that we already had in spades with our world's finest single-engine fighter F-16s.

For my BFM sortie, I was tasked against a MiG-21 Fishbed. With its delta-wing configuration, we had always been taught that the MiG-21 had an outstanding initial turn-rate capability, but would bleed off airspeed quickly. That's exactly what happened.

When I was on offense, I broke with him initially as he made his defensive turn, then took it up slightly into the vertical to spiral down inside his expanding turn circle for the eventual gun kill. On defense, I essentially did the same thing; I gave him a hard 9-G bat turn, briefly accelerated away, then took it up into the vertical once again to effectively negate his threat. It was the same result—our F-16s were far better than the MiGs we might face.

For the ACT sortie, my wingman was Trigger, as good a fighter pilot we had in the 496th. Once again, we were not told what type of aircraft we would be fighting; the scenario was simply an intercept to an engagement, and we would have to positively identify the bandits and react accordingly. At the "Fight's on," call, we quickly established radar contact, got a clean radar sort—"I've got the east guy, you've got the west" —and as they attempted to break our radar lock with one of their jets aggressively descending out of their altitude block, Trigger got a visual tally on both bandits.

We continued with our visual sort, identified our adversaries as Floggers, and shot both of them pre-merge. We maintained visual with each other throughout the engagement, quickly rejoined, and started to set up for another set when the Floggers called bingo for being low on fuel and returned to Dream Land. A short-but-sweet duel in the desert; we had flown our own tactics perfectly, collected two quick kills and returned overwhelming in confidence and swagger.

The rest of the guys had similar results. Constant Peg was one of the Air Force's great training programs. While we thankfully didn't end up having to face off against the Soviet Union and the Warsaw Pact, we did encounter enemy MiGs and pilots trained in Soviet tactics during Desert Storm, Deny Flight, Deliberate Force, and Allied Force.

As Dr. Daniel L. Haulman states in his work, *No Contest: Aerial Combat in the 1990s*, "During the 1990s, U.S. Air Force pilots shot down 48 enemy aircraft. In the same decade, enemy pilots shot down not one U.S. Air Force aircraft. In the field of aerial combat, there was no contest."

Ultimately, until its final sortie in March 1988, 5,930 USAF fighter pilots were exposed to the training provided by Constant Peg. Hats off to the 4477th TES Red Eagles! (For more on the 4477th, I recommend the book *Red Eagles: America's Secret MiGs*, by Steve Davies.)

We moved on with our eight jets to Tyndall AFB for WSEP after a quick stop for refueling at Carswell AFB in Fort Worth. As we approached Panama City, we were notified of thunderstorms in the area. Being unfamiliar with the traffic pattern at Tyndall, we split off for individual instrument approaches.

As I left the final approach fix in preparation for landing, I entered a huge rain squall, stronger than any rain I had ever experienced while airborne. It was like flying in a waterfall. I took the jet down to the landing minimums and still couldn't see the runway. I had to execute a missed approach.

I couldn't believe it—three years of flying out of Hahn's worst weather in the Air Force, never having had to go missed approach, and here I was in sunny Florida in the summer not being able to find the dang runway.

The seven jets behind me had no problem landing, and by the time I was vectored around again for another instrument approach, the squall had passed, and the weather was clear-in-a-million. At least at Hahn, you knew the weather was probably going to be lousy. Here at Tyndall on the Gulf Coast, you never knew what to expect weather-wise, except that whatever presented itself would probably pass quickly.

There are three WSEP programs: Combat Archer, for air-to-air weapons, Combat Hammer, for air-to-ground weapons, and Combat Sledgehammer, for nuclear weapons. Our wing was participating in Combat Archer—strictly air-to-air.

WSEP evaluates weapon systems in their entirety, including aircraft, weapon delivery system, weapon, aircrew, technical data, and maintenance, so the Air Force can assess operational effectiveness, verify weapon system performance, determine reliability, evaluate capability and limitations, identify deficiencies, and pursue corrective actions. It also gives crews valuable practice with actual weapons.

We were scheduled to be at Tyndall for two weeks. In addition to our WSEP missions, we were also going to fly DBFM, DACM, and DACT (dissimilar) sorties against the 325th Fighter Training Wing F-15s stationed there. Flying air-to-air for two weeks on the white sandy beaches of Florida. Not a bad gig.

On top of that, my parents were going to make the three-hour drive down from their home near Wetumpka, Alabama, to spend the weekend with me in a rented condo on the beach. I hadn't seen them since their visit with us in Germany for Christmas, so it was a real treat.

While we were all looking forward to firing a live air-to-air missile, we were disappointed to learn that most of us would be firing an antiquated AIM-9 Papa. The AIM-9 Sidewinder is a short-range, heat-seeking missile, and the only air-to-air missile carried by the F-16 until the early 90s when F-16s were modified to carry the AIM-120 AMRAAM (Advanced Medium-Range Air-to-Air Missile). However, in 1987, our primary missiles were the AIM-9 Lima and the AIM-9 Mike versions of the Sidewinder. Both the Lima and the Mike were all-aspect missiles, but the Papa was rear-aspect only. The Papa was a leftover from Vietnam, and we assumed the Air Force was simply trying to deplete the inventory of this older missile, hardly in use anymore by active-duty fighter squadrons.

Before we departed Hahn, those of us scheduled for WSEP loaded dummy AIM-9Ps and flew a sortie and several simulator rides just to get used to the unique missile tone and its rear-aspect limitations. Still, a live Papa is better than no live missile at all.

I was scheduled to be one of the first guys out of the chute to fire a live missile. This wasn't just a joy-ride. In addition to WSEP evaluating weapons systems, the pilots participating would also be graded on their effectiveness, and the Papa, with its rear aspect restrictions, was a much more demanding missile to employ than the Lima or Mike. I felt significant pressure to perform well, represent Hahn, and not screw up.

The scenarios were all essentially the same; we would launch single-ship with a WSEP instructor flying in chase, enter the live fire area, and wait to perform a stern-intercept on a QF-4 Phantom remotely-controlled aerial target drone for a rear-quadrant shot. Once you had completed the intercept, the chase pilot would call out, "Turn the drone!" and the QF-4 would break either left or right. You would then fly your jet to weapons parameters and employ your live missile.

These live AIM-9 Sidewinders for training were equipped with proximity fuses and were not teeth-hair-and-eyeballs missiles; most of the time, the QF-4 was not blown out of the sky. An explosive device was placed in the QF-4 to destroy the aircraft if it inadvertently became uncontrollable, but most of the time, even after onboard sensors registered a hit, it was able to be remotely flown back for a landing to be used again.

Everything was going like clockwork. I completed my stern intercept, heard the chase pilot declare, "Turn the drone!" and the QF-4 broke right. I maneuvered into the kill zone, got a decent growl tone from the missile, and fired. There was a slight delay—what the heck???!!—then the missile soundlessly came off the rail of my right wingtip.

To my dismay, it immediately started to dig hard to the right, actually ahead of the line-of-sight to the QF-4. I thought the missile was going stupid, but lo and behold, the missile was simply tracking lead on the drone, and I saw it detonate to the rear and slightly below the QF-4.

"That's a hit!" I heard the chase pilot call, much to my relief. Once back on the ground and in the debrief, we were provided detailed computerized data on our intercept, employment parameters, and detonation results. I was glad to get it over with and spend the next ten days killing F-15s. Much easier.

Overall, that three-week deployment for Constant Peg and WSEP was one of the highlights of my 30-year career. Being the Wing Project Officer brought additional pressures and responsibilities, with nearly three months of planning, preparation, and briefings to the higher-ups, but we returned to Hahn in triumph with everyone and everything intact.

BRAVO DELTA DELTAS

That summer, the 496th went through several big changes. One was the final completion of constructing a new squadron bar. Previously, we didn't have one of which we were proud, but with the help and inspiration of some of our more talented guys, we built a dandy. We christened it Trevor's Bar, after the guy who led the charge in the rebuild.

During that same period, we changed our squadron patch from the Electric Chicken blue patch back to the original 496th Squadron patch designed by Walt Disney. Disney designed nearly 1,200 squadron patches during and immediately after WWII. The new-old patch depicted a hound dog riding a missile with a sword in its hand, on a yellow-gold background. Someone said, "That looks like a Big Dick Dog!" and of course, the name stuck.

Accordingly, we changed our F-16 tail flashes to yellow-gold and changed our nametags to reflect the new color scheme. In addition, we updated the traditional squadron toast:

> To the envy of the 10th!
> The protectors of the 131th!
> The pride of the 50th!
> The World's Finest... Big Dick Dogs!

Hear, Hear!

To preserve some semblance of political correctness, we usually referred to ourselves as The Big Dogs, or Bravo-Delta-Deltas, but everyone knew who we were.

To celebrate the new patch and the new bar, the squadron had a huge blowout inauguration party that 4th of July. Wives and other squadron comrades from the 10th and 313th were invited. Grilled brats and burgers, Kirner Pils, from our newly-installed taps, songs, hilarity, and chaos ensued. The R-B-Double-A-Bravos performed, and I chose the occasion to introduce "The Big Dog Rap":

We're the Big Dick Dogs, and we're so bad.
We're the best lovers, baby, that you've ever had.
We can drink more gin in a single night
than you can in a year—ain't that right!
We can fly and fight, drink and sing,
and rock all night, baby, that's our thing
When you see us coming better step aside,
some men didn't—some men died.
We come on hard; we come on mean,
and in the air, we're a killing machine.
Ivan knows, and he's filled with dread.
If they mess with us, they know they're dead.
We're the Big Dick Dogs, in for the kill.
The 496th is King of the Hill.
Say yeah! (Yeah!)

The party went well into the night, and when it was time to go home, Wendy and I both found ourselves a bit more incapacitated than we normally would have been. The squadron was located in a secure area, and alarms were set when the squadron building was closed every night. So, Wendy and I spent that night sleeping on the couches in my little flight commander's office.

Bright and early the next morning, Sunday, Tex came over, disarmed the alarm system, and let us safely and soberly exit for the drive home, where we promptly went to bed again.

About six weeks later, Wendy called my office and told me she was at the commissary, had just left the hospital, and I would have to start cleaning the kitty litter from now on.

"Why?" I asked.

"WE'RE PREGNANT!!!"

I let out a war-whoop of joy, and made a big-voice announcement on the squadron comm system that the rabbit died!

Wendy and I were so very, very happy and excited. We had been trying—or rather, not-not-trying for nearly a year, but it seemed I was often away somewhere with all of our TDYs and deployments when it was prime time.

Finally, a few of the squadron wives sat down with Wendy, and together they calculated the best dates for baby-making and marked our calendars appropriately.

We called all the parents in the U.S., who, in turn, called each other to celebrate the good news. Wendy and I were planning a big road trip vacation through England and Scotland within a few days, so the timing was perfect. We were going to be a Mom and Dad!

We had been anticipating our road trip through Britain for quite a while. Though we had been to London several times, we had never really traveled through the rest of the island. I particularly wanted to see Scotland and attend the Edinburgh Tattoo.

Our 11-day self-designed itinerary had us driving to Calais, catching the ferry to Dover, and continuing through Canterbury on the way to London, where we would stay a few days with our friends Mark and Linda. We would then work our way north with overnights at Oxford, Stratford-Upon-Avon, York, then up to Edinburgh, making all of the mandatory tourist stops along the route. After two nights in Edinburgh for the Tattoo, we would continue up north to Inverness, in hopes of seeing the Loch Ness Monster. Then, a quick drive back through England and ferry back home the way we came.

Everything pretty much went as planned. Driving a German-standard Toyota with the steering wheel on the left, just like in the States, presented challenges driving in Britain. I nearly killed us at least once every other day, driving on the wrong side of the road. On top of that, Wendy began to experience her first pangs of morning sickness and nausea. She basically vomited her way up to Loch Ness and back. The Tattoo was as epic and glorious as we hoped it would be, and Loch Ness was as dark, mysterious, and creepy as we expected, and no, we didn't spy Nessie. Despite first trimester symptoms, it was an awesome trip.

While we were in Edinburgh on the day of the Tattoo, I bought a book of baby names in a local book store. Wendy and I enjoyed a picnic lunch in Princes Street Gardens while we contemplated what we were going to name our child. Wendy had always loved the name Walker, so we decided on David Walker if it was a boy, and we would call him Walker. We agreed on Claire Morgan if it was a girl. I liked Claire Morgan well enough, but I knew it was going to be a boy.

EXCALIBUR II

In October, HQ USAFE announced another Excalibur bombing competition. Excalibur was similar to the Air Force-wide Gunsmoke competition, except it only involved fighter wings in USAFE. HQ USAFE would pick one flight from each wing at random to represent their wing.

The 4-ship scenario included an aerial refueling over the North Sea followed by a designated TOT (Time-Over-Target) for an individual 30-degree pop-up attack on a controlled bombing range target. After rejoining the 4-ship over the range, there would be another 30-degree, two 20-degree, and two 10-degree passes on the main pylon from the standard range pattern, followed by low-angle strafe. Enroute to the range, flights would be opposed by air-to-air F-15 units from Bitburg and Camp New Amsterdam, and points would be deducted from flight members killed.

The selected flight would have one day prior to the Excalibur date to practice together, but they could not practice on the designated range for this competition—Nordhorn Range, in Northern Germany.

The first Excalibur had been held at Bardenas Range in Zaragoza and was won by the flight from Torrejon. For this Excalibur, the awards banquet and Crud competition—see Appendix: Culture, Customs, and Craziness—would be held at Hahn after all the teams had completed their missions. There would be a big blowout at the Officer's Club, and our ramp would be full of visiting and competing jets.

I prayed my flight would be selected, and even though, with four flights in each of the three squadrons at Hahn giving us 12-to-1 odds for being chosen, I just had this feeling that we would be the one. Sure enough, two days prior to the competition day, I was returning from a sortie and giving my inflight report to the ops desk when the Ops Supervisor said, "Congratulations! B Flight has been selected for Excalibur!"

Participants for the competition had to be formally assigned to the selected flight, and I had already chosen my guys. As the flight commander, I would naturally be the Flight Lead; #2 would be Rookie, #3 would be Ziggy, and #4 would be Sammie. Since they were all assigned to B Flight, I had flown with each of them many times, and they were among the best in the squadron. Rookie, in fact, had been a member of Hahn's most-recent Gunsmoke team, which had finished second overall in the Air Force-wide contest at Nellis AFB the year prior.

As per the rules, on the day before the competition, we scheduled two sorties to practice together. Range space was hard to come by, but we managed to secure Vliehors (Cornfield) Range in the Netherlands for the morning launch, and Helechteren (Pampa) Range in Belgium for the afternoon launch.

We absolutely killed it. It was a bad weather day, particularly at Vliehors, which was on an island in the North Sea just off the coast of the Netherlands. The crosswinds were strong, and the rain was blowing sideways, but we managed more Delta Hotels (Direct Hits, or Bullseyes) than misses, and all of our bombs were decent scores. The same held true for our afternoon sortie to Helechteren.

After landing and debrief, we spent the rest of the day planning the mission, developing the best route to take advantage of the low level opportunities in Low Fly 1 and Low Fly 3 airspace to avoid being detected by the opposing F-15s, finding the best update points to keep our Inertial Navigation Systems (INS) tight, and calculating our timing. We left the squadron that evening bursting with confidence, and I was already proud of the boys from B Flight.

The next day was sunny, clear, and beautiful—we couldn't have asked for better weather conditions for the contest. Start, taxi, and takeoff were uneventful, and we easily made our way to rejoin on the tanker in the North Sea and hooked up right at our designated refueling time slot. We left the tanker on time, dropped down into Low Fly 1 in our 4-ship battle box, and pressed toward the target area at 250 feet and 480 knots. We received no threat calls from Magic radar control, and we didn't pick up anything on our own radars.

As we transitioned into Low Fly 3 and approached the IP (Initial Point) for entry into the range, we took spacing for our individual first-run attacks into Nordhorn. We purposely selected two easy-to-see crossroads as steerpoints to perform INS updates, which I executed. Still raging at 250 feet, none of us having any threat indications, I contacted the range, accelerated to 540 knots, and began my IP-to-Target run.

As I left the IP, things didn't look quite the way I expected them to. I had been to Nordhorn several times before, but I wasn't thoroughly familiar with the range, especially going that low and that fast. I had this gnawing suspicion something just wasn't right, but this was no time to worry. I was seconds away from my planned pop-up point. Up I went for the climb, and I immediately saw I was way off.

Although my INS told me I was exactly where I was supposed to be, I could see visually that I was several miles to the west of where I should have been. I called, "I'm late!" to the guys, but I could already see Rookie starting his attack.

"How late?" he yelled.

"Press on, I'll be high and dry," I called, and told the range controller that #1 would be passing overhead dry on the first-run attack.

I was stunned—what the heck happened? I could see my INS was off by a couple of miles; I tried hitting cursor zero to take out any inadvertent INS slews a dozen times, but nothing changed. There was nothing I could do but transition to bombing manual, without INS assistance—always a challenging event.

We continued our range work, and per the rules, the range controller could not transmit our bomb scores. However, I could see I was throwing bombs all over the place. The other guys were doing great, but I was hopeless. After we finished our strafe passes, we safed our weapons systems, exited the range, and quietly made our way back home. My INS continued to be way out of whack, but I could still navigate well enough by map and navaids to lead us back in. It was one of the most horrible feelings I had ever felt.

After landing, the Wing Commander, Director of Operations, and the entire 496th were there at engine shutdown, eagerly awaiting the news on how we did. When I told them what happened—still not knowing why—I could see the massive disappointment on their faces. I had let the side down. I had personally failed the 50th Tactical Fighter Wing, the 496th Tactical Fighter Squadron, and my comrades. It was absolutely soul-crushing.

At the banquet that night, I tried to keep my chin up. During the Crud tournament, I was the last man standing on my team before finally being eliminated, but we still lost. The R-B-Double-A Bravos performed again, and while we tried to maintain our usual enthusiasm and gusto, our hearts just weren't in it. Scores weren't posted, but winners were announced, both in the individual and team categories. We didn't win anything. The overall winner was the team from Ramstein; their flight commander also won the Top Gun Award for the competition.

No one ever really said anything to me about it later in the squadron; it was just a subject that didn't come up in my presence. I agonized over what could have gone wrong, and I deduced that I had probably performed an INS update on the wrong steerpoint just prior to entering the range; I essentially told the INS it was somewhere it really wasn't. A completely boneheaded mistake in the heat of battle, and totally my fault.

We all received participation plaques for competing in Excalibur II. I am staring at mine right now; it still hangs on my wall with the rest of my Air Force mementos, and I've had it hanging in every office I had for the rest of my Air Force career as a reminder that no matter how good you think you might be, your could still fail on any given day.

Of all the mistakes and errors I made in my 30 years in the Air Force—and believe me, I made plenty—Excalibur II is still the one that haunts me the most.

PARENTHOOD

That November, we took off for our standard fall WTD to Zaragoza. Tex had departed the squadron for the HQ USAFE staff as Chief of Assignments, and our Operations Officer, Cobber, was the new commander. The departure of Tex was felt deeply by the squadron and signified the end of the R-B-Double-A-Bravos, but we all loved Cobber and were delighted that he was our new commander.

Our Zaragoza deployment was highlighted by Thanksgiving in Barcelona. We chartered a bus to take us there for a 3-day weekend. We spent the first night on the Ramblas, where we celebrated Thanksgiving together with a huge Spanish feast. On Friday, we moved on to the beaches at Sitges, where our favorite hang-out was an alley-dive bar, owned by an American Navy expat.

Before departing Zaragoza in early December, we had our traditional Flight Suit Dining-In and Naming Ceremony, which had the usual frantic fun, chaos, and brotherhood spirit. I knew it was going to be my last trip to Zaragoza with the squadron, and it felt bittersweet.

When I got back to Hahn and rejoined Wendy, we were lying in bed that first night home when Wendy took my hand and placed it on her belly. I felt a little squiggle-movement—BABY! It was a wonderful feeling. I couldn't stop laughing and rejoicing that I was actually going to be a father, Wendy was going to be a mother, and we were actually going to have a child together.

The squadron held our annual Christmas party at a hotel on the Mosel River. Having just returned from another WTD, there were fun skits and songs, both from the pilots and the spouses. Then, Cobber stood up to announce the recipient of the first-ever 496th Top Dog Award.

Cobber informed us while we were at Zaragoza that the squadron would present this new award every six months to a worthy individual voted by members of the squadron. The criteria were somewhat vague—the squadron's true informal leader, the guy we would follow into battle, and the guy we would follow to the bar.

When Cobber announced my name, the whole squadron burst into loud cheers and applause. I was moved beyond words. Here I was, the guy who had just so spectacularly failed the squadron at Excalibur II a mere two months before, and now they were giving me the greatest honor I had ever received in my lifetime up to that point. I was truly speechless; I choked back tears as I accepted the plaque, which also still hangs on my wall. All I could do was give a wave of acknowledgment, sit down, and hold Wendy's hand.

There are a thousand reasons to love flying fighters and being in an operational combat squadron with like-minded men and women dedicated to something greater than themselves. But the love and fellowship shared between warriors is something extraordinary, and is cherished beyond measure. When you ask former fighter pilots what they miss most, many of them will answer the camaraderie. On that evening on the Mosel, my squadron mates gave me a precious gift I will never forget.

The year 1988 began with big expectations for Wendy and me. Overseas assignments typically lasted three years for accompanied service members, but I had been allowed to extend for a fourth year. We knew that in addition to our child being born, we would also receive a new assignment. We loved living in Europe, but the only way to remain there would be for me to take a non-flying staff job, or an Air Liaison Officer (ALO) job for two years with the Army.

Neither of those options really appealed to me, and with a new baby in tow, Wendy and I thought it best to return stateside so the new grandparents could spend some time with their grandchild. The odds of being assigned to another operational fighter squadron were virtually nil, since I had already had two flying assignments and was coming off a 4-year operational tour, so my only really good option was to apply for an F-16 Instructor position at Luke AFB—back to RTU, but this time, as an IP. Through conversation with the assignment folks at HQ AFPC at Randolph AFB, I learned that's what they planned as well, so the die was cast.

Towards the end of January, Wendy had an ultrasound performed to check on the status of the baby growing in her belly. The little hospital clinic on Hahn AB didn't have ultrasound equipment, so it was outsourced to a German civilian doctor in Oberwesel on the Rhine River. His little office had a beautiful picture window overlooking the Rhine, not too far from Wiesbaden, where Wendy and I had grown up.

With Wendy on the table and me watching with anticipation, Dr. Benkert explained the images on the screen: "Here is the head. Here are the arms. Here is the back. And here is the penis!"

"WOO-HOO!!" I yelled, pumping my fist in the air while Wendy lay on the table with her belly still exposed, laughing and crying at the same time. A Son! David Walker White! As we left the office, we literally danced down the street to a pizzeria where we enjoyed lunch and rejoiced in the healthy baby boy who was scheduled to arrive on-time on-target in mid-April.

At this point, I was one of the older grizzled veterans in the squadron, and the guys had taken to calling me Papa Kilo. My duties as a flight commander and instructor continued, and I spent much of my time flying with the new guys and getting them proficient and comfortable with flying in Central Europe and their new assignments to Hahn.

When I received word in February that I had been promoted to Major, the feeling that I was now one of the senior guys was magnified. I had also made the School's List, meaning that it was the Air Force's intent to send me to Intermediate Service School (ISS) somewhere and at some point in the next three years. Accordingly, we assumed that my assignment to Luke would be short-lived—two years at the most.

In March, we headed back down to Incirlik for my last WTD with the squadron. It was pretty much business as usual, but not without a few surprises. I was getting a checkride leading a 4-ship, and we had just completed our simulated attack when we got a call from squadron ops to contact the GCI controller frequency.

I sent the flight to the freq, and was informed that a Syrian MiG-25 Foxbat had penetrated Turkish airspace, had flown over Incirlik, and was speeding its way back south to the Turkish-Syrian border. Did we have enough fuel to engage?

"Well, heck yeah," I replied. But we were configured with two wings tanks, two empty SUU bomb dispensers, and an ECM pod. We also had cold guns; even if we could catch this guy, what were going to do when we got there? Anyway, they wanted us to try, so we gamely accepted GCI vectors and tried to climb up to altitude to at least threaten the MiG. We never got close, of course, but it was certainly a break from the normal routine.

On our third week at Incirlik, one of our new pilots, a major, came walking back in the ops building after having stepped to his jet for an upgrade mission around 20 minutes prior. I was pulling squadron supervisor duties at the desk.

"I can't do this anymore," he muttered. "I can't keep up this pace. If I keep going like this, I'm going to crash and kill myself or somebody else. Take me off the schedule."

Wow. That was a sobering moment. We took him off the schedule, and after spending some time with Cobber, we sent him back to his family at Hahn to receive counseling and to cool off for a while. He eventually returned to flying in a somewhat limited capacity, but it was a reminder of some of the hazards in the fighter business.

During my time at Hahn, we lost five jets and had three fatalities. While we lost a jet in the 496th, the pilot, Bubba, safely ejected, so we hadn't lost a pilot. But the impact of those lost lives was felt by everyone in the wing.

I didn't realize how much stress that puts on the spouses, and on Wendy in particular. I found out later that when I went to work every morning, she prayed a worried silent prayer for my safety, and that when she heard me drive back in the evening, she said a relieved prayer of thanks. Our families make a big sacrifice in allowing us to do that thing we love so much.

On our return from Incirlik, we had our typical Welcome Home party. The dress code was to arrive in some kind of Turkish attire—easy to do since most of us always loaded up with Turkish pants (the infamous Seven-Day-Shitters, or later more conservatively called MC Hammer pants) and other Turkish accouterments. As a joke, Wendy, who was 8-months-heavily-pregnant, decided to come as a belly dancer. When she attempted to do a belly dance in her costume, she threw her back out. It was funny and not funny at the same time since she had to stay a couple of days in bed.

In early April, we got a call one weekend from John Portelli, Wendy's cousin. John was the current tour manager for AC/DC, one of my all-time favorite bands. "Hey!" John said. "We are in Frankfurt for the show tomorrow night. Why don't you and PK come up? I'll get you backstage passes, and you can get a chance to see the show and meet the band."

Holy Smokes! What an opportunity! I was so excited, but Wendy just shook her head. "Thanks, John, but I am due to give birth any day now, so it's probably not a good idea!"

She was right, of course, but I was devastated. In my mind I pictured Walker being born backstage at an AC/DC concert—how cool would that be? Not a good idea, obviously, but Walker probably doesn't know how close he came to being named Angus Malcolm White.

I often tell people that the real reason we only had one child was because I had such a rough pregnancy. Wendy breezed through it after that first trimester's nausea; she loved being pregnant and was the perfect expecting mom-to-be. I, however, was a nervous wreck. If Wendy whispered a little groan while slowly getting off the couch, I would bark, "Oh my gosh, what's the matter??? Are you okay?? Do we need to go to the hospital??!!"

If Wendy got up in the middle of the night for a bowl of cereal, I got up and ate a bowl with her. If she wanted pickles and peanut butter, I wanted pickles and peanut butter. I had all the bags packed by the door for the trip to the hospital, and I constantly reviewed inventory to ensure nothing was left behind. As a result, it's no wonder that Wendy asked her mother, Dolores, to come to Hahn to help with the birth of her grandson. Wendy knew that I would be a mess. With much relief, I picked Dolores up at the Frankfurt Airport on Saturday, April 16th.

Walker's scheduled due date was April 14th, but he was taking his good sweet time about it. Coincidentally, the 50th TFW's NATO TACEVAL—an operational readiness inspection that would include both our conventional and nuclear combat roles was scheduled to begin Monday, April 18th. After discussions with Cobber and the squadron leadership, we agreed that if Walker was born as scheduled, there would still be enough time to get Wendy and him safely at home to allow me to be a full participant in this critically important inspection.

However, if he was born much later, all bets were off. So, on Sunday, April 17th, I was at the squadron, helping make final preparations for the TACEVAL while Wendy was at home with her mother. I was back in the weapons vault when I heard over the Big Voice speakers: "PK White!! Baby Scramble, Baby Scramble! Walker White is inbound!"

Some of the guys lined up and gave me high-5s as I exited the squadron and raced to the base hospital, which was only minutes away. I got there before Wendy and Dolores did. I was waiting anxiously in the waiting room when the door flew open. It was windy and raining outside—Dolores stood there, the wind blowing her raincoat and hair, and with her model/actress background, dramatically shouted, "We're Having A Baby Here!!"

Wendy was in labor for about four hours, and Dolores and I were with her throughout the process. When Wendy was having a particularly bad surge of pain, I held her hand, stared into her eyes, and softly sang "Stand By Me" by Ben E. King. It made some of the nurses cry watching us together—it was a cherished moment. Walker was born at 9:53 PM; an 8-pound, 5-ounce healthy baby boy with a head full of copper-blonde hair like his Daddy, and bright blue eyes like his Mama. It was the second greatest day of my life—the first being the day I married Wendy.

Much to the nurses' amusement, I had already prepared a mini-poster, which I taped to Walker's bassinet. It had lyrics stolen from George Thorogood and the Destroyers:

On the day I was born,
the nurses gathered 'round
And they gazed in wide wonder
at the joy they had found.
The head nurse spoke up,
And she said, "leave this one alone!"
She could tell right away
That I was bad to the bone.

The squadron very generously excused me from participating in the TACEVAL, so I was able to spend most of my time at the hospital until Wendy and Walker were discharged.

The hospital was being evaluated during the TACEVAL as well as the other units, so visitors were not allowed. The morning after Walker's birth, we heard a knocking at the window outside Wendy's room. We looked outside, and there was a gang of 8-9 of the squadron wives with balloons and cards demanding to see Walker and checking to see if Wendy was doing okay—another indicator of the closeness common in overseas fighter squadrons.

After paying our $9.00 fee to the hospital for medical care—we often joke with Walker that he cost less than our pet cats—we drove home in the rain with Walker wailing in the back strapped in his new car seat. We were terrified.

We put his crib in our bedroom and checked on him throughout the night every 15 minutes or so—is he still alive?? Since it had worked so well with Wendy, I sang "Stand By Me" to Walker as a lullaby; it worked on him, too. He was a good baby, not cranky, not colicky, and generally slept through most of the night.

While we were learning to be parents, we also spent the next weeks preparing and packing for the move back to the States and my assignment to the 312th TFTS Scorpions at Luke AFB.

I handed my flight commander duties over to Lenny, my replacement as the B Flight Commander, and continued mostly flying upgrades with the new pilots. My finis flight was on July 19th—a BFM sortie, which was perfect.

In typical fashion, the squadron met me after landing and engine shutdown by hosing me down with fire extinguishers and spraying me with champagne. It was time to move on.

The squadron threw a big hail-and-farewell party about a week before our departure. We welcomed the new guys, said goodbye to Mac and his family, then the squadron said goodbye to Wendy and me. The spouses made several very gracious speeches to Wendy, and some of the senior leadership to me.

The guys put together a video montage, entitled "This Is How PK White Sees Himself." There were numerous clips of heroic speeches from war movies: *Henry V* at Agincourt, Chard at Rorke's Drift from the movie *Zulu*, Travis's Victory or Death speech at *The Alamo*, the John Wayne cavalry charge from *She Wore A Yellow Ribbon*—you get the idea. It was all in good fun, of course, and Wendy and I loved it.

When it was my turn to speak, there was a box of tissue on the podium labeled PK Wipes, making fun of my habit of getting emotional during speeches. I made good use of those tissues. I thanked everyone and spoke of the greatness of the squadron, and mentioned how incredibly awesome it was to have received the Top Dog Award after letting everyone down at Excalibur II. I ended by doing the "Big Dog Rap" one last time.

Saying goodbye to the 496th, after four years of laughing, living, fighting, and traveling together, was hard; they were truly as close to us as family. More than 32 years later, we are still in close contact with many of the friends we were with during our time at Hahn. It was my first fighter squadron, we were back home in Germany, and it was the place where our son was born. It will always be very, very special.

The Assistant Ops Officer, Hulio, drove us to the airport at Rhine-Main Air Base in Frankfurt—Hulio later went on to command the 10th, and led them to glory during Desert Storm. Wendy cried all the way; it was breaking her heart to leave Germany after four years, all of our wonderful and fun experiences, and all of the good times we had with friends and comrades.

As for me, I was leaving with a great deal of satisfaction. When we arrived in 1984, I wasn't sure if I was even truly good enough to be an F-16 fighter pilot. Four years later, I was leaving as a flight commander with all the flying qualifications I could possess. I had earned the respect of my peers, and I had been promoted for my efforts. I was ecstatically happily married to a beautiful, loving, smart, and talented wife, and I was returning home the father of a handsome, healthy baby boy who was already changing my life in ways I could not have imagined.

As our plane lifted off and we said goodbye to Hahn, I thanked God for blessing us so abundantly, and for the adventures yet to come.

Hobart, OK's Top Gun, 1958   Uhuru, Wiesbaden, Germany, 1974

Commissioning, Troy State University, AL, 1978

T-38s, Williams AFB, AZ, 1980

T-37 FAIP, Sheppard AFB, TX, 1982

Somewhere Over North Texas, 1981

Randolph AFB Chapel, TX, 1983   Flight Suit Dining-Out,
Hahn AB, 1985

Air Refueling, Somewhere Over the Med, 1986

Welcome Home, Hahn, AB, 1986

Prepping for RCP Taxi Ride for Wives Day, Hahn AB, 1986

RBAABs—PK, Rev, Skull, Tex— Hahn AB, 1987

496th Tac Fighter Squadron Bravo-Delta-Deltas,
Zaragoza AB, 1987

Finis Flight, Hahn AB, 1988

POSTSCRIPT

1988–2009

"Times change, the technology changes, but the man in the cockpit must remain that same brave warrior every age has counted on in times of peril... Fighter pilots understand the fundamental law of wartime negotiations. You negotiate with the enemy with your knee in his chest and your knife at his throat."

—Brian Shul

When I first decided to write this book, it was my original intention to address my entire 30-year career, with a particular focus on flying jets. However, as I got deeper into writing and including all of the detail I wanted, I realized that it might turn into an 800-page tome that only close family members would be even remotely interested in reading.

Accordingly, I scaled back the scope to relate only my coming-of-age as an F-16 fighter pilot during the Cold War, the end of which was symbolized by the fall of the Berlin Wall a year after we left our Hahn assignment.

After leaving Hahn in July 1988, I spent another 21 years in the Air Force. A synopsis of the rest of my Air Force career follows.

312th Tactical Fighter Training Squadron
Luke AFB, Arizona
August 1988 - December 1989
Position held: Chief of Squadron Scheduling

We lived on base at Luke. Wendy enjoyed it well enough; living on base, day-to-day living was much more convenient than it was at Hahn, especially with a newborn baby. Being back stateside after four years, we were able to spend some quality time with family and friends.

I, however, was not truly happy. Flying with students was fine, even from the occasional rear cockpit, but I sorely missed the camaraderie and spirit of an overseas operational fighter squadron. At Luke during this time, it seemed that most everyone was more intent on studying and testing to get the ratings they needed to punch their ticket to fly for Southwest Airlines than staying in the active-duty Air Force and being fighter pilots.

Instead of gathering at the Officer's Club on Fridays, most seemed more intent on going home and cleaning their swimming pools. The warrior culture just seemed to be missing. Fair enough—but it wasn't for me, and although I was expecting to be selected for an Intermediate Service School assignment, I jumped at the chance to leave Luke early when it was offered.

F-16 Security Assistance Program
Hellenic Air Force (HAF), Nea Anchialos AFB, Greece
January 1990 - December 1990
Position held: U.S. Point of Contact to develop combat capability for Greece's only F-16 tactical fighter wing

We had trained the initial cadre of Greek F-16 pilots in the 312th at Luke, so I knew most of the guys and had flown with them. When TAC put out the word that they needed two pilots to spend a year in Greece, providing the HAF advanced combat training, I quickly volunteered. Even though it was considered a remote tour, which I needed to get out of the way at some point anyway, I took Wendy and Walker with me, since Walker wasn't yet of school age. While living in Greece had its occasional challenges, it was a great year for family time.

I flew with an air-to-air squadron; the flying schedule usually had the last landing down by 2:00 PM, and they didn't fly on Fridays, so I was able to spend much more time with Wendy and Walker as he was growing into toddlerhood than I would have otherwise. I enjoyed flying with the HAF and the people there. They were extremely hospitable, and we also made friends with U.S. contractors who were providing maintenance and simulator support. Flying air-to-air every day over the Aegean Sea was fantastic. I also hoped that being stationed back in Europe would provide a gateway to a follow-on assignment with a return back to USAFE.

The highlight of my tour in Greece was a fly-off competition between their U.S. F-16s and French Mirage 2000s. The Greek government wanted to determine which aircraft would best suit their needs in the future, so they designed a competition to be held at Nea Anchialos AB.

The competition involved BFM, ACM, and intercept scenarios. Just prior to the event, I received a call from Joe Bill Dryden—a well-known F-16 test pilot flying for General Dynamics. Over the phone, he coached me on how best to employ our Vipers against the Mirages, "Don't let them start the fight below 400 knots, and don't let them start at line abreast!"

I passed his words on to my HAF F-16 comrades and even flew a few sorties during the competition. In the end, it was no contest—even the HAF Mirage 2000 pilots agreed, being especially impressed with the F-16 radar. As a result, Greece invested in another huge F-16 buy. Later, I was sad to hear of Joe Bill's death in 1993 during a test flight. Nickel in the grass.

HQ 17th Air Force Operations Division
Sembach Air Base, Germany
December 1990 - May 1993
Positions held: Chief of Weapons & Tactics, F-16
Standardization-Evaluation Flight Examiner (SEFE)

I made some calls to USAFE assignments shortly after arriving in Greece; as a Major, it was time to consider a staff assignment. When I learned of a flying staff position available at 17th Air Force, I quickly submitted my resume. Luckily, folks there knew me from my Hahn days, and I was hired.

I sent Wendy and Walker home from Greece in October to spend some family time with the grandparents and to arrange for shipment of our car and household goods to Germany.

However, in mid-November, I received a congratulatory letter in our personal mail—which we picked up once every 3-4 weeks from the U.S. Embassy in Athens. The message was from a 2-Star general officer in EUCOM congratulating me on my selection to attend Marine Corps Staff College in Quantico starting the summer of 1991.

Somehow, my supervisors at the Office of Diplomatic Cooperation in Athens had not gotten the word and neglected to inform me when the official message was released nearly a month prior, so I was in a dilemma.

We already had our household goods and car halfway across the ocean on their way to Germany, I was scheduled to report to 17th Air Force in three weeks, and had verbally agreed on a house.

I called HQ AFPC. They informed me I had three choices. I could extend in Greece for another seven months, although my replacement had already been named; I could report immediately to Quantico and serve on casual status for seven months until my class started; or, due to my situation, I could decline the school slot without prejudice.

Given that Desert Storm was about to commence, I received a rare flying staff job—I would be attached to the 512th TFS Dragons in Ramstein for flying purposes—and we would be returning to Germany, I elected to decline the ISS slot. Most everyone, including my father, told me I had committed career suicide, "You're turning down a joint school slot for a Numbered Air Force staff job!!??"

We never regretted our decision. We loved living in our tiny village of Breunigweiler, and we made good friends on and off base. The 512th wasn't tasked for Desert Storm, so I stayed behind with the rest of the squadron.

However, over the course of my time at Sembach, I deployed three times with the 512th to Incirlik for Operation Provide Comfort, patrolling the skies of Northern Iraq to defend the Kurds from Saddam Hussein in the aftermath of Desert Storm.

During my first deployment in April 1991, my sole job was to train the initial cadre of Turkish F-16 pilots in aerial refueling from our KC-135 tankers. I also later attended a NATO Weapons Planning course at Oberammergau in Bavaria, not a bad gig, where again, I took Wendy and Walker with me. We traveled extensively and enjoyed raising Walker and watching him develop his fun personality and delightful sense-of-humor.

In those days, the Air Force conducted what was known as Return-To-Fly boards for pilots who were coming out of staff positions. Even though I was actively flying F-16s with the 512th, I was still required to meet the board. I was rated #1 in USAFE for majors meeting the board, so I had a high level of confidence that we would be able to stay in Europe, either at Ramstein or Spangdahlem.

Wrong. When I finally got the call from HQ AFPC, I was offered Osan AB or Kunsan AB in Korea, or any number of Guard Advisor jobs at various Air National Guard bases in the States. That was it.

I was deeply disappointed, but I leaned towards Osan because I knew there was a strong possibility I could take Wendy and Walker with me, and I would be flying in a front-line operational fighter squadron.

But Wendy wasn't convinced; she had heard all of the wild west stories of remoteness and debauchery from others who had been stationed in Korea, was worried it might not be a great place to raise a child and preferred a return to the States at a small Guard base where I would have less chance of a lengthy deployment, and we could be closer to our families.

We prayed about it one night before going to bed. The next morning, Wendy woke up, looked at me, and said, "Let's go to Osan!" God bless her!

51st Operations Support Squadron, 51st Fighter Wing
Osan Air Base, South Korea
August 1993 - January 1995
Positions held: Operations Officer, Wing Chief of Safety

The 36 FS Flying Fiends at Osan flew the LANTIRN-equipped Block 40 F-16s and flew a large portion of their missions at night. Therefore, before we reported to Osan, I had to complete the F-16 Block 40 Transition Course back at Luke AFB.

This provided Wendy and Walker another great opportunity to spend some time with the grandparents while I was back at Luke once again.

When we finally arrived at Osan in late August, we were shocked! It was a beautiful base with nice housing, excellent facilities, and off-base was nothing like we expected. Downtown Songtan was full of interesting shops and restaurants and bustling with life. The people were warm and friendly, and we fell in love with Korea immediately. We happily moved into our 930 sq ft apartment on base in Mustang Valley Village. Walker was pleased to have so many kids to play with, and playgrounds and sports fields where he could run wild.

I was disappointed to learn that I would be assigned to the 51st OSS instead of the 36 FS, but as at Sembach, I would be attached to the 36th for flying. As the Ops Officer for the OSS, I was also designated as the Night Mission Director on the Battle Staff for the once-a-quarter base-wide exercises held at Osan, with the North Korean threat being a mere 7-minutes away in flying time.

Combat operations in Korea are high-speed. The threat is real, including chemical and biological warfare, so you are in a constant state of readiness. I learned much as the Mission Director that would serve me well in future assignments.

After seven months, I was moved to the Wing Chief of Safety, given my training and background as a Safety Officer. In addition to flying safety, I was also responsible for ground and weapons safety on the base.

One Saturday, the Wing Commander called me on the brick (hand-held radio)—I was Mustang 9—and Mustang 1 told me to meet him outside our housing building. I had just been informed I had been promoted to Lt Colonel and had made the Senior Service Schools list, so I suspected that's where the conversation might be leading.

When I got in his car, we started to drive around the base, and he asked me, "So. What are your plans for your next assignment?"

I told him I would like to keep flying, and hopefully, get an Operations Officer position somewhere.

He answered, "I can probably get you an Ops Officer job at Kunsan."

Kunsan AB was located south of Osan, and was a genuine remote assignment; no families were allowed. Although it had an excellent reputation as a flying wing, I was not interested in being assigned anywhere without Wendy and Walker, and I told him so.

"Well," he said as he dropped me off back at our apartment building, "Don't feel bitter when you later realize you failed to grab the brass ring."

"Well, that's that!" I thought to myself, again, without regret. I started searching the Want Ads assignments pages for a potential follow-on assignment out of Osan. I found a position as the Assistant Attache in Singapore that required a pilot on flying status, and after talking it over with Wendy, we agreed to go for it. I made a few calls, and it was looking highly favorable when one day not too long after that, I got a call from the new OSS commander.

"Hey, P.K.! The Operations Group commander from Misawa is here and said he was looking to interview anyone who might be interested in an Operations Officer position with the 14th Fighter Squadron there. Are you interested?"

It was there that I met Nordo for the first time—one of the most inspirational and influential officers in my career, who later went on to earn 4-Star rank.

14th Fighter Squadron, then
13th Fighter Squadron, 35th Fighter Wing
Misawa Air Base, Japan
January 1995 - June 1998
Positions held: Operations Officer, 14 FS;
Commander, 13 FS

I had been attached to squadrons and flying as a Mission Support (MS) pilot for nearly five years; it was great to actually be back flying as a full-up Mission Ready (MR) fighter pilot. The 14th FS Fightin' Samurai were just starting their conversion from Block 30 F-16s to Block 50 Wild Weasel F-16s. Managing the transition, with the training and logistics involved, was my primary focus as the Ops Officer.

Morale was high, and the pilots and maintenance crews were top-notch. I took command of the 13th Fighter Squadron Panthers in June 1996, days before the Khobar Towers incident, where 19 airmen were killed.

The 13th was already scheduled to be the first PACAF fighter squadron to deploy to the Iraqi AOR, in early July. Our initial task was to assist with the cleanup of the extensive damage to Khobar Towers. We then took part in Desert Strike, flew the first missions in the newly-expanded No-Fly Zone for Southern Watch, re-opened operations at Prince Sultan Air Base, relocated to Sheik Isa Air Base in Bahrain, and ended up staying six months for what was originally planned as a 90-day deployment.

We, the 13th, also had the first engagements with Iraqi Surface-to-Air Missile (SAM) sites since the end of Desert Storm.

In late 1997, I learned I had been selected for the U.S. Air Force Lance P. Sijan Leadership Award in the senior officer category. It was probably the greatest honor I received in my career, all thanks to the incredible hard work and sacrifice of the pilots, maintainers, and weapons troops of the 13th Fighter Squadron.

The Air Force flew Wendy, Walker, and me out to the Pentagon for the awards ceremony, where we were joined by my parents and other family members and friends. We proudly laid claim to the title of World's Greatest Wild Weasels (WGWWs), and the 13th still defends that title today. Being a fighter squadron commander is the best job in the Air Force.

Senior Service School (SSS)
Washington Institute for Near East Policy (WINEP)
Washington D.C.
July 1998 – July 1999
Position held: National Defense Fellow

Following squadron command, I knew I would attend SSS somewhere. It would be the first non-flying assignment in my 19 years in the Air Force, but I accepted the inevitable. I didn't want to attend the Air War College, since I had already completed it by correspondence, so I applied for a National Defense Fellow (NDF) position. The Air Force gives out about 30 NDF slots per year.

The purpose is to serve for a year with a D.C. or university Think Tank to allow a mutual exchange between military and civilian ideas and concepts.

WINEP is a pro-Israel think tank focused on the foreign policy of the United States in the Near East. The only SSS requirement for National Defense Fellows is to develop an academic study/paper worthy of publication. While there, I wrote *Crises After The Storm: An Appraisal of U.S. Air Operations In Iraq Since The Persian Gulf War*.

WINEP published it as a book, and it became required reading at the School of Advanced Aerospace Studies (SAAS). Later, excerpts of the book were printed in Joint Forces Quarterly magazine, which in turn were incorporated into the Air War College syllabus.

Just prior to leaving WINEP, I learned of my promotion to Colonel.

Joint Staff, J-5 Strategy Division
The Pentagon
July 1999 - June 2001
Position held: Strategy Planner

Wendy, Walker, and I enjoyed living in Washington, D.C. well enough, and we didn't want to move again after only a year, so I began searching for staff jobs at the Pentagon.

Once again, Nordo came to my rescue. He was then serving as the Executive Assistant to the Director of the Joint Chiefs of Staff, and he arranged for an interview for me with the chief of the J-5 Strategy Division.

I was hired, and my primary responsibilities were planning and oversight of the Joint Strategic Capabilities Plan (JSCP), which directs planning tasks and apportions forces to the CINCs and Services, and the Contingency Planning Guidance (CPG), which provides guidance and objectives to the Combatant Commanders for specific contingencies. Both plans are TOP SECRET.

Much to my surprise, I didn't hate working at the Pentagon, and I learned much about how our senior leaders, both military and civilian, run the military machine and make decisions. Still, I was ecstatic when I came out on the Operations Group Command-select list. I would be going back to the cockpit—somewhere.

51st Operations Group
Osan Air Base, South Korea
July 2001 - August 2003
Position Held: Commander

The family was delighted to be returning to Osan AB, the most forward-deployed fighter wing in the Air Force, and to a country, installation, and mission with which we were familiar and enjoyed.

As the Ops Group Commander, I had oversight of the 36th Fighter Squadron F-16s, 25th Fighter Squadron A-10s, the 51st

Operations Support Squadron, and a C-12 Squadron. It was a great assignment; it gave me the opportunity to learn and understand senior officer duties and responsibilities in a high-tempo, combat-oriented environment.

It was a real meatgrinder, however. It was the only assignment in my career where I truly worked 14-hr days or more, and I was tied to the brick as Mustang 3, constantly responding to radio calls and events requiring decisions and actions.

While there, we dealt with the fallout of 9/11, a visit from President George Bush (43), Class A Mishaps on one of our F-16s and a U-2, whose squadron shared our runway, a Class B Mishap of an A-10, and numerous hostile provocations from North Korea that caused us to constantly alter our alert posture.

In April 2003, I came out on the Air Base Wing Commander list, which meant I was eligible to be the commander or vice-commander of an Air Base Wing (ABW). Air Base Wings, obviously, are not Fighter Wings; they generally provide support for major command functions such as senior service schools, training centers, etc., and as such, are usually not flying billets.

Naturally, I was a little disappointed, but given my background—I didn't attend ISS; I never served as a general's exec or aide; I had only one below-the-zone promotion (to colonel); and I didn't play golf! I knew I was never really on the fast-track to begin with. Nevertheless, I was excited when I learned I had been selected to be the Vice Wing Commander of the 36th Air Base Wing at Andersen AFB in Guam.

36th Air Base Wing, then
36th Air Expeditionary Wing
Andersen AFB, Guam
August 2003 - July 2005
Positions held: Vice Wing Commander; Wing Commander

Almost immediately after our arrival in Guam, we learned that the current Wing Commander had been promoted to Brigadier General, so I would soon be getting a new boss.

Andersen AFB mainly served as a bomb storage facility for Pacific-related contingencies, and a stopping place in the middle of the ocean for refueling aircraft on their way to somewhere more important.

In December, I was shocked when the 13th AF Commander informed me I was going to be the new Wing Commander, and as such, in charge of the transformation of Andersen AFB from an Air Base Wing to an Air Expeditionary Wing.

Right away, I tripled patrols in our weapons storage area, outfitted our security forces at the main gate in full battle rattle, placed an Armored Personnel Carrier just inside the gate, and decreased the amount of civilian personnel authorized access to the base by 20%.

I increased our operational readiness exercises to quarterly, and totally reconstructed our Base Operations facility to more readily assume a combat operations posture.

I gave notice to everyone on the island that Andersen was no longer a sleepy little base, virtually open to the public—we had the knife in our teeth, and we meant business. These were not always popular actions for the people of Guam and elsewhere, and I ruffled a few feathers, but it had to be done, given our growing posture.

As an Air Expeditionary Wing, we were now going to have a constant rotation of fighters, tankers, and bombers, so we also had to modernize and update operations facilities and billets to accommodate the increased presence. By the time we departed Guam, we had turned a remote Air Base Wing noted mostly for gas-and-go's to the premier combat wing in the Pacific.

There were no permanently assigned aircraft at Andersen; we had a different squadron roll in every three months. However, as a rated wing commander, I had the privilege of sandbagging sorties in a variety of jets. I picked up nearly 30 hours in the right seat of B-52s—folks, let me tell you, that beast is not easy to fly, especially aerial refueling. I had two backseat sorties in F-18s off the *Kitty Hawk*, where I experienced a carrier landing (insane!). My last flight in an F-16 was with one of my old squadrons, the 14 FS Samurai; the front-seater let me fly most of the mission from the back seat, for which I was very grateful. Finally, my finis flight was in the right seat of a B-2—a pretty cool way to end the flying portion of my Air Force career.

One added bonus to our Guam assignment was that the Commander, U.S. Naval Forces, Marianas, whose headquarters was also in Guam, was RADM Arthur Johnson.

Artie was one of my best friends in high school in Wiesbaden; he lived on the top of a hill on Arizona Strasse, where I would pick him up on the way to school. We had kept in close contact throughout the years, and now he was the Naval forces commander, and I was the Air Force wing commander together on Guam. I suspect the Navy and the Air Force never worked so closely together as they did when Artie and I were stationed there at the same time.

AFROTC Detachment 910
The University of Washington, Seattle, WA
July 2005 - June 2009
Position held: Commander

When it became clear that the Air Force wasn't going to promote me to Brigadier General, rather than accept another high-stress job back at the Pentagon or even HQ PACAF in Hawaii, and after discussions with Wendy and Walker, I decided to compete for an AFROTC commander billet at a university.

We knew it would be my last assignment, so we wanted to find somewhere that we hoped would be an attractive retirement location.

The Colonel's Group was very encouraging, informing me that I had a good shot at getting my first choice. Looking over the choices available, I narrowed it down to three: Embry-Riddle Aeronautical University in Daytona (where I could fly again), Massachusetts Institute of Technology (MIT) near Boston, and the University of Washington in Seattle.

Wendy and I always thought that when we retired, we'd probably like to retire somewhere in New England, where the weather, flora, and fauna were similar to Germany—hence MIT. However, the Seattle area offered the same environment.

So, since I had moved Wendy and Walker all over the world to serve my career ambitions and desires, I told them that they could choose where our final Air Force assignment would be. I made out a list of pros and cons for each and awaited their decision.

For both of them, Florida was immediately out; humid, muggy, hot temperatures with a constant hurricane threat and they didn't really want me flying anymore. MIT and the Boston area had its attractions, but Wendy had visited Seattle when she was in college and loved it. Walker was a budding rock star, and Seattle was one of the Rock-N-Roll Capitals of The Universe. So, we chose the University of Washington.

We instantly fell in love with the Pacific Northwest, and immediately decided to make it our retirement home. It was a great four years and an easy eventual transition to civilian life.

I enjoyed teaching and spending time with the cadets. Dealing with university officials was often a pain; the anti-military sentiment was high, especially with George Bush still president, but we excelled. Our entire detachment staff was outstanding, and it was largely due to our superb NCOs and civilian secretary that we were awarded the 2007 Right-of-Line trophy for the Best Large Unit AFROTC Detachment in the Nation.

For my retirement ceremony, my good friend RADM Artie Johnson flew in to officiate. My parents, other family members, and more friends from high school and my military career also were present. I said goodbye as best I could.

FINAL COMMENTS

I finished my Air Force career in 2009 with 3,500 total flying hours—2,250 hours in the F-16, 1,100 hours in the T-37, and 150 hours in various other jets. I accumulated 210 hours of combat time, mostly Wild Weasel missions, all over Iraq. Since my finis flight in the B-2 at Guam in 2005, I have not flown an aircraft where I am at the controls.

While I was at the University of Washington, I got a call out of the blue, asking me if I would be interested in interviewing to work for a multi-billionaire living in the Seattle area who owned a vast, private fighter jet collection. The job involved nothing more than flying the jets and keeping them airworthy. How cool would it be to simply take some vintage and modern-day jets up for a spin every day? But after a short time thinking about it, I declined.

After 30 years, I discovered something about myself. What I enjoyed about flying wasn't simply slipping the surly bonds of earth. What I loved most was employing the weapons system—taking three other like-minded brother-warriors, planning an attack, and executing it to perfection, blowing the heck out of something big, and destroying any adversaries that flew in our path.

This job sounded more like doing loops to music over the flag pole; as attractive as it sounded, I wasn't really interested.

I have been asked on several occasions, especially having been a successful Wing Commander under challenging circumstances, why I wasn't promoted to Brigadier General. The simple and honest truth is that there were others more qualified and deserving than me, period. Was I disappointed? You bet. But like most fighter pilots, being a fighter squadron commander is what I truly wanted to be, and it was everything I had ever dreamed of and more. Everything else was icing on the cake.

I also realized the higher I rose in rank, the less fun it was. Being a fighter squadron commander was a blast, but after that, less so. As a Wing Commander, I used to joke that once I had been solely concerned with how to kill and survive; now, I was worried about enough diapers in the commissary. An exaggeration, to be sure, but herein lies a grain of truth. Also, the added stresses and pressures on Wendy as the spouse of an Ops Group Commander, and much more so as a Wing Commander, were substantial. Wendy was not comfortable with the never-ending expectations and living in a fish-bowl; she often says her favorite moments at Guam were the times she was scuba diving, where no one could reach her or beseech her.

Walker had similar demands on him and often ended up with a scuba tank underwater with his mama. For my family and me, the Air Force made the absolute right choice, and I am grateful.

I'm also frequently asked, "What was your favorite assignment?"

That's a tough one.

Most fun? Flight Commander, Hahn.

Most rewarding? Squadron Commander, Misawa.

Most impactful? Wing Commander, Guam.

But I can honestly say that we enjoyed every one of our assignments.

From my childhood to the present, the Air Force has given my family and me—my parents, my wife, my son—a wonderful life, and I wouldn't change a thing.

I still stand at attention when I hear the Air Force song. I still get excited when I see a flyover at a football game. I still look to the sky when I hear the sound of a jet flying overhead. I get in arguments on the internet over which is the greatest fighter jet.

Being a fighter pilot will always be a large part of who I am. And in my dreams, inside the turn circle is still where I want to be.

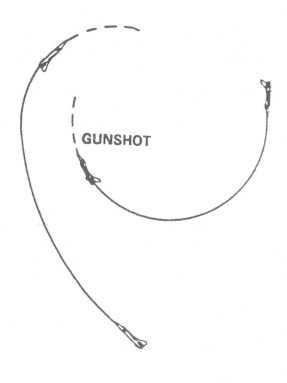

DEADBUG—A TRIBUTE TO FIGHTER PILOTS

As we get older and we experience the loss of old friends, we begin to realize that maybe we bullet proof Fighter Pilots won't live forever, not so bullet proof anymore. We ponder -- if I was gone tomorrow, did I say what I wanted to my Brothers? The answer was no! Hence, the following few random thoughts.

When people ask me if I miss flying, I always say something like -- "Yes! I miss the flying because when you are flying, you are totally focused on the task at hand. It's like nothing else you will ever do (almost). But then I always say "However, I miss the Squadron and the guys even more than I miss the flying." Why you might ask?" They were a bunch of aggressive, wise ass, cocky, insulting, sarcastic bastards in smelly flight suits who thought a funny thing to do was to fart and see if they could clear a room. They drank too much, they chased women, they flew when they shouldn't, they laughed too loud and thought they owned the sky, the Bar, and generally thought they could do everything better than the next guy. Nothing was funnier than trying to screw with a buddy and see how pissed off he would get. They flew planes and helos that leaked, that smoked, that broke, that couldn't turn, that burned fuel too fast, that never had auto pilots or radars, and with systems that were archaic next to today's new generation aircraft. All true!

But a little closer look might show that every guy in the room was sneaky smart and damn competent and brutally handsome! They hated to lose or fail to accomplish the mission and seldom did. They were the laziest guys on the planet until challenged and then they would do anything to win. They would fly with wing tips overlapped at night through the worst weather with only a little red light to hold on to, knowing that their Flight Lead would get them on the ground safely. They would fight in the air knowing the greatest risk and fear was that another fighter would arrive at the same six o'clock at the same time they did. They would fly in harm's way and act nonchalant as if to challenge the grim reaper.

When we went to another base we were the best Squadron on the base as soon as we landed. Often we were not welcomed back. When we went into an O club we owned the Bar. We were lucky to have the Best of the Best in the military. We knew it and so did others. We found jobs, lost jobs, got married, got divorced, moved, went broke, got rich, broke something and the only thing you could really count on was if you really needed help, a fellow Pilot would have your back.

I miss the call signs, nick names, and the stories behind them. I miss the getting lit up in an O'club full of my buddies and watching the incredible, unbelievable things that were happening. I miss the Crew Chiefs saluting as you taxied out the flight line. I miss the lighting of the afterburners, if you had them, especially at night. I miss the going straight up and straight down. I miss the cross countries. I miss the dice games at the bar for drinks. I miss listening to bullshit stories while drinking and laughing till my eyes watered.

I miss naps in the Squadron with a room full of pilots working up new tricks to torment the sleeper. I miss flying upside down in the Grand Canyon and hearing about flying so low, boats were blown over. I miss coming into the break Hot and looking over and seeing three wingmen tucked in tight, ready to make the troops on the ground proud. I miss belches that could be heard in neighboring states. I miss putting on ad hoc Air Shows that might be over someone's home or farm in faraway towns.

Finally, I miss hearing DEAD BUG being called out at the bar and seeing and hearing a room of men hit the deck with drinks spilling and chairs being knocked over as they rolled in the beer and kicked their legs in the air, followed closely by a Not-Politically Correct Tap Dancing and Singing spectacle that couldn't help but make you grin and order another round!

I am a lucky guy and have lived a great life! One thing I know is that I was part of a special, really talented bunch of guys doing something dangerous and doing it better than most. Flying the most beautiful, ugly, noisy, solid aircraft ever built. Supported by ground troops committed to making sure we came home again! Being prepared to fly and fight and die for America. Having a clear mission. Having fun.

We box out the bad memories from various operations most of the time but never the hallowed memories of our fallen comrades. We are often amazed at how good war stories never let the truth interfere and they get better with age. We are lucky bastards to be able to walk into a Squadron or a Bar and have men we respect and love shout out our names, our call signs, and know that this is truly where we belong. We are Fighter Pilots. We are Few and we are Proud.

I am Privileged and Proud to call you Brothers.
Push It Up! & Check SIX!

—Author Unknown

APPENDIX

CULTURE, CUSTOMS, AND CRAZINESS

FRIDAY FOLLIES IN FIGHTER SQUADRONS

This appendix lists some of the typical activities that took place on Friday nights at O'Clubs and fighter squadrons everywhere, but especially during deployments. As one might guess, the further away from home, the more rowdy the activity tended to be.

Squadrons based stateside would tend to be more conservative than squadrons based overseas, and squadrons at the remote locations in Korea occasionally tended to take these work hard, play hard activities to the extreme. Each squadron had its own versions of many of the activities listed here, but overall they were fairly universal.

Sadly, many of these traditions have been driven out of existence. However, a few remain, standing as a reminder that building a team of warriors who are willing to risk it all, to give their lives for each other, is not built on a 9-to-5 ethic.

THE SQUADRON BAR

In addition to an O'Club bar, most fighter squadrons have their own private bar as well. Squadron bars have existed as long as men have been flying fighters. One can easily recall the movies with the chaps gathered 'round a dingy bar somewhere in France during WWI singing cheerfully about the poor blighter who rode one in.

The bar is usually stocked and operated by the LPA (see the LPA section), and generally has an ample supply of mostlymicrowaveable food and beverages handy for folks to consume on the premises throughout the day.

Most squadron bars are just separate rooms located inside the operations building, but some squadrons have full-up hooches like the Juvats and Pantons have at Kunsan.

Alcohol is available, but the Beer Light cannot be lit until the last landing of the day has occurred. Rules for bar conduct are usually posted, with the last rule declaring that anyone caught reading the bar rules must buy a round. Another common rule requires anyone receiving a phone call from their spouse while in the bar to also buy a round.

Squadron bars are strictly small-time money-making endeavors for the unit but are sometimes frowned upon by O'Club managers and Mission Support commanders who consider the squadron bar a competitor to the O'Club bar, which it may be, depending on the current atmosphere at the O'Club.

I have seen Security Forces parked specifically outside squadron bars on Friday nights, with the hopes of busting some slightly-over-the-alcohol-limit fighter pilot (and thereby ruining his or her career). However, besides making money for the squadron, the bars also allow the lads and lasses to blow off some steam in a manner not always appropriate for the O'Club.

Many squadron commanders put a time limit on how long the squadron bar will be open, thereby encouraging the squadron to proceed to the O'Club after the general craziness has concluded.

In short, both the O'Club and the squadron bars serve a useful purpose. Squadrons are very proud of their bars, and they are a great forum for historical displays, nametags, plaques, flags, and other related paraphernalia.

NAMEAGE

If you've seen *Top Gun*, you know all about Maverick, Goose, and Iceman. Nicknames and Call Signs are generally officially bestowed during an elaborate ceremony once a fighter pilot becomes Mission Ready.

They are usually based on a variation of someone's last name (Stilly Stilwell, Mac McCarthy, Gruve Gruver); a well-known nickname (Muddy Waters, Buck Rogers, Dusty Rhodes); an act of buffoonery (Plow for a guy who ran off the runway, Cortez for a guy who got lost, Planet for, well, a guy who seemed to be living on his own planet); a general description of a character trait (Wedge, as in the simplest of tools, Kelvin, as in absolute zero, Nail, as in always getting pounded); some physical trait (Ears, Beak, Foot, Airbus, HairClub, Horse); some semi-humorous variation of the last name (Tootsie Roll, Short Order Cook, Duck Teal); or sometimes simply something that just sounded cool (Ace, Guns, Killer).

Typically, during the week before the Naming, a roster would be hidden in the secure weapons vault with a list of potential names for the prospective new guys, or suggestions might be made in the highly-classified Squadron Hog Log (see the Hog Log section).

During the ceremony, there are all kinds of rules for the actual naming process, but generally, once you get a name, it is yours for life. There are many guys I know today only by their nickname.

The Nameage Ceremony itself can be quite an ostentatious affair. It is usually conducted by a squadron Mayor—an individual elected by the squadron for his leadership and talents as a Master of Ceremonies. It is a huge honor to be chosen as the Mayor, typically a senior captain in rank, and he runs the Nameage Ceremony, sometimes called A Show of Colors, with an iron hand.

The event begins with a Roll Call, to ensure all squadron members are present and accounted for. If there are guests present, and sometimes guests were not permitted, they would be introduced and welcomed with style.

Roll Call is usually followed by a series of toasts, to fallen comrades first, then for whatever the Mayor decides to accept. He will then bring forward the new candidate(s) for naming with a big flourish and begin accepting nominations from the crowd.

Someone would be acknowledged by the Mayor. Then this person would stand, and with great formality and fully utilizing the 10% Rule—only 10% of what you say must be true—explain why the candidate deserved to be bestowed such-and-such a name. Eventually, the Mayor presented a name for a vote from the squadron, and based on a majority-rules decision, declare the new name on the candidate. So let it be written—so let it be done!

It is a huge mistake for a new candidate to lobby for a call sign; that is generally one way to guarantee you will NOT get that name. Sometimes, the Mayor may try and lure the new candidate into making that mistake, much to the derision of the crowd. Once, at the 496th TFS in Hahn, an individual was asked, "Well, what would you like to be named?"

The newbie replied, "I don't care what you call me, as long as it's not Shithead or something like that!"

You guessed it—we immediately christened him Shithead, and he proudly still goes by that moniker today. Another demanded that he be named Thor. He was named Barney, for Barney Fife of *The Andy Griffith Show* fame, instead.

Sometimes, the Mayor may accept a bribe from the new candidate, in an attempt by the newbie to influence the crowd to bestow a cool or favored name. The bribe may be several cases of beer, bottles of scotch, or something of that nature to replenish the stock of the squadron bar.

The best bribe I ever saw was with the 14th Fighter Squadron in Misawa. When the new candidate was asked to present a bribe, he exited the room briefly, then returned with the large wooden Panther mascot he had stolen in the dead of night from the rival 13th Fighter Squadron next door. Perfect.

Once the name is bestowed, the new candidate must then accept it with some kind of standardized ceremony. In the 14th FS, it was to drink from a bottle of whiskey and make 14 bubbles as you swallowed (1! 2! 3!...). In the 13th FS, it was to drink from an over-sized bottle of whiskey that contained a large dead lizard, purchased from a bar in Thailand (Tongue The Lizard!!!!). There was a non-alcoholic version, with the same kind of lizard, but with coke instead of whiskey; however, while the whiskey preserved the lizard, the coke actually accelerated the decaying process, so it was a brave pilot who elected the non-alcoholic option.

In the the 36th FS, it was to shake the stick, an F-16 stick mounted on a wooden plaque, and yell, "Welcome to the 36th

Fighter Squadron!" Each squadron has a different tradition, each unique in its own way.

I was actually given the name P.K. during my first naming ceremony with the 496th, to my relative dismay. Even though it is my real name, P.K. stands for Probability of Kill in fighter pilot-speak. The guys thought that was pretty cool, so I basically kept my real name. Later, at Osan Air Base in 1993 with the 36th Fighter Squadron Flying Fiends, I was named Sting—I played bass, had spiky-blonde hair at the time, and they thought there was a resemblance. I kept the call sign Sting for the rest of my career.

Originally intended to mask the identities of aircrew in case they ejected behind enemy lines, nicknames have taken on an additional function. When you are assigned a call sign in an ATO (Air Tasking Order) or frag, it is only for that specific mission for that specific day. You may be Chevy 1 on one day, or Buick 3 the next day. However, in the heat of battle, in certain situations, you may want to be able to get your wingman's attention in a hurry. If I hear Chevy 1, I'll likely process that info quickly and easily, but with the never-ceasing chaos and chatter on the radios during air combat, if I hear, "Sting! Break left!" I am in the break instinctively.

On Fridays, while the bar beer light was lit, most squadron commanders allowed their pilots to wear name tags bearing their nicknames on their flight suits. It was common for pilots to wear their colored squadron t-shirts on Fridays as well. A squadron's colors were generally based on the fin flash on the tails of their jets, so a red fin flash meant your squadron nametags and t-shirts were also red.

When the squadron was TDY or off-station, it was also common on Friday nights at the bar to wear fake nametags, mostly so you couldn't be named if the shenanigans got too far out of control, which was not uncommon. John Doe, of course, was popular. Some squadrons took to everyone wearing identical nametags, like Race Bannon, ensuring everyone would take the fall if the security police showed up (I'm Spartacus!). The F-111 guys from the 48th Liberty Wing from Lakenheath often wore Friday nametags with Dupp as the last name; you got an assortment of Mess Dupp, Gussy Dupp, Screw Dupp—you get the picture.

Naming Ceremonies sometimes took place during Squadron Dining-Ins, as opposed to more formal Dining-Outs, which included spouses. Dining-Ins have their own set of formal rules of behavior, violation of which usually involves trips to the alcoholic grog bowl or the much-worse non-alcoholic variety. At any rate, a loud and proud party might come pretty close to describing a typical Naming Ceremony.

With all that said, there can be a dark side to the whole Nameage culture. Here is how one fellow fighter pilot, who I admire and respect deeply, put it:

> I've been in squadrons where the Naming Ceremony turns into a burning, alcohol-fueled runaway train, which generally turned out to be funny as hell. HOWEVER, the final adjudication and sanity check of the call sign came from a thumbs-up or thumbs-down from the commander. I've also been to a few places where the commander hands that power over to the masses. In every one of those namings, someone's feelings got hurt, the crowd sensed blood in the water, which only egged them on more, and which, in some instances, eventually led to a renaming. However, there were good pilots that ended up with embarrassing names who hated but endured their call sign for the rest of their careers simply because no one thought a level deeper than 'it seemed funny at the time'.

In recent years, the whole Nameage culture has been examined, especially given the politically-correct environment that currently exists.

Clearly, squadron commanders need to take some responsibility, and lines need to be drawn, as they always should have been. It's a judgment call, but having good judgment is one of the criteria for being selected as a squadron commander in the first place.

However, guys and gals are going to get named, whether through formal squadron ceremonies or by discussions over beers at the bar. Call signs are not going away.

THE SQUADRON TOAST
Every squadron has one, usually reserved for special occasions like dining-ins/outs, hail-and-farewell events, etc. However, if you were new to the squadron, you might be spontaneously called upon to lead the toast at other more informal gatherings, so you had better learn it quickly and correctly.

PARTY SUITS
This tradition tended to be limited to the Pacific squadrons, especially the Korea-based squadrons, where it was easy to walk downtown to the nearest tailor and get your individualized party suit, a modified flight suit, made in a few hours.

Party Suits were generally only worn during special squadron events, like Nameage Ceremonies and Roll Calls. Each squadron had its own special colors, patch requirements, and rules to go with them.

The Party Suit tradition began during the Vietnam War—one of the reasons they primarily remain a thing for the Pacific-based squadrons. When I was in the 13th Fighter Squadron in Misawa, Japan, we researched the old 13FS Party Suits from the Vietnam War days and tried to make it a tradition again.

I don't think it lasted much past my tenure, but I still have my party suits from the 36 FS Flying Fiends in Osan and the 13 FS Panthers in Misawa.

THE LPA
The LPA, or Lieutenants Protection Association, existed in every fighter squadron in one way, shape, or form and consisted of newly-assigned lieutenants who tended to be somewhat abused by the older guys. Surprise!

The squadron commander was always an automatic member of the LPA, and at most formal functions, the LPA would be seated with the squadron commander at the head table. The members of the LPA provided the manpower for operating the squadron snack bar, setting up parties, and doing most of the grunt work no one else wanted to do.

Many LPA members have special patches made up for wear on Fridays and wear them with pride. One could always count on a member of the LPA to initiate some of the buffoonery listed here. God bless 'em.

While most LPAs were designed as primarily defensive organizations, they often had no fear of going offensive as well. Some LPAs were very potent groups, instigating organized, stealthy, and much-feared Graded Hospitality Checks (see the Hospitality Checks section).

When they pounded on the door to initiate the Hospitality Check on some unsuspecting comrade, they started a stopwatch and pulled out a clipboard with a modified Form 8 Checkride Evaluation form.

Quality standards were enforced: One minute to door opening, three minutes to drinks poured, seven minutes to snacks served. One could get a Bust for no beer, warm beer, or no ice for the cocktails. Jeremiah Weed (see the Jeremiah Weed section) was, of course, mandatory.

Exceptionally Qualified grades were given for hot preprepared snacks within 10 minutes, and ratings for the quality of music played. These were real programs, with results posted in the Hog Log.

The LPA could and did make lives miserable for those who failed to measure up, but mostly, they raised the quality of squadron life and camaraderie. Still—they had to be scrutinized and controlled as best as commanders were able.

SQUADRON MASCOTS

Nearly every fighter squadron has some kind of mascot, symbol, or figure that represents them, and it is cherished and protected.

During the Vietnam War, the 13th Fighter Squadron had a real black panther they named Eldridge, and stories about Eldridge abound to this day. After the war, Eldridge was shipped to the Phoenix Zoo, and legend has it that he sired 13 baby panthers of his own. The 13th kept a large wooden panther in Eldridge's likeness; after it was stolen by the 14th FS, as related earlier, the Panthers kept it under lock and key, but it still managed to vanish occasionally.

The 14th FS had Sammy, a wooden statue of a Samurai Warrior, and the squadron also had a full set of Samurai armor they would have someone, usually from the LPA, wear for various occasions.

The 525th Tactical Fighter Squadron Bulldogs at Bitburg kept a real bulldog named Apex in the squadron; Apex would go home with families scheduled to watch him over the weekends.

Mr. Bones, a full-sized skeleton displayed at the 95th TFS at Tyndall AFB, is another well-known mascot.

The theft of squadron mascots was a constant activity, especially if there were only two fighter squadrons on the base that continuously competed against each other.

The 36th Fighter Squadron at Osan had a large F-16 model displayed outside their operations building; it would disappear about once a month, and could usually be found hanging in the 25th Fighter Squadron bar.

The 25th (Pilsung!!!) was an A-10 squadron; sometimes, they would hang the F-16 model from one of the A-10 pylons and post the photo worldwide for all to see.

Squadron commanders constantly had to be on the lookout, not only to protect the mascots but to discourage particularly evil plots of revenge contemplated by the LPA, usually towards the end of a long Friday night's revelry. Sort of like the Mutually Assured Destruction strategy during The Cold War.

CRUD

The game of Crud is a team game played on a pool table with only a cue ball and a striped ball. Most squadron bars have an old, beat-up-and-abused crud table, and most O'Clubs have pool tables, so games are easy to arrange.

Two teams, usually from four to eight players each, play sequentially until they are eliminated. A referee is required, often someone of higher rank with some semblance of authority in settling the inevitable dispute and discouraging fisticuffs.

The side pockets are plugged with rolls of toilet paper. The rules are complex, but the goal is to knock the striped ball into one of the pockets before it comes to a complete halt, thereby claiming the life of the adversary team member currently on the table.

A player is eliminated after losing three lives, and the game continues until one team loses all its players—the losing team having to buy the winners (and the referee) a round of beverages.

Squadrons often formed teams that would practice with deadly seriousness to prepare for facing off against other squadron teams, whether during Crud Tournaments at your home base, or at WTDs like Incirlik and Zaragoza.

Crud is Canadian in origin, and in full accordance with a nation that invented ice hockey, is a full-contact sport of blood, mayhem, and downright fun. Gentlemen's rules exist, but those rules generally fall by the wayside in the heat of battle, especially if both sides agree to Combat Crud rules, meaning hardly any rules whatsoever.

It was not unusual to see one of your squadron mates reporting to the Flight Surgeon the night of or the morning after a Crud match. I have seen black eyes, broken ribs, and blown knees resulting from Crud. Not for the fainthearted. Highly recommended.

THE DOLLAR BILL GAME

As with most games played in the bar, this one also involves who buys the beverages. It's usually played with at least four, but hopefully, as many as 12 players—"Are you in?"

The last guy who lost and was the one to buy the last round was usually designated The Hammer. He produced a dollar bill and looked at the 8-digit serial number on the bill. "First two or last two?" he asked a person of his choosing. If the first two were chosen, he'd use the first two numbers of the 8-digit serial as the shack number.

He then began going around the circle; the first player must choose a number between 0 and 99. Let's say that first-two-number on the dollar bill is 41—if the first player says 66, The Hammer will announce 66 is high.

The guessing continues around the circle, with The Hammer indicating high or low until someone guesses or lands on 41.

That person is shacked and must buy the round for all the players.

The fun was in wondering if The Hammer was lying. As The Hammer, you could shack anyone you want, whether a player lands on the hot number or not. The dollar bill in question remained secret and in possession of The Hammer, usually tucked in a tight roll behind an ear, unless the player shacked announces a challenge.

If The Hammer is proven to be lying, The Hammer has to buy the round; however, if The Hammer was telling the truth, then the player issuing the challenge must buy double. Most players choose not to issue a challenge unless the particular Hammer is known for lying, and many are.

It also matters where you are in the player's circle. When a dollar bill game begins, you will see the wiser participants jockeying for position, since a shack statistically tends to land on player #6 or #7. Like most bar games, the dollar bill game takes some skill and experience, but the lure of a free cocktail is hard to resist for most fighter pilots.

DICE GAMES

In most bars frequented by fighter pilots, you will find a table with several guys sitting around and a cup containing five dice. You may find money, usually small denominations, but pots can grow as the night continues, in a pile in the middle of the table, unless they are playing for drinks, which is also common.

The most popular games are Liar's Dice and 4-5-6. I won't discuss the complex rules here—you can Google them if you want the details. Suffice to say that you really need to beware before you sit down at a dice table for a friendly game with a bunch of fighter pilots. It is fairly easy to gang up on an unsuspecting player and take his/her money. Watch, learn, and maybe practice a bit in private before you partake in an innocent game of chance.

THE SINGING OF SONGS

Another grand tradition, borrowed mainly from the Royal Air Force and English Rugby teams, is the singing of songs.

As the night rolls on and the alcohol takes effect, someone will start bellowing out a well-known song, and the whole bar may start singing in unison. "The Balls of O'Leary," "Dear Mom, Your Son Is Dead," "Adeline Schmidt," "Mary Ann Burns," "The Bloody Great Wheel," "The Friar's Song," "Swing Low Sweet Chariot (ptooey!!)" All were well-known songs passed down from generation to generation.

Dick Jonas, a retired Air Force Lieutenant Colonel and former F-4 pilot, performs throughout the country and runs his own record label to produce albums of many of these songs.

Many fighter squadrons have published songbooks, which tend to remain classified due to the occasional X-rated nature of some of the lyrics.

In recent years, there has been a crackdown at most O'Club bars prohibiting the singing of songs due to their non-PC content.

It is a tradition that is dying out as the Air Force makes exponential efforts not to offend anyone, so nowadays songs are typically reserved for singing at the members-only squadron bar, or often at Naming Ceremonies.

Admittedly, some of the older traditions probably needed to go away; the public singing of X-rated songs is one of them. Still, keeping some of the songs going in the relative secure isolation of the squadron bar is a good thing.

If you haven't heard Dos Gringos, a band started by two Viper pilots, Chris "Snooze" Kurek and Rob "Trip" Raymond, you owe it to yourself to give them a listen. They have released four albums about their mostly hilarious experiences in military life, and as fighter pilots—"Two's Blind" is a classic! But be warned, many of their lyrics are R-rated or worse.

DECEASED INSECT

"Dead B_g!!!" is a phrase-that-shall-not-be-mentioned, unless in deadly earnest, at a bar, with the intent of forcing someone to buy a round.

Generally, only the last person who had to buy has the right to yell, "Dead B_g!" He will then observe to see which person was the last to assume the position—on your back, on the floor, with your arms and legs sticking up in the air. The last person down has to buy the round.

Most fighter pilots have a Pavlovian response to the phrase, "Dead B_g." You could be at a 4-Star classified briefing in the Pentagon, and if someone uttered the phrase, chances are that 4-Star AF general officer would be on his back before he had time to think about it. Therefore, the term Deceased Insect is reserved for the phrase-that-shall-not-be-mentioned. It is considered extremely poor form to yell, "Dead B_g" at a bar unless you are prepared to buy the round yourself. FYI—you can see a tame version of Deceased Insect in the movie *Animal House*. Amateurs!

COIN CHECKS

Carrying a squadron coin, or RMO (Round Metallic Object), was a tradition that began with fighter squadrons in the Pacific and later spread to almost every unit in the military. Almost every squadron/group/wing has its own RMO now, and if you are or were a member of that unit, you must possess it at all times.

If someone initiates a coin check, usually signified by someone taking out their RMO and banging it on a table, everyone must present their personal RMO. If you are without it, you are deemed not worthy and must buy the round for the house. Some squadrons place a time-limit on presenting the RMO, i.e., the 10th TFS allowed one minute to come up with the goods.

Once, this time-limit rule resulted in near-disaster. While at the O'Club bar at Hahn one Friday night, someone from the 10th TFS initiated a coin check. A guy named BoomBoom realized his RMO was in his car, so in an effort to meet the one-minute criteria, he went flying out of the Club into the parking lot.

However, in his haste to return within the time limit, he forgot to actually open the door and crashed through the glass door of the Club, shattering it beyond repair. He was cut up pretty badly, but lying on the floor, bleeding, sweating, and panting, he feebly held up his RMO. It cost him a trip to the hospital and payment for a new O'Club door, but his effort was deemed worthy by his squadron mates, and a legend was born.

Coin challenges could happen in the most unlikely places. I was once in the middle of a swimming pool in Bahrain, when I spied an old wingman of mine I had flown with in Germany in the 512th about ten years previously. He swam towards me with an evil grin on his face, and sure enough, right there in the middle of the pool, he whipped out the RMO from our old squadron.

On another occasion, I was refueling from a KC-10, and one of my squadron mates was performing Supervisor of Flying duties in the tanker and watching us refuel from the boom position. I glanced upward after I was hooked up to the boom, and saw him smiling and banging his RMO on the observation glass. I tried in vain to stay on the boom and refuel while trying to get into my flight suit pocket via my survival vest, G-suit vest, and poopy suit, and present my RMO. I finally gave up trying, as it was much more embarrassing to fall off the boom, which would also cost you a round, than to have to buy a round due to a failed RMO check.

Unit RMOs have become such a thing that if you were not careful, you could end up with a pocketful of big metal coins in your flightsuit, clanging your way down the hallway and weighed down with all the heavy metal.

It has gotten to be such a fad that in Korea, you can buy a glass-topped coffee table, or smaller showcase table just to contain all the RMOs you might collect over the course of your career. My table was full when I retired, and I donated it to the AFROTC detachment at the University of Washington.

However, I have kept all of my assigned squadron RMOs displayed on a wooden rack made for that purpose, just to be ever-ready for a challenge from an old comrade.

SOCK CHECKS

Believe it or not, for a period of time during the 80s, the Air Force tried to impose a strict rule on what color socks you could wear with your flight suit and combat gear.

Most pilots elected to wear thick, white athletic socks for comfort and sweat protection, but the Air Force insisted you wear their standard-issue thin black sock, that was uncomfortable, unhealthy, and inefficient. Most of us ignored this rule, as did most commanders.

However, occasionally, you would find a commander, usually a non-aviator who had a thing for those arrogant fighter pilots, who became very interested in what color sock you were wearing with your flight suit. As a result, it became not uncommon for someone on a Friday night at the club to stand up and yell, "Sock Check!" at which point every pilot would stand, unzip their flight suit, and let it drop to their ankles, thereby revealing your socks, and your underwear, and anything else you may or may not have been wearing underneath.

If a female pilot was in the bar, you could almost guarantee that someone was going to call for a Sock Check at some point. It didn't take long for most commanders to realize that the Sock Witch Hunts needed to be terminated, but occasionally someone would still initiate a Sock Check at the O'Club bar just for the sheer naughtiness of it.

SWIRLIES

Sometimes, even by fighter pilot standards, someone might get just a little too obnoxious at the bar on a Friday night. If the poor behavior continued, the individual might find himself the recipient of a swirlie.

Three or four guys would sweep down on the unsuspecting victim, drag him to the Men's Room, hoist him upside down, put his head in a toilet, and flush (sometimes repeatedly) until the offender agreed to more closely monitor his conduct.

It was sort of an early version of waterboarding. You can see an example of a swirlie in the movie *The Great Santini*, where Bull Meecham accidentally selects a corporal for a sneak attack.

BAT HANGING

This was a popular activity for awhile. The object was to find someplace you could hang upside down, maybe from the banister over a balcony, or over the bar with your legs held up by the guys. Then comrades poured beer or a mix of tequila and triple sec into your open mouth for you to guzzle—again, upside down. It's harder than it sounds.

CARRIER LANDINGS

Obviously, an activity borrowed from our Naval Aviator brethren, and not much practiced (wisely, just like real-life carrier landings) in most AF bars.

However, especially at a Dining-In, someone might come up with this great idea. Basically, you set up three or four long tables—splash the tables with the most handily available liquid, often the pitcher of beer in your hand—grab a table cloth, and have two guys stretch that table cloth at the end of the tables to simulate a cable on an aircraft carrier deck.

Then you line up, and one by one, take a running jump and slide across the tables and try to hook the table cloth cable with your feet before sliding off the end.

You had the option of doing bad weather landings, whereby you would be continuously doused with beer as you slid across the tables. Or you could opt for night landings where you would have to perform the feat with the lights out.

It was not unusual for someone in their inebriated state to miss the initial jump altogether and catch the edge of the table with their knees or noggins, bringing the whole apparatus crashing down, followed by a trip to the flight surgeon. Again, not a common activity, but one that (thankfully) only occurred every now and then.

THE VALVE STEM GAME

Fighter pilots are notoriously cheap, and the older you are, the better you become at finding creative ways to vector the tab to the younger pups.

When drinking is involved, driving is taboo, so taxi cabs are often the logical choice. At the end of the trip, the guy riding shotgun in the front seat asks the cabbie to wait one minute while the passengers check the position of the valve stem on their assigned wheel. The valve stem closest to the 6:00 position loses and has to pay the cab fare. Shotgun owns the front-right wheel, back-left and right-seat get the corresponding wheels. Backseat middle gets the drivers-side front wheel.

And if you were unfortunate enough to be the fifth passenger (which happens more often than one might care to admit), you get the spare tire. Everyone jumps out and calls the position of the valve stem on their assigned wheel. Honesty is usually the order of the day since the actual position is readily apparent.

WALLING

If you were on a squadron TDY somewhere, you stayed in squadron-assigned hooches or VOQs. Billeting tended to put the entire squadron on one floor or in one general location, which worked best for everyone concerned. If you called it an early night on a Friday night and were trying to get some much-needed rest after a hard week of flying, you were apt to become a target.

The boys would come stumbling in after the Club closed, looking to continue the hijinks and festivities. While most guys tended to keep their VOQ rooms unlocked, nearly everyone knew it was a good technique to lock your room on Friday nights, or you might get walled.

Walling involved four or five sweaty fighter pilots bursting into your room, whooping and hollering, and as a team grabbing your mattress and hoisting it against the wall, with you still in it. They would then rush out of the room to much rejoicing, leaving you to straighten up your bed and put everything back together again. Sometimes, it just made more sense to sleep curled up on the floor and clean everything up in the morning.

The following story was related to me from a guy who flew with the 81st F-4G Wild Weasels at Spangdahlem.

They were at a WTD at Zaragoza, and one of the pilots had his family drive down all the way to Spain to meet up with him and embark on a vacation after the WTD concluded. The pilot, his wife, two kids, and their pet dachshund were staying in one of the bigger family-friendly VOQs, all sleeping soundly, looking forward to departing for Madrid the next morning.

As should have been predicted, nearly the entire squadron came crashing into the room. First, they walled the unsuspecting pilot and his wife. Then, they walled the two kids (much to their delight). The dachshund was cowering in his little wicker doggie bed—but not to be neglected, they walled the dog, too.

I was in Incirlik one late Friday night, in my room trying to sleep when the guys came calling. My door was locked (no fool, I), so they banged away, yelling my name; I felt like Vincent Price in *The Last Man on Earth*—"Come out, Morgan!!!"

I just smirked to myself, rolled over, and tried to go back to sleep when I heard my window slide open. Next thing I knew, someone had shoved a garden hose through the window, and sure enough, a cascade of water came pouring in. I rushed outside in my underwear to turn off the spigot to the joy of the crowd. At least I didn't get walled.

HOSPITALITY CHECKS

At the end of a Friday night, after the O'Club closed its doors, the lads and lasses weren't always ready to end the evening's activities. That is generally the time when someone, usually from the LPA, would decide that a hospitality check, or roof stomp, was in order, most often at some unsuspecting squadron/group/wing commander's home.

The idea was to use stealth; 15-20 slightly inebriated souls trying to quietly (haha!) sneak up on some squadron comrade's roof, begin stomping and yelling simultaneously, and then be invited inside to continue the party that had just ended at the O'Club.

Most guys usually welcomed such an intrusion—it was a sign of affection, after all—but not all spouses tended to be as enthusiastic when subjected to a Hospitality Check. Most commanders kept a special refrigerator well-stocked with food and beverages in the event the inevitable Roof Stomp would occur. How well you responded—Enough food? Enough beverages? Good music? Good attitude?—could influence your reputation in a big way.

One of my son Walker's earliest childhood memories was to be awakened in the middle of the night, around 1:00 AM, by a tap-tap-tapping on his window.

It was in the middle of winter, in Misawa, Japan, and snow and ice covered everything. Walker's room was on the second floor of our on-base house. "Walker! Open the window! It's the Doc!"

Yes, our squadron flight surgeon was on the roof of our ice-encased house, precariously trying to make his way into our home with a dozen fighter pilots slipping and sliding on the icy ledge behind him.

Naturally, Walker happily flung open his window, and in came a gaggle of hootin' and hollerin' fighter pilots assaulting our bedroom while their spouses waited impatiently outside by the front door to be let in.

On another occasion, again in the dead of winter in Misawa, we had just concluded a week-long exercise whereby a deployed Marine AV-8 Harrier Squadron had supplied adversary support. Having had our way with them for the most part, I invited the Harrier squadron commander and his troops to Roof Stomp the Wing Commander's house with us. They happily obliged.

In typical Japanese fashion, the Wing Commander's wife wisely insisted that we take off our shoes before entering their home, so there was a pile of about 40 pairs of flight boots and wive's shoes stacked outside the door in the snow.

The Marines left shortly thereafter (wimps!), but when it was time for all of us to depart at around 2:00 AM, all of our shoes had disappeared. We found them lining the street in front of the Wing Commander's house, one-by-one in a trail leading back to the O'Club.

We had to walk in the snow in our stocking feet to find our shoes, and all flight boots look alike. The Harriers had got their revenge with style. HARRUMPH to them.

JEREMIAH WEED

The story of Jeremiah Weed, a sublimely tasty bourbon liqueur, is well known and will not be repeated here. However, it is worth knowing that no self-respecting fighter pilot will be caught dead without a bottle of Weed in the freezer, for toasting with old comrades, or in preparation for a hospitality check.

THE SQUADRON PENALTY JAR
Most squadrons had a system of fines set up where penalties were paid based on the infraction. The penalty jar was usually a large plastic pretzel jar sitting on the squadron bar or the more secure weapons vault, and the money was used by the Snackos to replenish bar supplies.

Fines were usually for some inflight anomaly; for instance, you might get fined a dollar for every pass on the range where your airspeed was too slow, or you pickled below minimum altitude. You might also get fined a dollar for calling a kill in an air-to-air engagement that was later invalidated during a video review.

Some squadrons fined five dollars, or more, for a fratricide episode. Others took fines to the nth degree; you might get fined a dollar for saying head instead of cranium, as an example—don't ask me why.

During the nineties, it became fashionable to say, "so to speak" (chuckle chuckle) after any reference that might have any kind of remote sexual innuendo. It got to the point that one sentence might have three or four "so to speaks" thrown in, even during formal briefings; it became very tedious after a while.

Finally, one squadron commander had enough and started fining a dollar each time someone said, "so to speak." The squadron penalty jar got pretty full for a while until everyone learned to eliminate the phrase from their vocabulary. So to speak.

THE HOG LOG
Every squadron has one—everyone in that squadron will deny its existence. Sometimes called the Doofer Book, it is usually kept back in the secure weapons and intel vault, so only squadron members have access to it (since one was stolen and exposed by a visitor several years back, and all hell broke loose due to its occasional non-PC content).

The Hog Log is a confidential squadron journal that allows every member of the squadron to write whatever is on their mind: document the buffoonery of another squadron member, comment on activities and/or people on the base or in the news, complain about the Air Force, the President, the Wing Commander, etc.

Generally, the Hog Log serves as a written Facebook-type document that allows everyone to express themselves without restriction or filter. The foundation of many call signs come from Hog Log entries, and as always, the 10% Rule firmly applies.

Some former comrades of mine have gone on to become congressmen, astronauts, and CEOs. If the content of some of those old Hog Log entries was ever revealed...

FINAL NOTE

Flying fighters is a demanding, deadly business, and almost every fighter pilot I ever met regarded the 12 hours from the bottle to the throttle rule very seriously. One might have the occasional beer after flying, or a glass of wine with dinner, but the consumption of alcohol was mostly reserved for Friday nights after the long week was over, and a weekend of rest and relaxation could be anticipated.

We all knew that an aircraft mishap of any kind would result in a blood-alcohol test, and a failure meant the end of the career you had fought all of your life to achieve. The same applied to driving under the influence.

It is also worth noting that you didn't have to drink to have a good time at the squadron or O'Club bar. I know many fighter pilots who are teetotalers, and the best dice player I ever saw never touched a drop—a real tipoff, eh?

Flying fighters requires that you be at your best mentally and physically, and if you don't have a healthy dose of self-discipline, you are in the wrong business.

The BL: no one I knew would willingly risk their life or their career by abusing alcohol, and commanders at every level made a concerted effort to ensure that their troops conducted themselves appropriately. Check Six!

GLOSSARY

AAA	Anti-Aircraft Armament
AAFCE	Allied Air Forces Central Europe
AAR	Air-to-Air Refueling
AB	Afterburner
ABW	Air Base Wing
AFB	Air Force Base
AFROTC	Air Force Reserve Officer Training Corps
ACM	Air Combat Maneuvers (DACM is ACM vs dissimilar aircraft)
ACMI	Air Combat Maneuvering Instrumentation
ACT	Air Combat Tactics (DACT is ACT vs dissimilar aircraft)
AFIT	Air Force Institute of Technology
AFN	Armed Forces Network
AFPC	Air Force Personnel Center
AGTS	Aerial Gunnery Targeting System
AHC	Aircraft Handling Characteristics
AMU	Aircraft Maintenance Unit
ANG	Air National Guard
AOA	Angle-of-Attack
AOR	Area of Responsibility
ATC	Air Training Command
ATO	Air Tasking Order
AWACS	Airborne Warning & Control System
AYA	American Youth Association
BDDs	Bravo-Delta-Deltas (Big Dick Dogs)
BFM	Basic Fighter Maneuvers (DBFM is BFM vs. a dissimilar aircraft)
BINGO	Out of fuel (or out of ammo), time to return-to-base

BIT	Built-In Test
BL	Bottom Line
BLIND	Lost visual contact with a friendly flight member
BOQ	Bachelor Officers Quarters
BUC	Back Up Control (for the F-16 engine)
BX	Base Exchange
CAP	Combat Air Patrol
CAPs	Critical Action Procedures
CAS	Close Air Support
CATA	Collision Antenna Train Angle
CCIP	Continuously Computed Impact Point
CCRP	Continuously Computed Release Point
CINC	Commander-In-Chief
DME	Distance Measuring Equipment
DNIF	Duty Not Including Flying
DOC	Designated Operational Commitment
DTC	Date Transfer Cartridge
DTE	Data Transfer Equipment
DTOS	Dive-Toss
EDA	Escape Distance - Actual
ECM	Electronic Counter Measures
EDR	Escape Distance - Required
EPU	Emergency Power Unit
ENJJPT	Euro-NATO Joint Jet Pilot Training
FAA	Federal Aviation Administration
FAC	Forward Air Controller
FAIP	First-Assignment Instructor Pilot
FCNP	Fire Control Navigation Panel
FLCS	Flight Control System
FNG	Funny New Guy
FOL	Forward Operating Location
FPC	Final Progress Check
FPM	Flight Path Marker
FRAG	Fragmentation from an explosion, or -
FRAG	Fragmentary Order, unit portion of an Air Tasking Order

GAF	German Air Force
GCI	Ground Controlled Intercept
GIB	Guy In Back (Rear Cockpit)
GLOC	G-Induced Loss of Consciousness

HAF	Hellenic (Greek) Air Force
HAS	Hardened Aircraft Shelter
HUD	Heads Up Display

IAF	Israeli Air Force
IFF	Identification Friend or Foe
IFR	Instrument Flight Rules
ILS	Instrument Landing System
INS	Inertial Navigation System
IP	Instructor Pilot
IPC	Initial Progress Check
ISS	Intermediate Service School
I/Q	Instrument/Qualification

LADD	Low Angle Drogue Delivery
LANTIRN	Low Altitude Navigation Targeting InfraRed Night
LCOS	Lead-Computing Optical Sight
LIFT	Lead-In Fighter Training
LLLD	Low Level Low Drag
LLS	Low Level Strike
LPA	Lieutenants Protection Association

MAC	Military Airlift Command
MCAS	Marine Corps Air Station
MFD	Multi-Function Display
MIMSO	Military Indoctrination for Medical Service Officers
MIL	Military, or 100% Full Throttle
MR	Mission Ready
MS	Mission Support
MTT	Multi-Target Track
MQ	Mission Qualification

NDF	National Defense Fellow
NWS	Nose Wheel Steering
OAP	Offset Aim Point
OSS	Operations Support Squadron
PAA	Primary Assigned Aircraft
PAL	Permissive Action Link
PAR	Precision Approach - Radar
PIO	Pilot-Induced Oscillation
PIT	Pilot Instructor Training
PLF	Parachute Landing Fall
RAF	Royal Air Force
RBAAB	Red Blooded All American Boys
RCP	Rear Cockpit
ROE	Rules Of Engagement
RLD	Radar Laydown
RLOFT	Radar Loft
RSU	Runway Supervisory Unit
RTB	Return To Base
RTU	Replacement Training Unit
RWR	Radar Warning Receiver
REO	Radar Electro/Optical Display
SAC	Strategic Air Command
SAM	Surface-to-Air Missile
SAT	Surface Attack Tactics
SEFE	Standardization-Evaluation Flight Examiner
SERE	Search, Escape, Resistance, Evasion
SFO	Simulated Flame Out
SMS	Stores Management System
SOF	Supervisor of Flying
SOS	Squadron Officer School
SSS	Senior Service School
STT	Singe-Target Track
TAC	Tactical Air Command

TACAN	Tactical Air Navigation System
TALLY	Visual sighting of an enemy aircraft
TD Box	Target-Designator Box
TDY	Temporary Duty (Travel)
TFS	Tactical Fighter Squadron
TFTS	Tactical Fighter Training Squadron
TFW	Tactical Fighter Wing
TLP	Tactical Leadership Program
TLQ	Transient Living Quarters
TOT	Time-Over-Target
TRA	Temporary Reserved Airspace
UFC	Up Front Controls
UPT	Undergraduate Pilot Training
USAF	United States Air Force
VAC	Victor Alert Facility
VFR	Visual Flight Rules
VICTOR	VHF Radio
VOQ	Visiting Officer Quarters
VR Routes	Designated air routes requiring Visual Flight Rules (VFR)
WSEP	Weapons Systems Evaluation Program
WTD	Weapons Training Deployment
ZAB	Zaragoza Air Base

Top hole. Bally Jerry pranged his kite right in the how's your father. Hairy blighter, dicky-birdied, feathered back on his Sammy, took a waspy, flipped over on his Betty Harper's and caught his can in the Bertie.

—Monty Python, "Pilot Banter" Sketch

ABOUT THE AUTHOR

P.K. and Wendy White are retired and live in the Seattle area. They are both active in their messianic synagogue. P.K. plays guitar in the Ezekiel's Bones blues band.

Made in the USA
Middletown, DE
21 December 2020